MRN

VIET-NAM AND THE WEST

VIET-NAM
and the West

RALPH SMITH

Cornell University Press
ITHACA, NEW YORK

First published, 1968
First published in U.S.A., 1971

International Standard Book Number 0-8014-0636-6
Library of Congress Catalog Card Number 78-148717

PRINTED IN THE UNITED STATES OF AMERICA
BY VAIL-BALLOU PRESS, INC.

Contents

Preface   vii

A Note on Vietnamese Names   ix

Prologue   3

PART ONE

    I.   The Vietnamese Tradition   11

    II.   The Tradition Challenged   25

    III.   Government and the Villages   40

PART TWO

    IV.   The Nation   57

    V.   Religion   70

    VI.   Constitutionalism   86

    VII.   Revolution   98

    VIII.   War and Partition   114

PART THREE

    IX.   The Quest for Modernity   125

    X.   Communism   138

    XI.   Non-Communism: The South   151

    XII.   An American Solution?   168

Epilogue   183

Notes   191

Index   203

Maps

The Expansion of Viet-Nam, 11th to 18th Centuries   61
Political Unrest in Viet-Nam *c.* 1930   105
Population Density and Rice Land in Viet-Nam *c.* 1950   131

Preface

FOR most Americans 'Viet-Nam' represents an episode of foreign policy, in what used to be called the Cold War between East and West. In judging what has happened in Viet-Nam, 'hawks' and 'doves' alike make their assessments in terms of the rights and wrongs of United States policy, in relation to a pattern of world-wide conflict. The 'hawks' consider Viet-Nam as an example of 'Communist insurgency' which is deemed to have a potential for expansion or contraction depending on how the United States reacts to it. Very little thought is given to the point of view of the Vietnamese themselves, to the fact that, first and foremost, the Vietnamese war is a crucial stage in the history of Viet-Nam.

The principal purpose of the present essay is to show how this most recent phase of Vietnamese history fits into the longer-term perspective, to show how it is the culmination of that country's tragic relationship with the West. It will look in particular at the period from 1858 to 1963, slightly over a century, in which Viet-Nam moved from the last days of monarchical independence, on the eve of French conquest, to a situation of divided independence in which the two halves of the country were at war with one another. The war itself, whose origins go back to 1957 but which did not reach a level of great intensity until after 1963, must be the subject of another book. It is still much too early to attempt a detailed assessment of that war, which in all its cruelty and horror is still being waged. But the question why such a war should have begun at all is one which men are already asking, and which can perhaps be given a tentative answer. It is inconceivable that either side at the start expected it to be so bitter and intense as it became; nevertheless the war itself already existed in the logic of the situation of 1963. And from the point of view of the Westerner, the fact that the war had to be fought at all must count as a tragic failure, whatever may be the outcome of the conflict.

To write the history of one's own country, though never easy, is a relatively uncomplicated task: whatever the difficulties of source material and interpretation, one is at least writing about people and institutions belonging to one's own cultural tradition. To attempt to write the history of a country as different from one's own as is (for an Englishman) Viet-Nam, is an undertaking so difficult that it might be called rash. For the subject of such a history must be viewed across a cultural gulf as wide as any that exists within the species of mankind. The problems are not merely those of language; they concern the whole framework of assumptions within which men live and have their being. For this reason, if for no other, the present essay sets out to be something more (as well as something less) than a mere chronicle of political decisions and their results. It seeks to bridge the gap between the study of politics and that of culture or civilization, and to relate the record of events to the framework of thought and belief, ideas and institutions, of the Vietnamese. Such an undertaking is as hazardous as, in the present state of the world, it is necessary. I am conscious that this essay does not do full justice to the subject: it does little more than scratch the surface of problems whose true complexity will only be appreciated when a vast deal more research has been done, and when many more minds are able to contribute to their elucidation. But a beginning must be made somewhere, and whilst there is some truth in the historian's dictum that 'interpretation must wait on scholarship', it is sometimes the case that interpretation will itself inspire scholarship.

The present study would have been impossible without the help and encouragement of a great many friends and colleagues. In view of the controversial nature of the subject, I shall not risk anyone embarrassment by recording his name in apparent association with points of view he may not wholly share. My gratitude is none the less deep for being expressed in general terms. I would mention especially my debt to colleagues at the School of Oriental and African Studies, University of London; to those who participated in the 'China and the World' study group at Chatham House, London, between 1963 and 1967; and most important of all, to my Vietnamese friends in Paris and Saigon.

R. B. S.

London, England
March 1971

A Note on Vietnamese Names

VIETNAMESE, unlike most Asian languages, does not present serious problems of transliteration. Although it was originally written in characters similar to those of Chinese, a standard Romanized form was developed by Christian missionaries from the seventeenth century, and during the twentieth century this has become universally adopted by the Vietnamese. Very few people know the old characters.

It is not however possible, using English type, to reproduce all the diacritical marks which are necessary in the Romanized script of Vietnamese to indicate differences of tone. In the present work I have not attempted to do so, though I have included the circumflex mark where appropriate, whose purpose is to indicate vowel quality.

Nor is it possible to indicate the difference between the Vietnamese Ð and D. The name Ngô Ðinh Diêm, for example, is pronounced Ngô Dinh *Ziêm* (in the Tongkingese dialect; the Cochinchinese pronounciation of the last name is something like *dYiêm*). The name Duy, often found as a middle name, is pronounced *Zwee*. It is impracticable to try to explain here all the subtleties of Vietnamese pronunciation, but one common name which often gives trouble is Nguyên: it should be pronounced *Ng-wi-en*.

In referring to one another Vietnamese normally use the third of their three names, which is the personal name. The only exception occurs in the case of a very distinguished person where it is appropriate to use the first (family) name with a special honorific title. Thus Hô Chi Minh (a pseudonym anyway) is never known as Minh; and while he lived Ngô Dinh Diêm was sometimes known as President Ngô. In order to avoid confusion I have (with the exception of Hô) adhered to the standard practice of using the personal name. No disrespect is intended to such revered figures as Phan Bôi Châu and Phan Châu Trinh, both of whom appear in Vietnamese writings as *cu* Phan.

PROLOGUE

The Bodhisattva Mahasattva wrapped his body in divine garments, bathed it in oil, made his last vow, and thereafter burnt his own body. . . . And the eighty Lords Buddhas all shouted their applause: Well done, well done, young man of good birth, that is the real heroism which the Bodhisattvas Mahasattvas should develop; that is the real worship of the Tathagata, the real worship of the Law.

Saddharma Pundarika (The Lotus Sutra).

Prologue

On the twentieth day of the fourth month, in the year of the Cat, tenth of the decade, a monk named Quang Duc was covered with oil and burnt himself alive at Saigon.

THE traditional Vietnamese style of chronology, being cyclical and lacking a continuous era, does not distinguish the absolute uniqueness of events. Ten numerals and twelve animals allow for a cycle of sixty years; then one must start again.[1] Consequently, described in this way, the self-immolation of Quang Duc might belong to any of a number of years of the Cat, stretching across several centuries: perhaps, for example, to 1363. The occurrence of such an event in that year would not be of great interest to most Western readers; only the student of the esoteric would probe deeper. He would find that it was not without parallel in the history of Asian Buddhism. In 1034, for instance, two monks are said by the chronicles to have set fire to themselves in the old Vietnamese capital of Thang-Long (the modern Hanoi), their ashes being enshrined in a special temple by the king Ly Thai-Tông. Again, in Bangkok a Buddhist monk sacrificed himself in this way in 1791, and another in 1817. And as recently as 1930 a Vietnamese monk burnt himself alive at Biên-Hoa. Buddhism is a religion in which men seek to escape all sense of attachment to a bodily self and a personal life, and the complete destruction of his body by a monk is applauded by several sacred texts. The monk who takes this extreme step does so in the confidence that his rebirth will be into a higher state of being. Ultimately he hopes to attain *Nirvana*, a state so empty of existence in any sense materialist Westerners can understand that it is neither 'being' nor 'non-being'.[2]

But the year of Quang Duc's self-immolation was not 1363, it was six centuries later; and the event was not of merely esoteric interest. Immediately it caught the imagination of a world which was watching every detail of the political crisis then unfolding in South Viet-Nam. During the months which followed there was much debate in American circles about the significance of the 'fire-suicides' and the attitude to be adopted towards them. The opinion which prevailed at the time was that they signified a Vietnamese 'public opinion' near to breaking-point. Accordingly the government of the United States withdrew its support from President Ngô Dinh Diêm, and in November of the same year, 1963, he was overthrown by a military coup.

More recent, and more cynical, commentators have suspected that this interpretation may have been too simple.[3] Appalled at the chaos which followed the coup of 1963, they have detected in the situation of that year a clever political manoeuvre designed to make foreign journalists dramatize the Buddhist opposition to the government in Saigon, and so to encourage the Americans to take decisions which would ultimately benefit their enemies the Communists. They find evidence of a careful calculation of the effects the 'fire-suicides' would have on world opinion; and they point to the elaborate public relations system of the Buddhist organization, which ensured that whenever such a spectacle took place Western newsmen with their cameras were quickly on the scene. The sacred bonzes, it would seem, were not men totally withdrawn from worldly life, but clever politicians who knew what they wanted and how to achieve it. The American diplomats and journalists fell into their trap.

To choose between the two interpretations is not easy; a characteristic Western reaction would doubtless be to suggest that the truth lies somewhere in between. But the truth is more complex. For neither of these views takes into account what must surely be the most important question about the immolations: that is, how a kind of action which if it happened six centuries ago we should regard as of purely religious significance, should in our own day and age come to be regarded as primarily political. Neither of the interpretations just outlined allows for the cultural significance of these events. Yet surely, whatever their political importance, these acts of self-destruction demonstrate more clearly than anything else the fact that culturally Viet-Nam is quite beyond the normal range of occidental comprehension. This fact is in itself of immense political significance.

Suicide is a deed not lightly undertaken, and in any society its occurrence will reflect fundamental themes of belief and culture. By Christian standards, to take one's life is a sin against the creator God, in whose sight every man should strive for living perfection on earth in order to be worthy of salvation in a life to come. The only view of suicide which such belief allows is that of an ignoble desire to escape: even the non-Christian humanist in the West condones suicide, he does not praise it. But in Viet-Nam, as in other countries of East Asia, to withdraw from the world is a means of proving virtue. Suicide can even be a way of proving superior virtue in face of a powerful but unvirtuous enemy. At that point, it can become not merely an escape but a weapon of considerable force. In 1963, a few weeks after the death of Quang Duc, another Vietnamese took poison in Saigon: the celebrated novelist Nhât Linh. He was about to be put on trial for opposition to the Diêm government, and his suicide was a more eloquent defence than anything he could have said in words. Quang Duc, as well as following a religious precedent, was speaking the same language as Nhât Linh. It is a language which most Westerners find utterly unfamiliar: so much so that in the summer of 1963 their first reaction to the fire-suicides was to over-dramatize them, and to exaggerate their significance. Inevitably this initial horror led in time to a reaction, and eventually many American observers came to conclude that fire-suicides have no significance at all.

But if the language of the suicides was unfamiliar, their context was even more so. The most important question for the Americans —journalists and policy-makers alike—was not *why* the monks were burning themselves, but how important the monks were in relation to the rest of Vietnamese society. It would seem that the Americans knew little about the nature of Vietnamese Buddhism before the crisis erupted; unfortunately it is not a subject which can be studied with profit at a moment's notice. It is not my purpose here to argue the question whether the American decision to withdraw support from Ngô Dinh Diêm was the right one, but merely to observe that it was taken almost in a cultural vacuum. Part of the tragedy of the American experience in Viet-Nam has been that a great deal in the political culture of the country and of its people is not readily intelligible to the Western mind. To say that this or that particular failure of cultural understanding has been of a decisive nature would be misleading. The self-immolation of Quang Duc is simply an illustration of a problem of communication which has pervaded the relationship between Americans and Vietnamese since 1954. The government of the United States has found itself becoming more and more deeply involved in the consequences of events whose causes or motivation it does not properly understand. That such a situation should befall the country whose boast is that its wealth and resources make it the most powerful in the world is galling indeed.

For Europeans to criticize Americans on this score however is not entirely appropriate. It so happens that in Viet-Nam the United States has become more deeply involved than any other Western power; but American involvement is only the most recent chapter in Viet-Nam's relations with the West. The current conflict there is the culmination of a developing relationship which began in earnest with the French attack on Da-Nang in 1858. It is in the complicated nature of that relationship, rather than in any specific decision of contemporary politicians, that we must seek the origins of the present situation.

Like all other Asian countries, Viet-Nam has a quality and character of its own, which must not be blotted out under the weight of sweeping generalizations about 'the East'. It must be accepted as unique among the nations of the world. By European standards moreover, it is by no means a small country: taking North and South together it has a population of thirty millions, more than double that of Australia; and in surface area its extent is about equivalent to that of the whole British Isles including Eire. Its recorded history goes back as far as our own, to the first or second century before Christ. Even if it had not become the focus of an international crisis, it would be a country worthy of study in its own right.

True, Viet-Nam is not one of the great centres of creative civilization radiating impulses in all directions, like India or China or Greece. The Vietnamese character is poetic before it is analytical, and for ideas capable of becoming the basis of institutional organization the Vietnamese have tended to borrow from other areas of the world. In particular, down to the nineteenth century they borrowed from the Chinese; and the relationship of Vietnamese to Chinese culture is in consequence an extremely subtle one. During the thousand years before about A.D. 900, when Viet-Nam was the southernmost province of a Chinese empire, the peoples of the 'Indonesian' civilization which had previously flourished in the area were greatly influenced by the Chinese who came to inhabit and to govern their country. The position of those peoples in relation to their conquerors was not unlike that between the British and their Roman rulers at about the same period in time. The subsequent development of the relationship might also have been paralleled in the West, if the Roman Empire had recovered its unity after the fifth century but had never again succeeded in reconquering the British Isles.[4] But just as the Britons were never completely Romanized, so the Vietnamese were still not wholly Sinicized when, about A.D. 900, the break-up of the T'ang empire brought about their independence.

In the thousand years that followed, they created and defended a state of their own in the South, calling it first Dai-Viêt (meaning 'Great Viet') and later Dai-Nam ('Great South'). From time to time they were threatened with incorporation into a reunified China, but on four occasions they succeeded in resisting or in quickly terminating Chinese attempts at reconquest. Although they sent periodic tribute to the Chinese capital, their king or emperor was ruler in his own right, making his own sacrifices to Earth and to Heaven. He and his officials continued to use the Chinese language for administrative purposes—and for classical literary composition—down to the nineteenth century: just as Latin was employed by clerics and lawyers in England and France long after the decline of Rome. The principles of Vietnamese government were based on those of the Confucian classics, and current Chinese literature was readily available to those who knew the characters.[5]

The parallel with England and France must not however be taken too far. The cultural gulf between Viet-Nam and the West, which became apparent in the nineteenth century, was much more than a gulf between 'traditional' and 'modern' societies. To think of traditional Viet-Nam as *culturally* comparable to medieval France or England would be a serious error. The nature of Western social and intellectual traditions made possible, from about the seventeenth century, developments which in time were to place European and Asian culture still farther apart: the 'scientific' and 'industrial revolutions'. Whether such developments could have ever taken place, given time, in

China or Viet-Nam is a question beyond our power to answer; for with Western expansion the traditional frameworks of East Asia were interrupted and forced to respond to Western influence. Conquest by France compelled the Vietnamese to turn away from China, at least for the time being, as their principal source of culture inspiration, and to turn towards the West. They accepted Roman script as a medium for writing their own language, and they were exposed to a wide range of new ideas and techniques in all spheres of activity.

Viet-Nam is possibly the most 'un-Western' of all Asian countries to have been conquered and ruled for a time by a European power. At the same time its colonial masters were probably the most eager of those powers to impose Western civilization on their Asian subjects. This coincidence has made Viet-Nam's relationship with the West culturally as well as politically dramatic. French rule has undoubtedly left its mark upon the culture and civilization of Viet-Nam, especially on those individuals who were so completely educated in French that they were accepted as virtually Frenchmen in France. Yet despite several decades of chanting 'nos ancêtres les Gaulois' there is no question that even the most Gallicized of them remain in essential respects Vietnamese.

In the past century or so, therefore, the philosophy of harmony derived from China was challenged by the philosophy of achievement brought by the Europeans. The encounter is not yet over, and those tempted to make too hasty a judgment of its outcome might do worse than to recall the reply of a Chinese scholar to a question about the effects of the French Revolution: it is much too early to say.

PART ONE

Our Great Viet is a country where prosperity abounds,
Where civilization reigns supreme.

Mountains, rivers, frontiers and customs,
All are distinct between China and Viet-Nam.

Triêu, Dinh, Ly and Trân
Created our nation,
Whilst Han, T'ang, Sung and Yuan,
Ruled over theirs.

Over the centuries,
We have been sometimes strong, sometimes weak;
But never yet have we been lacking in heroes.
Of that let our history be the proof.

> Lê Loi's proclamation of independence
> after driving out the Ming, 1428.

I

The Vietnamese Tradition

THE temples and palaces of the 'Great Within' (the *Dai-Nôi*) of the imperial city at Huê are preserved as a national monument, much as the French Republic preserves Versailles and Fontainebleau. It is permitted to ordinary citizens, and even foreigners, to wander through pavilions and gardens once sacred and forbidden. They may inspect the *Thê-Miêu*, the temple built by the second emperor of the Nguyên dynasty in veneration of the spirit of his father who in 1802 had united Viet-Nam under a single dynasty. They may visit the imperial throne hall, where emperors were first enthroned at the beginning of their reign and received the allegiance of their highest officials; prostration before the emperor on such occasions was abolished only in 1932. None of the buildings is impressive by its height, for the Vietnamese did not share the urge of the Indianized peoples of South East Asia to build upwards to the sky; but their spacious serenity reflects the search for harmony which pervaded all Vietnamese religion.

Not all however is preserved. When the visitor arrives at the centre of this inner city he will find no trace of the forbidden palaces of the imperial residence itself. At one edge of the area where they stood, the burnt-out shell of a minor pavilion bears witness to the destruction of the rest by fire. The destruction occurred early in February 1947, when the *Viêt-Minh* set fire to the palace before retreating in the face of reoccupying French forces. They had been virtually the government of this part of Viet-Nam for a period of eighteen months, since the seizure of power in Hanoi by Hô Chi Minh's provisional government. The last emperor of the dynasty, Bao-Dai, had abdicated on 25th August 1945; this destruction of his palace (and also, as far as is known, of the imperial seals) was a dramatic symbol of the transition from monarchy to republic.

The transition was not really so sudden, however. The Vietnamese monarchy had failed its subjects sixty years before in

allowing the French to establish their 'protectorate' over Annam
and Tongking. Although the French preserved the formalities of
rule by a Confucian court and its officials, the reality of power lay
with the Résident-Supérieur. Even those opponents of French
rule who wanted, in the early decades of this century, to put on
the throne a new monarch in place of the French nominee,
recognized that it would not be enough merely to restore
an independent Confucian regime. Their model was Japan,
whose monarchy had successfully responded to the Western
challenge by developing a constitutional government. As for
those who, after 1911, looked to China for inspiration, their aim
was to establish a republic of Viet-Nam and to have done with
monarchy altogether.

The forbidden palace at Huê had thus ceased to be the focus
of national life long before it went up in flames. Moreover
this decline and final collapse of the monarchy was a spiritual
as well as a political change, and it left a hole in traditional
society far greater than the lacuna on the ground at the centre of
the Huê citadel. The sanctity of the ruler had been central to
that society. But it could not survive untarnished the disaster of
material defeat at the hands of barbarian invaders. There was no
sharp distinction between politics and other aspects of life in the
Vietnamese tradition, and the Confucian monarchy had been
the keystone of a cultural edifice whose very foundations were
shaken by the victories of the West over the Middle Kingdom.
The whole traditional conception of the universe was called in
question by the failure of the monarchy, both in China and
Viet-Nam, to respond successfully to the challenge of the West.[1]

The fundamental contrast between the traditional culture of
Viet-Nam and that of the countries of Western Europe is readily
apparent if one compares their respective views of the individual
man, and their very different ideals of personal behaviour. In
Viet-Nam, the complete self-abnegation of Buddhism was demanded only of the minority of people who entered that religion.
But in the more 'secular' religions of Taoism and Confucianism,
the ideal was still one of restraint and personal detachment. Vietnamese children were (indeed still are) brought up to regard it
as very inferior behaviour to show any sign of their inner feelings

in their relationships with others. The Confucian *quan-tu* (Chinese *chün-tzu*)—a word very inadequately rendered into English by 'gentleman'—was one who had penetrated the moral order that embraces both man and nature and so knew how to live in harmony with it. He was admired for his self-control, his ability to keep silent and at the same time to apprehend the reality of things. To show emotion was to lose face, to reveal a weakness unworthy of the cultivated man. Nor was this ideal limited to Confucianism; it was shared by the Taoists, who sometimes spoke of the *phong-luu*: literally a man who would allow water to flow past him, by implication one who would remain unperturbed.

The historical figures most admired by the Vietnamese include not only men of action, like Trân Hung Dao and Lê Loi whose heroism lay in defeating the Chinese, but also men who knew how to wait. Among the most celebrated of these men of inaction was Nguyên Binh Khiêm, who rose to a position of prominence as a successful young scholar, but then in 1542 retired from the court and refused to become involved in the conflict between the Mac usurpers and the clans who wanted to restore the deposed dynasty of the Lê. He lived for forty years in his 'refuge of the White Cloud', from time to time giving advice to the leaders of both sides; and when he died, having achieved only the peace of his own mind, a temple was erected in veneration of his spirit. Such a career recalls to mind the advice of the *Tao Te Ching*:

> Know contentment and you will suffer no disgrace. Know when to stop, and you will meet with no danger. You can then endure.[2]

This philosophy of withdrawal and of personal harmony is alien to the modern Western outlook, in which only positive achievement commands unstinted praise. Nor would it have been very much more acceptable to the medieval Christian: for despite its great diversity the Christian tradition has as its central theme belief in grace and salvation in the sight of a personal and omnipotent God, a divine legislator whose judgment is the ultimate reality. To obtain that grace, men must be actively good. It must not be imagined however that the Vietnamese tradition never allowed for any action at all. One might say rather that, by contrast with the Western tradition, it gave equal weight to the inner and outer spheres of human existence, to inner response and external activity. This was the essence of the Confucian philosophy which, as it developed over the centuries, became the foundation of both Chinese and Vietnamese society. The Confucian state was held together by the belief that when men act according to the universal moral order, virtue is sure to prevail; when they assert themselves against it, there is chaos. The *Great Learning*, one of the most important classical texts from the twelfth century onwards, says that:

> When things are investigated,
> then true knowledge is achieved.
> When true knowledge is achieved,
> then the will becomes sincere.
> When the will is sincere,
> then the mind sees right.
> When the mind sees right,
> the personal life is cultivated.
> When the personal life is cultivated,
> then the family life is regulated.
> When the family life is regulated,
> then the national life is orderly.
> When the national life is orderly,
> then there is peace in the world. [3]

The person, the family, the nation. These were the three levels of existence, of participation in the moral order, which mattered to the Confucian scholar. The regulation and good order of all three were proof that universal harmony prevailed, and that Heaven would prosper the realm. The way to ensure this order was through the fulfilment of obligations: that of the son to his father, that of the pupil to his master, that of the subject to his ruler. It might have been possible to interpret the Confucian philosophy in a spirit of rebellion, for if the personal life of the emperor or of his officials was lacking in virtue and sincerity, then surely their fitness to rule was called in question. But in practice, Confucianism was essentially conservative. It was true that a ruler might lose the 'Mandate of Heaven', but if he was then deposed it was less a matter of human choice than of an impersonal decree of Fate. There is nothing in the classics about the person as an individual, possessing inalienable rights. The universal moral order sanctioned only obligations.

The Confucian monarchy was nevertheless quite different from the Western conception of absolute autocracy. The foundation of the Confucian order was neither human reason nor divine authority: it was the very nature of the universe itself. The continued harmony of the universe depended upon regular sacrifices to Heaven: therefore there must be an emperor, and as the Son of Heaven he must be obeyed as the highest of all human beings. In the West on the other hand the traditional king was first and foremost a maker of laws, and he derived his authority from an analogy between the king in his kingdom and God in His Heaven. The whole attitude to action and achievement which characterizes Western civilization is rooted in the tradition of Christianity. Western man has tended to imitate his omnipotent God, and has sought to be both legislator over society and master of the natural laws which govern the physical world.[4]

The same conception of God did not exist in traditional China or Viet-Nam. To say that their tradition had no personal God at all would be misleading: it would be more precise to say that they distinguished (in practice, not in theory) between two levels of the supernatural, Heaven and the spirits. Personality was an attribute not of Heaven but of spirits, which were legion. Often they were the souls of departed men: in the cult of the ancestors it was incumbent upon every man to venerate the spirits of his own forebears, and any man who was unfortunate enough to have no progeny to perform rites for his soul after death would become a 'wandering soul', a burden to himself and to the world. Not all spirits were regarded as inevitably good; wandering spirits indeed were capable of positive harm to man, whilst the spirits of mountains and waters had to be correctly appeased or they would become wayward. Certain spirits however were especially beneficent, and men would appeal for protection to their wisdom and virtue. Every village had its protective spirit: sometimes an ancestor of one of the village clans, sometimes a famous hero with local connections. The kingdom as a whole was protected by the ancestral spirits of the imperial dynasty, in whose honour there were elaborate temples in the precincts of the capital. In addition there were special hero cults associated with the spirits of men like Trân Hung Dao or Nguyên Binh Khiêm, whose virtue in life gave his soul great power after death. Not surprisingly, people came to regard Confucius, or the mythical Lao-Tzu, or the innumerable manifestations of the Buddha, as spirits of a very high order. The nearest the Vietnamese tradition came to a religion like Christianity was in the sects which venerated some spirit as supreme over all the rest. But they do not appear to have seen their protector as a judge: rather, his virtue made him infinitely compassionate, and salvation through him called only for devotion and faith. Such was, and still is, the nature of Amidist Buddhism, in which the spirit worshipped is that of the former Buddha Amitabha.

For the educated Confucian Vietnamese, however, the supreme position was reserved for Heaven, whose Way was the highest possible way of virtue. This supremacy, over spirits and men alike, was not that of a personal legislator, but of an impersonal moral force. Heaven was simply 'there', transcending all conflicts and activity, the source of infinite harmony, uniting in itself both the positive and negative elements of the universe. The decree of Heaven was not seen as a code of laws so much as a chain of Fate. Fate made sense of the experiences of the individual, and prevented the diversity and apparent contradictions of earthly life from interfering with his search for harmony.

In the medieval West of course, the power of making earthly laws was not that of the king alone: authority was divided between Church and State, in accordance with the doctrine of 'Render unto Caesar'. Conflicts between King and Bishop (or Pope) paved the way for a theory of limited sovereignty: it became natural for Westerners to think in terms of an authority that had more than one arm. This too was quite alien to the Confucian system: one might say that system was monolithic, whereas that of medieval Christendom was 'duolithic'. The contrast finds a curious symbol in the game of chess. In Western chess the centre of the board is shared by two pieces, the king and his consort; and power is divided between them. In Vietnamese (that is, Chinese) chess a single piece occupies the central position, the general flanked by his two scholar-advisers.[5] Yet there is irony in this comparison, for the general does not combine the power of both king and consort in the Western game. He stands alone, but he is confined to the eight points closest to his own spot. It was the West, and not East Asia, that produced the idea of absolute state power, in which the authority of Church and State were mercilessly combined. Perhaps the reason was that the Western king was forced to compete with the Church for the loyalty of his subjects. Eventually he would assert his own temporal power and deny the spiritual claims of the Church to be the guardian of absolute truth. When royal absolutism produced its own reaction, a new conflict developed between the totalitarian and the democratic views of the state: a conflict which is held by many to be the most important single theme in modern Western history. But it was a conflict which would have been utterly unintelligible to the traditional Confucian ruler or scholar.

Those who have sought to explain 'oriental despotism' in the same terms as occidental totalitarianism, of the kind practised by Hitler or Stalin, have failed to take account of all this, and also of the fundamental difference between Eastern (that is, Chinese and Vietnamese) and Western modes of logic.[6] The traditional mode of logic found in the West, from Aristotle onwards, has had as its fundamental aim the desire to arrive at some definitive truth: in other words, to eliminate contradiction. The archetype of the method is the syllogism, in which the apparent contradiction between two statements is resolved by a third. To say that the syllogism never occurred in traditional Chinese thought would be tendentious, and would beg a number of difficult questions about the interpretation of Buddhist and Mohist texts. But the syllogism was certainly not characteristic of Chinese and Vietnamese logic, and it is not found in the Confucian classics which were the staple diet of the scholar's education. The characteristic mode of logic there was 'conditional', embracing two statements rather than three: for example, in the text just quoted, 'when things are investigated, then true knowledge is achieved'. It seems to have been generally true that when the Chinese or the Vietnamese scholar was faced with two ideas, he was always far more interested in discovering how they complemented one another than in exploring possible contradictions between them. Contradictions were resolved by Heaven: by man they must be simply accepted.

Thus Confucianism contained no philosophical basis for an insistence on the conformity of men's minds to one absolute truth. As a political orthodoxy Confucianism all but deified the emperor. But it did not compel him to defend and develop his power against a rival source of authority, nor did it lead him along the path of the modern dictator to seek control over his subjects' every thought and deed. The harmony upon which the supremacy of the emperor was based was the harmony of the universe, not a man-made harmony created by the elimination of contradiction from human minds. Being itself absolute, universal harmony had no need of absolutism.

Obligations to parents and to emperor were the cement of the Confucian order; but specific obligations were not hereditary. In this respect the Sino-Vietnamese tradition was much less severe on the individual than Hinduism, for there was no rigid caste system in Confucianism. In order to govern according to the universal moral order, the monarch had not only to be himself a man of virtue, but he had to choose virtuous men from all quarters of his realm to assist him. The measure of virtue was not birth, nor wealth, but learning. Consequently imperial officials were selected by means of regular examinations in the Confucian classics, to which all men of landowning families were allowed access. (And in a society where partible inheritance was the rule, a great many people had land.) The ownership of land in itself conferred nothing: to belong to the 'aristocracy' or 'gentry' of traditional Vietnamese society a man had to be educated and had to prove his education. Even in times when titles were sold by the court, the highest dignity and probably the highest offices were accorded only to those whose learning was genuine and who had passed the examinations.

The emperor and his hierarchy of scholar-officials took the place of both Church and State in traditional Vietnamese society. This left no room for any other 'established' religion, either Buddhist or Taoist. There was no officially recognized Buddhist *Sangha* such as existed in the Theravada countries like Burma and Siam.[7] Taoist 'masters' and Buddhist monks were either quite isolated from one another, or they were grouped into sects whose character was more analogous to the Vietnamese clan than to a Western Church. The master of the sect occupied the position of the clan-chief, and the duty of the pupil to his master was as binding as that of filial piety within the clan. Moreover, just as the clan would tend to divide into separate branches after a number of generations, so too a sect which prospered and grew was very likely to divide into two or more smaller sects after the death of its master. Thus Taoism and Buddhism lacked the kind of institutional framework of discipline that was necessary to hold together as one body all those who shared the same beliefs. And where there was no framework for orthodoxy, there was no problem of heresy.

Once again the contrast between East and West is very striking, for Christianity is very much a religion of orthodoxy. More, it is a religion of conversion and proselytizing, which means that it immediately identifies a man as either one of the faithful or not: Christian or pagan, orthodox or a heretic. Religion thus tends to define the community, and in medieval Christendom at least, it was the pastor and his cure of souls which tended to hold the local community of the parish together. In East Asia, on the contrary, it was the community which defined religious activity and there were many cults in which only a man born into the community (or initiated into it) could really participate. Thus the member of a clan had his own ancestors, the member of a village his own protective spirit to venerate. Likewise the member of a sect had his own teacher to follow, and acquired his beliefs from his master. There were many sects and there appears to have been no strong tendency for any one of them to claim the supremacy of a proselytizing religion. There was room for the eclectic attitude to religion which so often strikes the student of Chinese or Vietnamese society. 'Let a hundred flowers bloom, let a hundred schools of thought contend.' But the contention was not a matter of absolutes: the Vietnamese saw no philosophical necessity for one school to triumph over all the rest.

Thus there was no philosophical reason why Confucianism, the religion of the state, should find itself incompatible with the more personal religions of Taoism and Buddhism. There was nothing in the religions themselves to prevent a scholar from being a Confucian in his public life and a Buddhist or Taoist at home. A favourite Vietnamese illustration of the harmony between the religions, albeit one drawn from an early period, is the story of the emperor Trân Thai-Tong (1228–58). Wishing to escape the complexities of court politics and the heavy responsibilities of government, he left his palace one night early in his reign, and went secretly to the hills to become a pupil of the Zen master Truc-Lâm. But the aged monk advised him: 'Buddha is not in the mountains, Buddha is in the heart of man. When your mind is calm and clear, Buddha appears.' Summoned back to the capital, Thai-Tong returned to become both a Confucian

monarch and a patron of the Buddhism of the Bamboo Forest.[8]
The sphere of Confucianism was the external order of society;
the inner life of the person was left to the other religions.

But now we must face a paradox. For there were times when
religions other than Confucianism appear to have been persecuted
by the court. More than that, the whole history of Viet-Nam
shows a society often quite incapable of living up to its ideals of
good order and social harmony. It is a history full of dynastic
conflicts, rebellions and wars. Quite apart from wars against
external enemies—China in the north, Champa and Cambodia
in the south—there have been periods when the country has all
but disintegrated from within. Clan against clan, region against
region, the conflicts fill the chronicles of Viet-Nam from the
sixteenth to the nineteenth centuries. How is this paradox to be
explained?

Part of the explanation lies in the nature of the Confucian
hierarchy itself. In theory at least, the official career was open to
talent: therefore learning itself had to be open to talent. The
effect of the examination system in practice was that there were
always some men who had more education than responsibility.
Knowledge of Chinese characters and of political principles was
not the monopoly of a caste or sect, or even of a successful elite.
There were village schoolmasters who had once hoped to become
high officials. Worse still, there were sons of mandarins who
failed to attain the same level of scholarship as their fathers and
were thus prevented from inheriting their influence within the
state.

Of course there was a compensatory distinction to be gained
in running the affairs of a clan or village. But for some that was
not enough. Sometimes they turned to religion, for in a religion
of small sects an ambitious individual might rise to a position of
some importance. In some sects it was necessary to become a
monk and to leave the civil life altogether; in others the priests
were hardly distinguishable from laymen, and the sect was
virtually a secret society with its own hierarchy of officials. It
is not easy to draw a hard and fast line between secret societies
whose character was fundamentally religious, and others whose
main concern was with politics or with banditry and crime.

The Heaven and Earth Society for example, which developed in China in the late seventeenth century, almost certainly had its roots in some kind of religious sect; but the story of its formal creation and early history is largely political since it became the vehicle of opposition in South China to the new dynasty of the Manchus. Later on, when its name and forms of initiation were taken overseas by the Nanyang Chinese in the nineteenth century, it became in many cases little more than an association of criminals and a protection racket. This same society had branches in Viet-Nam, and there were other societies of a similar kind.[9] If the leaders of such a society were truly religious, its character would be truly that of a sect. But if they were men of political ambition, they would make it into an instrument of political opposition; it might even sponsor an open revolt.

Beneath the surface of Confucian order therefore, there existed an underworld of secret societies and political revolt. Sometimes the opportunity for action was created by factions within the imperial court and bureaucracy: a crisis there might well be the signal for revolt in the country. In other cases the opportunity arose from the grievances of the peasantry, and a rebel leader might recruit a large following in a particular area, to create what amounted to virtually a private army. It was because secret associations were likely to become involved in this kind of activity that it was necessary for the Confucian court to keep a watchful eye on the sects of the Taoists and Buddhists.

From time to time decrees were issued insisting on correct principles in all branches of social life, and declaring that this or that sect should be suppressed. But what appears to us as religious persecution arose more often than not from political motives rather than from any desire to impose doctrinal ortho-doxy for its own sake. From the seventeenth century onwards, Christianity was liable to be treated in a similar manner, and in the decades after 1825 the persecution of Christianity became a regular policy of succeeding emperors. But it was not the religion of the missionaries that was under attack. The Vietnamese court simply regarded the Catholics as a new kind of sect, with foreign priests taking the place of the Buddhist monk or the Taoist master. Their fear was not for Confucianism as a religion or a philosophy, but for their own position in power. If there had been a single religious Order or Church, of whatever beliefs, it would have been relatively easy for the emperor or his ministers to control it by disciplining its leaders. But the smallness of the sects, and yet the speed with which they could combine under an able leader, made periodic persecution the only way of dealing with them.[10]

The apparent contradiction between the philosophy of harmony and the reality of political conflict does not seem to have troubled Vietnamese scholars. To oppose the idea of harmony on the philosophical plane would have been almost to oppose Fate itself. Nor did successful rebellion lead to serious ideological conflicts. A new ruler who emerged from a rebellion, whatever its original religious character, would tend very quickly to take over Confucian institutions and would use the theory of the Mandate of Heaven to justify his new position. The period since 1500 has seen at least four occasions when rebellion and civil war grew out of the kind of circumstances just described, three of which led to the establishment of new dynasties.

To a Westerner the Vietnamese tradition seems to abound in paradox. It is perhaps necessary therefore to reiterate the importance of Fate as the unifying force of everything under Heaven. The Vietnamese conception of Fate is best revealed in the 'national poem', *Doan Truong Tân Thanh*, usually known as the *Kim Vân Kiêu*.[11] Its theme is the conflict between talent and Fate. Thuy Kiêu, a beautiful and talented girl of good family, falls in love with the equally gifted Kim Trung. But in order to save her father from the clutches of a cruel mandarin, she sells herself in marriage to a stranger. Her exemplary filial piety is rewarded with nothing but suffering for fifteen years, for she discovers that she has sold herself into prostitution. How could such a thing happen, the author asks? How could Heaven fail so conspicuously to reward virtue by success?

> Everything here below flows from the will of Heaven. It is Heaven which assigns to every human being his Fate.
> Why does it distribute favours as it does, giving to one person both talent and destiny?
> In order that he who has talent shall not use it to glorify himself.
> If a heavy *karma* weighs down our destiny, let us not accuse Heaven of injustice.

The root of goodness lies in ourselves.
Let us cultivate that goodness of heart which is worth more than talent.

Kiêu's fate is that she must suffer for the heavy *karma* she has acquired by her sins in a previous existence: Buddhist and Confucian beliefs are accepted here as part of a single system of morality. When Heaven is satisfied that she has expiated her sin, only then is she allowed to return to Kim Trung. Heaven is judge, but not in a spirit of salvation or damnation once and for all: the chain of existence is virtually unending. Fate is unmoved by human suffering, but it is not blind to human virtue; and there is virtue in the very acceptance of Fate rather than in struggling against it.

Nguyên Du, author of the poem, was a man who himself suffered deeply. Having supported the unsuccessful Lê dynasty of Hanoi at the end of the eighteenth century, he was condemned by his own destiny to witness the triumph of the new emperors of Huê, and to be forced to offer allegiance to Gia-Long. Rather than rebel, he accepted the decree of Fate and retired to the seclusion of his home village in Ha-Tinh province. Withdrawal was not however the only answer to adversity or challenge of which the Vietnamese were capable. It would be truer to say that Fate, the arbiter between success and failure in any human enterprise, was the deciding factor between action and inaction. If Fate seemed unfavourable, it was better not to act: Nguyên Du's withdrawal was characteristic of a man who felt himself defeated by Fate. But a man who believed that destiny was on his side would act with determination and courage.

This helps to explain the importance in traditional Vietnamese society of geomancers and astrologers, and of spirit mediums. Such people had special powers to enable them to discover what Fate intended in any situation. The *thây-phap* (whom the French called a 'sorcerer') was universally respected as a man who could site houses or tombs in such a way as to protect them from evil spirits, or who could calculate a man's horoscope so that he may avoid unlucky encounters or unpropitious times to act. That role extended moreover to politics. Rebel movements were very often led by men who claimed supernatural powers, whether as Buddhist monks or as Taoist masters, because men of that kind had the best chance of convincing their followers that Heaven, or the stars, or the spirits, were on their side.[12] In warfare too, armies would join battle only when one at least of the commanders was convinced that he was destined to victory; the horoscope of a superstitious general might play as important a part in his campaign as military skill. To risk a conflict against the will of Heaven was not only to court disaster but to act against the whole moral order of the universe.

When the French conquered Viet-Nam, the first reactions of the scholars were what one would expect from the nature of the tradition. Some followed the example of Nguyên Khuyên, a famous poet who withdrew to the seclusion of his native village in Tongking. Others, like Phan Dinh Phung, refused to accept that Fate was against them, and fought on for ten years and more.[13] But gradually a small minority of intellectuals came to see the French as something more than conquerors whose cause had been temporarily espoused by a cruel Fate. They began to see them as men of a new kind, whose success stemmed from a philosophy which rejected Fate altogether, and which therefore presented a challenge to the whole of Vietnamese civilization.

II

The Tradition Challenged

'OUR hearts are like iron and stone: they will never tremble.'
In those words the poet Phan Van Tri, writing in the 1860s,
defied the barbarians of the Western Seas. They occurred in the
course of a celebrated literary exchange between himself and his
contemporary Tôn Tho Tuong. Both men were natives of the
Vietnamese provinces which were ceded to France in 1862, but
whereas Phan Van Tri withdrew to his village and lived as a
schoolmaster after the conquest, Tôn Tho Tuong chose to serve
the French, and continued to do so until his death fifteen years
later. It was in order to justify this choice that Tuong wrote a
series of ten poems, to which Tri replied line for line.[1] The contrast
between their points of view was one which was to recur throughout the period in which the French ruled Viet-Nam. Tuong had
been to Europe, and saw the futility of attempting to resist a
foreign power which derived its strength from long lines of telegraph wires and from powerful engines emitting great clouds of
steam and smoke: he advised his countrymen to make peace for
the time being, in order to learn from their enemies. Tri, less
impressed by feats of technology, saw the issue solely in terms of
spirit: the only hope of eventual victory was to refuse ever to
admit defeat.

The two decades from 1860 to 1880, virtually the interval
between the first loss of Vietnamese territory to France and the
final establishment of a French protectorate over Tongking and
Annam, were a turning-point throughout East Asia. By 1870,
Japan had set out upon the road which led to a strong centralized
government and technological Westernization. In China too,
following the suppression of the Tai-Ping rebellion and other
disturbances, the 1860s saw the 'Tung-Chih Restoration' under
which men like Tseng Kuo-fan made their own attempt to
strengthen the country, but failed to establish sufficiently that
centralized control which was so important for the Japanese

success. In Viet-Nam, the reign of Tu-Duc (1848–83) was
the one period when the traditional monarchy might there too
have come to terms with the West, and possibly avoided the
fate of being the only country in the Chinese-speaking world to
be actually ruled by Europeans. Although that fate was not
avoided, it is to this period that we must look in order to find the
beginnings of the Vietnamese response to the Western challenge.

The first important embassy of the court of Huê to the courts
of Europe—in fact to Paris and Madrid—was that led by Phan
Thanh Gian in 1863. Its object, not achieved, was to secure the
return of the three provinces ceded to France by treaty in the
previous year. Its impressions of the West are recorded in the
diary which Gian kept from day to day, and which has survived
in the Huê archives.[2] The envoys were especially impressed by
the concrete achievements of French civilization: the speed of
travel by steamship and by railway, the artificial lighting in the
streets at night, and the many kinds of factories that they were
invited to inspect. But when one comes to the less material
aspects of French culture and institutions, it is less easy to gauge
their impressions. When referring in the diary to the dignitaries
and officials of the Napoleonic court, they made no attempt to
find a terminology that would indicate the differences between
French institutions and their own. They used Vietnamese titles
to designate the officials who received them, and they referred to
the Church as the Ministry of Rites. Although the diary reveals
hardly anything of the ambassador's innermost thoughts and
reflections, its content does not suggest that he or his colleagues
had any deep understanding of the institutions and ideas that
underlay Western engineering achievement.

The Vietnamese of this period who were most likely to develop
such an understanding were not the Confucian officials of the
imperial government, but the Catholics who had received an
education from the missionary priests. One such man, who in
fact accompanied the envoys to Paris and Madrid in 1863,
working as an interpreter for the French, was Petrus Truong
Vinh Ky. He had studied in a Catholic college at Penang in the
1850s, and although he too was making his first visit to the West,
he was going with some idea in his mind of what to expect, and
some realization of the cultural differences between his own
country and France. He stayed in Europe for several years, and

did not return to Saigon until 1867 when he took up a teaching position in the French school for officials there. In a long series of publications between then and his death in 1898 he took upon himself the task of trying to explain Western knowledge to the Vietnamese, and of providing more information about Viet-Nam for the French. For example, in 1867 he produced (in French) the first grammar of the Vietnamese language; and ten years later the first French history of Viet-Nam.[3]

Truong Vinh Ky, like Tôn Tho Tuong, chose to work for the French: their understanding of the West therefore, such as it was, was not a factor in the affairs of Tu-Duc's empire. There were, however, others with some knowledge of Western learning who chose to remain in the independent region of the country and who from time to time pressed the government to make reforms. Probably the most articulate of them was Nguyên Truong Tô, a native of Nghê-An province and a convert to Christianity. In 1859, at the age of about thirty, he was taken by his teachers to Italy and France, where he spent several years studying a wide range of Western subjects. He returned about the time of the first loss of territory to France. Never having passed any of the Confucian examinations (although he knew Chinese characters) he was not eligible for any important office; his only political position was that of private secretary to the governor of his native province during the 1860s. Nevertheless during the eight years preceding his death in 1871 he submitted to the throne at least fourteen memorials advocating a variety of policies of reform. He argued that to oppose France openly would lead only to disaster, whereas to seek French assistance and friendship would allow the Vietnamese to learn from the foreigners and eventually strengthen their own country by imitating France. He proposed that students be sent to France to learn new techniques in agriculture and industry, and to master new methods of warfare. He advocated policies to strengthen the economy by developing trade and manufactures. He himself was especially interested in mining and put forward detailed plans for developing the minerals of Central Viet-Nam. Some of his memorials reflect the same attitudes as the proposals put forward in China during the 1860s by Tseng Kuo-fan and Li Hung-chang, the most progressive of the new generation of officials serving the Ch'ing dynasty.

Nguyên Truong Tô's plans were not entirely without result.

He appears to have won over the governor of Nghê-An to his project for developing mines, and was on the point of recruiting French technicians for that purpose when hostilities were renewed in Cochinchina in 1867.[4] But the chances of the imperial court as a whole being converted to his ideas were very slender. There was little hope of action to implement such proposals as that for a sweeping reform of the bureaucracy to eliminate corruption, or a reorganization of judicial procedures to separate the power of magistrates from that of administrators. The court of Huê was dominated at this time by an older generation of men, set in their ways and unlikely to accept any deviation from Confucian orthodoxy. The most powerful minister was Nguyên Tri Phuong, whose influence was brought to an end only by his death in 1873 whilst fighting the French at Hanoi. In other circumstances it might have been possible for Phan Thanh Gian to emerge as the leader of a reform party, opposed to Phuong; for he was a man of the same generation as the arch-conservative, as well as having first-hand experience of the West. But following his return from Paris empty-handed in 1864, the remainder of his career was taken up by further efforts to oust the French from Cochinchina. When he failed to prevent their seizing still more territory in 1867 he took poison; and the following year he was deprived by the emperor of all his official titles and distinction. The man who might have been the reformer became the scapegoat for something which timely reform might conceivably have prevented.

Nor was very much more done during the 1870s, after the death of Phuong. In 1873, when the French seized Hanoi for a time, a younger official named Bui Viên was sent to Hong Kong to make contact with some Western power other than France, and from there he went to the United States.[5] He appears to have been well received by the American President; but with the (temporary) disappearance of the French threat, the Vietnamese did not pursue the relationship. Bui Viên was appointed to be head of naval transport, and devoted his energy to the suppression of piracy in the hope of making the South China Sea safer for trade. It was not long however before French pressure was renewed. In 1882 a French administration more ready to expand the colonial empire set in motion the policy which led to the virtual annexation of Annam and Tongking. In 1885, after a Franco-Chinese war in which the victories were by no means all on one side, the Chinese surrendered to France their claims to the 'protection' of Viet-Nam.

The French conquest brought to an end the period in which it was meaningful to talk of the possible 'self-strengthening' of Viet-Nam within a traditional monarchical framework. For the next two generations and more, modernization would be intimately bound up with the problem of obtaining independence. But within the framework of colonial rule, or 'protection', the old questions still demanded an answer: what attitude ought the Vietnamese to take towards their conquerors? Could anything be gained by co-operation with the West, by seeking to learn from the West? And if so, what was the proper relationship between the culture and institutions of the past, and the ideas and institutions to be borrowed from the West? The exchange of poems between Tôn Tho Tuong and Phan Van Tri, and the opposition between the Nguyên Tri Phuongs and men like Nguyên Truong Tô, were merely the first round of a debate on the relevance of foreign culture for Viet-Nam which was to last throughout the era of French rule, and which is in a sense still not concluded today.

It was of course impossible that Viet-Nam should make no response at all to the Western challenge. The cause of Phan Van Tri was doomed, once colonial rule was firmly established. But his spirit did not die: throughout the French period there were those who believed that whatever the West had to teach there should be no compromise with the particular Frenchmen who were governing Viet-Nam. They were very often those who believed that Asians could supersede the achievements of the West by means of a revolution which Europe itself had not yet experienced: their heirs are the present-day Communists. Opposed to them were those Vietnamese who believed in an adaptation to the culture and institutions of the Europeans. They did not necessarily favour political subservience to the French government, but they saw in their relationship with the West an opportunity to develop Viet-Nam's own potential for progress. Although the various anti-Communist groups in South Viet-Nam today do not claim direct descent from the Westernizers of previous generations, their willingness to accept American aid stems from a fundamentally similar attitude towards the West.

One finds an analogy with this conflict between different reactions to occidental culture if one looks at China's experience in the same period (since, say, 1860). Indeed, though it was never actually conquered by a single Western power, China faced many of the same problems as Viet-Nam, and given the Vietnamese habit of looking towards China for inspiration it is not surprising that some of the major Chinese thinkers of modern times have had considerable influence on the modern intellectual development of the Vietnamese. No apology is necessary therefore if we refer from time to time to the writings of those Chinese scholars which are better known in the West than those of Vietnamese, thanks to the efforts of American historians during the past few decades. Professor Levenson's study on the modern fate of Confucian China, in particular, draws together a number of conclusions of great relevance to Viet-Nam.[6]

What does Westernization mean in this context? The French colonial administrators, with their claims to a 'mission civilisatrice' and their philosophy of 'assimilation' (to be discussed in a later chapter), sometimes spoke as if they expected their Asian subjects eventually to become Frenchmen in all essential respects—though they provided educational facilities for only a small minority to do so in practice. But such a complete transformation of a whole population was out of the question; and in any case, with the exception of a tiny minority, the Vietnamese themselves did not want to become Westerners. What they wanted at the very most was to change, according to Western principles, the Viet-Nam to which they would always and inevitably belong. Westernization therefore involved some kind of interweaving of occidental and oriental cultures, not a wholesale replacement of one by the other.

Chinese Westernizers of the 1860s and 1870s, and perhaps too Vietnamese like Nguyên Truong Tô, saw the problem in simple terms. Their philosophy was one of *t'i-yung*: in Vietnamese *thi-dung*. They believed in imitating the West in matters of utility (*yung*), but in maintaining their own traditional values in matters of substance or essence (*t'i*). This was more reasonable than later critics of the philosophy supposed. The Confucian tradition had distinguished between the inner and the outer affairs of man, and had even allowed a man to be inwardly Taoist or Buddhist so long as he was outwardly a Confucian. Moreover, it was very much a tradition of pragmatism in material things, so that a man could be a Taoist at heart, a Confucian in politics, and still a very practical man in such fields as the building of dykes or the designing of gadgets. The type of man who was both a poet and a very practical administrator is well illustrated in nineteenth-century Viet-Nam by the career of Nguyên Công Tru (1778–1858). His poetry is full of the joys of living and the ephemeral nature of life. But in his career as an official under Minh-Mang he was responsible for one of the major engineering feats of pre-colonial Vietnamese history: the bringing under cultivation of about 10,000 hectares of alluvial rice land in the coastal province of Thai-Binh.[7] If the techniques of irrigation were independent of belief in Taoist meditation or Confucian institutions, then why should not Western steam engines and telegraph lines be seen in similar light? Why should it have occurred to the Vietnamese (or the Chinese) of the Tu-Duc period that the material achievements of their new enemies were inseparably bound up with a cultural and institutional milieu totally different from their own?

It was towards the end of the nineteenth century that the Chinese, or at least a few of them, began to appreciate that the West presented a challenge to their institutions as well as to their technology. One of their reasons for doing so was the success of Japan, where technological and institutional reform went hand in hand. The *t'i-yung* philosophy did not adequately account for the relationship between institutions and material strength: were institutions part of the substance, or merely an aspect of utility? Confucianism was both a system of government and a framework of values: indeed its strength derived from the fact that it related institutions directly to the nature of the universe as a whole. This made it difficult to attempt a purely utilitarian reform of institutions without undertaking a complete re-evaluation of Confucianism.

It was in response to this difficulty that in 1897 the Chinese scholar K'ang Yu-wei published his treatise *A Study of Confucius as a Reformer of Institutions*. He tried to replace the established conservative interpretation of Confucius' teachings by one which would allow for change: to demonstrate that the essentials of the Confucian canon were in no way incompatible with reform, but even demanded it. In the following year K'ang and his disciples captured the ear of the young emperor at Peking, only to be hounded out by a conservative coup before they had time to make any serious reforms. Following the Boxer 'rebellion' the regime began—under the pressure of still greater Western interference in China—to attempt its own modernization. K'ang Yu-wei, still out of favour, watched the attempt from Japan or from whatever part of the world he was visiting. But when the Chinese monarchy finally collapsed he was too much of a Confucian to support the Revolution. His last appearance on the political scene was as one of the promoters of the vain bid to restore the emperor in 1917.

K'ang's leading disciple however, Liang Ch'i-ch'ao, was prepared to follow the logic of institutional reform beyond the Confucian framework altogether. His most important writings belong to the years 1899–1905, when he too was in exile in Japan or travelling around the world; but he continued to be an influential figure in Chinese thought down to his death in 1929, for he was willing to accept that the monarchy was not the only possible focus of political life.[8] Like many young Chinese in the 1890s, Liang had been enthralled by the Chinese translation of McKenzie's *Nineteenth Century*, a Spencerian tract of little importance in the West but one in which an Asian could find reflected all the assumptions and prejudices of the popular occidental belief in progress. Liang's conclusion was that if China was weak it was because her cultural tradition had been paralysed by complacency, so that she had failed to progress. Evolution was the result of incessant competition between the peoples of the world, of whom only the fittest could survive. But China had fallen into the error of supposing that no other people had any civilization at all: that the rest of the earth was populated by inferior barbarians. Naturally she was overwhelmed when other civilized people appeared at her gates. The question for Liang's generation was obvious: how can China begin again to progress? Whereas K'ang could see only the possibility of reform within the Chinese tradition itself, Liang began to study the history and institutions of the West, and to think in terms of deliberate imitation of countries like England and France. For the superiority of the West must surely derive from the nature of occidental progress.

Liang attached the greatest importance not only to institutions but also to the role of thinkers in influencing institutional development. He traced the origins of Western progress to the intellectual movement of the seventeenth century, which overthrew the authoritarianism of the medieval schoolmen and set the scene for the eventual overthrow of traditional conceptions of political authority as well. The true heroes of these developments were not great kings or politicians, but men like Luther, Bacon, Descartes, and Rousseau: men who asserted their right to think for themselves. China must follow their example and so emancipate itself from the strait-jacket of ancient authority. In identifying K'ang Yu-wei with Martin Luther, as leader of a Confucian Reformation, Liang may have seen himself in the role of a Chinese Descartes.

Liang's writings were almost certainly very influential in Viet-Nam, where they contributed to a new kind of national movement that began in the first decade of the twentieth century. Phan Bôi Châu, who went to Japan in 1905 hoping to get help for the Vietnamese reformers, returned home with copies of Liang's writings and distributed them widely amongst his friends.[9] We must explore the development of this and other Vietnamese movements in a later chapter: they did not all remain under the influence of Liang for long, but the initial impact of his ideas was irreversible. When it came to proposals for action, Liang was a constitutionalist: at first he wanted a reformed monarchy, though later he was willing to work under a constitutional republic. But for much of the time his concern was not with precise forms of government but with China's conception of its place in the world. China must see itself as a single nation, one amongst many in the world, or there was a danger that the penalty for claiming to be more than a state would be to become less than a sovereign nation. Liang himself was present at the Versailles conference when the official Chinese delegation refused to sign a treaty that appeared to tolerate Japanese aggression in Shantung. Twenty years before that, he had written an essay on patriotism in which he identified loyalty to the nation as one of the most important sources of Western progress. This was especially relevant for the Vietnamese, whose place in the world had been transformed by the French conquest. Ought not Viet-Nam also to strive to become a nation?

The concept of the nation supplied what the *t'i-yung* philosophy had lacked: a focus for institutional reform. It was of course in itself a borrowing from the West, and moreover even in the West it was of relatively recent development. It grew out of the conflicts of the sixteenth and seventeenth centuries in which the kings of a number of major states in Europe succeeded in replacing the medieval principle of papal suzerainty in spiritual affairs by the principle of *cuius regio eius religio*. That victory was of the greatest importance for Asia; for it amounted to a secularization of the state, without which Western theories of politics and law would not have been readily intelligible to Asians. The Vietnamese, for example, would have made little sense of political doctrines couched in terms of the duality of supreme authority, for as we have seen such duality was alien to their own tradition.

Also during the sixteenth and seventeenth centuries, kings were in many cases able to destroy what remained of the power of their feudal nobility, and to replace the feudal concept of lord and vassal by the modern notion of the state as consisting of a prince and his subjects. By about 1700 European political theory had begun to move in the direction that was to lead to the principle of the sovereign equality of nations in international law. That principle found its fullest expression in the creation of the League of Nations in 1919, and the enunciation of the Wilsonian doctrine of national self-determination. It was no doubt intended at the time to apply primarily to the post-imperial situation of Central and Eastern Europe. But inevitably it had great appeal for Asians in search of new concepts that might satisfy their increasingly ambitious aspirations. In the atmosphere of the Versailles Peace Conference the Chinese felt bold enough to refuse formal concessions to Japan. Earlier that year, a young Vietnamese tried to present to the same Conference a cahier of his own country's claims to greater justice, but was refused a hearing. As Nguyên Ai Quôc and later Hô Chi Minh, the same young man was to play a prominent role in the struggle to create a nation of Viet-Nam by less gentle means than the submission of demands.

The desire for nationhood became for the Vietnamese a focus for their borrowings from the West. They need not swallow occidental culture whole: they now had a criterion for deciding whether any particular idea was useful to them or not. Anything that served to help Viet-Nam to become an independent nation was of value; other aspects of Western civilization could be rejected. There were in fact two themes in modern European thought which were of especial relevance to this aim of nation-building: first, the development of what might be called economic rationalism; second, the increasing concern of political thinkers with the need to relate the system of government to the aspirations of the people.

By economic rationalism, I mean the tendency to make decisions about livelihood according to the best available rational opinion, with a view to getting the highest possible return for one's efforts, and to do this consciously, though not necessarily in relation to any theory or plan. On the level of the family or the individual enterprise, this is what Weber and Tawney referred to as the 'spirit of capitalism'. On the level of the state it has led to a variety of economic philosophies whose central feature was the desire to increase the wealth of nations. The Chinese Westernizer Yen Fu, who translated Adam Smith's *Wealth of Nations* into Chinese in 1900, believed that the most important of all factors in the rise of the Western powers was their spirit of economic enterprise.[10] On a more mundane level, one finds that Asians tend generally to regard materialism as an essentially occidental view of life. But their eagerness to strengthen their own countries has led many of them to become extremely materialistic themselves. It is a fallacy to suppose that twentieth-century Asia rejects materialism out of some vague respect for a religious tradition which in earlier centuries probably did limit some men's eagerness for wealth. The tendency to measure success, especially political success, in terms of material achievement was one of the most penetrating effects of the Western impact on Asia, and it has transcended most of the differences of opinion and policy that have divided Asian politicians during and after the colonial period.

Those differences are very much more apparent when it comes to questions about the proper relationship between government and people. When the Vietnamese, or indeed any Asians, asked themselves what political system had accounted for the triumphs of the West, Europe did not answer with one voice.

The arguments of Rousseau for example could be used to justify polities as different as representational democracy or totalitarian dictatorship, whilst the ideas of Hegel about the importance of the nation-state led, by some strange logic, to the doctrines of Marx who regarded nations as of little import by comparison with the struggle between classes. In the twentieth century European politics and international relations became increasingly dominated by struggles whose basis was to a greater or lesser extent ideological. How then were Asians to decide which Western theories to adopt themselves? It is not surprising that they sometimes found themselves transferring to their own countries conflicts which the West had seemingly failed to resolve. But in every emergent nation in Asia some kind of decision on issues of this kind was essential. The reform of institutions could not take place without raising the question of the place of 'the people' in the new political system.

Amongst the Chinese thinkers who addressed themselves to these problems of economic change and political development in the early years of this century, one of the most important was Sun Yat-sen. Whereas Liang Ch'i-ch'ao had concentrated on the nature of progress and the institutional development of the nation, Sun's principal concern was with the material development of China, which he believed could only be achieved through revolution. Sun was apparently introduced to the idea of revolution as a political method by the Russian *émigrés* whom he met in London in 1896.[11] It is very likely that they were Populists rather than Marxists, which may explain why Sun was not deeply impressed by Marxism at this stage in his career. Not sharing Liang's preoccupation with progress, he was not particularly receptive to the dialectical theory of history—though he appears to have been familiar with Marx's work at this time. Nor was he willing to accept that class warfare was a necessary phase of social development: conflict of all kind was something to be avoided, a necessary evil perhaps but certainly not the basis for political idealism. In Sun's view, the purpose of the Chinese revolution would be to avoid, rather than to fulfil, the class war. He firmly believed that China could escape the internal tensions which had disrupted Western societies during their industrialization.

To that end he worked out a theory of how China should

industrialize, which was also a theory of political modernization. Of his 'three people's principles' (the *San-Min Chu-I*), the first stressed the solidarity and independence of the people; the second outlined the kind of constitution necessary for a proper balance between government and people; whilst the third related to the 'people's livelihood'. It was this which was Sun's real interest, down to about 1918. As early as 1894 he had stressed the importance of material improvement in a letter to Li Hung-chang, and incidentally had expressed a wish (never fulfilled) to study agricultural engineering in France. Eighteen years later, following the overthrow of the monarchy, he accepted a position in Yuan Shih-k'ai's government in which his chief responsibility was the development of a railway system throughout China. The plans for development which he worked out then and later deserve to count amongst the first serious essays in economic planning for developing countries. It was only with Sun's repeated failures to stay in power, after his flight to Japan in 1913, that he began to think out a new approach to politics and the nature of power. During the last seven years or so of his life (he died in 1925) he came gradually under the influence of Lenin's ideas about the role of the party in revolution, and the Soviet example of government by a revolutionary party.

Sun, like Liang, had a considerable influence on the development of political ideas in Viet-Nam, especially during the 1920s. The *Quôc-Dân Dang* party founded in 1927[12] had a programme based explicitly on Sun's ideas; but other parties at that period also owed some of their inspiration to the 'three people's principles'. The Chinese thinkers gave Vietnamese politicians an alternative source of ideas, quite separate from these of their colonial masters, which helped them to adjust to the situation in which Asians were dominated by Europeans. Some Vietnamese too, as we shall see, read the works of Rabindranath Tagore and M. K. Gandhi. We must explore in Part Two of this essay some of the political movements which resulted from their acquaintance with these new ideas.

The introduction into Vietnamese political thinking of such Western concepts as the nation, economic development, constitutional government, and revolution, represent a completely

new departure. But political concepts cannot be set entirely apart
from the cultural milieu of the men who use them. One may well
ask how far the Vietnamese really understood Western modes of
thought as a whole, and whether the concepts they borrowed
could possibly have had the same meaning for them as for the
Westerners who first produced them. It is interesting from this
point of view to ask, for example, how far they really understood
the ideas of a philosopher like Descartes, whom Liang Ch'i-ch'ao
so much admired and whose writings were familiar to Vietnamese
through their French education. Descartes would no doubt have
agreed with Liang's assessment of his intellectual importance,
for he was very conscious of being an innovator; and indeed his
mathematical method for describing the universe was highly
original. But was it Descartes the mathematician whom Liang
was praising? If, as seems likely, it was the Cartesian spirit of
inquiry rather than the content of his mathematical achievement
that impressed the Chinese, then perhaps we should conclude that
Liang greatly overemphasized Descartes' importance.

The 'scientific revolution' of the seventeenth century amounted
to the drawing together of two previously separate elements in the
Western intellectual tradition: on the one hand the empirical
observation of phenomena, on the other the rational system of
logic. Dr Needham has shown how much the former of these
elements had in common with the empirical outlook of the
Taoists;[13] what was not paralleled in the Chinese nation was the
occidental mode of logic, which insisted above all on the elimination of contradictions. Whilst Descartes must be credited with
having originated a new method within the framework of that
logic, the mode itself is very much older. The principles of logic
which the medieval schoolmen endowed with an absolute authority contained in themselves the seeds of intellectual growth,
which in the seventeenth century overthrew that authority.
Perhaps therefore the cultural and mental gulf between traditional
China and Viet-Nam on the one hand, and the modern West on
the other, was greater than men like Liang supposed. It was ultimately not unbridgeable, but its existence meant that only a very
small minority of highly educated individuals would be capable of
a complete understanding of the West. Even fewer perhaps would
be capable of Westernizing themselves to the extent that they
completely left behind all traces of the very different mentality of

their own tradition. In speaking of the political movements of modern Viet-Nam therefore, we must be careful not to assume too readily that we are as familiar with Vietnamese ways of thought as the familiarity of terminology might at first suggest.

III

Government and the Villages

THE French thought much more clearly than any other European power about the theory of colonial government, and their thought was pervaded by the notions of 'assimilation' and the 'mission civilisatrice'. Some colonial officials, it is true, held to these notions more steadfastly than others, but none could escape the necessity of either implementing them or reacting against them. The thoroughgoing assimilationist was conscious of belonging to a France which had inherited the civilizing mission of the Roman Empire. He believed that just as Rome had civilized Europe, including ancient Gaul, it was now the duty of modern Gaul to civilize the barbarians of Africa and Asia. Often this sense of a civilizing mission was combined with faith in Christianity. But not invariably so, for there were other assimilationists who saw themselves as heirs of the Enlightenment, and whose ideas of civilization centred around the 'principles of eighty-nine' and the creation of the Republic. The idea of assimilation was so deeply ingrained that it transcended many otherwise fundamental differences in French intellectual life.[1]

'Assimilation' had two rather different implications for colonial policy in practice. First, the 'mission civilisatrice' implied cultural assimilation: the education of native peoples and the inculcation of respect for French culture. But secondly, there were implications for administrative organization: the colonies must eventually be assimilated into the French Republic. Ideally French citizenship would be granted to all educated natives, the colonial communities would have full democratic representation in the National Assembly in Paris: and above all, these communities would be governed according to the laws of France, the Code Napoléon. It was the second implication which gave rise to the greatest difficulty. Cultural assimilation was inevitably a long-term aim, which required patient efforts over a long period: no one expected it to occur overnight. But the colonies had to be

40

governed immediately, which meant that a large number of villages had to be controlled and administered from the French cities created at Saigon and Hanoi. Administrative assimilation was fine in theory, but it depended on cultural assimilation for its success: the Code Napoléon would be fully intelligible only to Vietnamese thoroughly educated in French. This practical difficulty was to lead in due course to the emergence of a new theory, that of 'association', which allowed for some measure of cultural independence on the part of colonial subjects. In the meantime, it was necessary for the administrators to adopt policies which recognized the greater familiarity of those subjects with their own traditions of law and custom.

At the level of the colony or protectorate (Cochinchina became a colony, whilst Annam and Tongking were protectorates), and even more at the level of the Union Indochinoise created in 1887, it was possible to introduce French methods immediately. But at the level of the village and the district, rapid change was less easy. In Cochinchina, annexed between 1861 and 1867, the conquerors were faced with the problem of running a country whose former officials had for the most part fled. They were able to use a number of Catholic-educated Vietnamese like Truong Vinh Ky, and also men of the 'failed scholar' class, like Tôn Tho Tuong. But for the rest they had to either administer the country directly, or educate Vietnamese in French methods of government to do it in their place. In Tongking and Annam, on the other hand, the imperial officials were hardly able to flee and it was possible for the French to take over the traditional administrative system at all levels. The emperor himself was left on his throne but under the close control of a Résident-Supérieur.

This meant that the French went further towards administrative assimilation in Cochinchina than in the rest of Viet-Nam, and also (since they had to educate officials themselves) that Cochinchina proceeded more rapidly towards cultural assimilation. Whereas Cochinchina had a French administrative college as early as the 1870s, the old imperial examination system was left in Tongking and Annam until 1916. And whereas the French began to reform the Cochinchinese village system in 1904, they did not make similar changes in Tongking until 1921, and in Annam the village system appears to have remained largely unchanged down to 1940.[2]

Even so, both in Cochinchina and in Tongking-Annam, the French impact on peasant life in the villages came very slowly, and the cultural assimilation which made fairly rapid headway in the metropolis of Saigon or Hanoi never completely embraced the countryside. In order to understand the role of the villages in the modern political development of Viet-Nam it is necessary to look closely at their normal traditional structure, and if possible to penetrate the formal records of their organization to learn something about the social and political realities within the individual village.

The village as an institution was probably even more important in the traditional life of Viet-Nam than it had been in the medieval West. It and the clan were the most basic of all institutions, together perhaps with the sects and secret societies whose activity was especially important at the village level. The basis of the clan was the veneration of ancestors, a cult which also ensured some sense of attachment to the village, for it required each family and individual to keep in touch with the place where their forefathers were buried. In traditional Viet-Nam it was most unusual for men to lose the sense of belonging to a particular village, even if they lived in a town or at the imperial court. When families migrated they would still retain the sense of having moved away from some earlier home.

The relationship between the clan and the village might sometimes be a very complicated one. In South China, especially in Kwangtung, it was not uncommon for all the members of a village community to belong to the same clan and in such cases the clan was the more important institution. The clan elders would constitute the effective local government and the ancestral hall would be the focus of village life. But in Viet-Nam this identity between lineage and settlement units seems to have been relatively rare, and the village was correspondingly a more important institution. Responsibility for local government would lie with the notables of the village, and whilst each family or clan in the village had its own ancestral altars, a more important temple was the *dinh* which contained a shrine to the protective deity of the village. Whereas the clan was held together by ties of filial piety, the cement of the village community was the sense of being protected by the same spirits, and probably also the acceptance of common administrative responsibilities imposed by the central government. The most important unit of village administration in Viet-Nam was called the *xa* (Chinese *she*), or sometimes the *lang* (a purely Vietnamese word without Chinese equivalent). It is significant that the original Chinese word, *she* or *xa*, had two meanings: it might mean an association of people, or it might mean an altar to the spirits of the soil. At the same time the *xa* was the basic unit of local government.[3]

Each village had its own customs and rules of precedence, and there was considerable variation between regions and even from one village to the next. Thus in some places precedence at village meetings in the *dinh* was based on age, whilst in others it depended on scholastic attainment, so that students and scholars were given the highest place. There were also differences in terminology, and the subdivisions of the village were known by different names in different provinces. Even the appearance of the village was not the same in all parts of the country. In Tongking it was usual for villages to have thick bamboo hedges which provided an effective local defence against marauders, whereas in Cochinchina such defences are only rarely found. Generalizations based on the few studies of particular localities which have been made from time to time cannot therefore be regarded as in any sense definitive. Yet when one comes to compare what is known of these Vietnamese villages with our knowledge of traditional villages in England or France, it is possible to distinguish certain features which in a comparative sense may be regarded as typical of the villages in Viet-Nam.

To begin, the Vietnamese *xa* was not the property of any private individual or family, in the way that the English or French manor belonged to its manorial lord. It paid taxes, furnished men for the army, or performed corvée labour services, entirely by virtue of its obligations to the emperor; and if at a particular time the actual recipient of these dues was someone other than the emperor himself, that person derived his position entirely from an imperial grant. It was the custom for imperial officials to receive grants of the dues from certain villages for the duration of their official careers, but this did not amount to the creation of fiefs. Much land was of course owned by individual families, and a rich family might have a substantial estate and even tenants on it. But ownership never carried with it the administrative or judicial powers which pertained to feudal lordship. In Viet-Nam, village affairs were in the hands of a council of notables in each *xa*, whose principal officers were responsible for keeping order there and for ensuring the performance of the community's obligations to the state. They also looked after the village treasury, and administered the area of land which in almost all villages belonged inalienably to the *xa* as a whole, and which had to be regularly partitioned amongst the member families.

The formal rules governing village administration were determined partly by imperial decree and partly by local custom. Certain essential rules were laid down for the country as a whole: for the appointment of suitable officers and notables, for the regular revision of census and taxation rolls, for the procedures affecting division of communal lands, and so on. From time to time these rules would be changed or elaborated upon by an emperor anxious to reinvigorate the system or to render it better capable of meeting some new situation, and a long series of such decrees relating to Tongking from the eleventh century onwards has been preserved in a nineteenth-century administrative encyclopaedia.[4] In Annam and Cochinchina the *xa* system did not develop until rather later than in Tongking, for those areas were only settled by the Vietnamese from the fifteenth century onwards.

How far the decrees were acted upon in detail, and how far the administrative practices of Vietnamese villages were standardized as a result, are questions which cannot be answered without a great deal more documentary research. But it is thought that the fifteenth century was the period when the greatest degree of central imperial supervision over local affairs was maintained, at least in Tongking. During the seventeenth and eighteenth centuries there seems to have been some decline in the extent to which the details of village administration were supervised from above. By the nineteenth century provincial and district officials, both in North and South, seem to have interfered in village affairs much less regularly than had been the case in the fifteenth century. Perhaps that is the reason why the early French writers who described the *xa* in the years immediately after the conquest were so much impressed by the degree of autonomy enjoyed by the village notables. More recently Vietnamese writers have referred to this autonomy as evidence that their forefathers were familiar with the idea of democratic freedom at the local level long before the coming of the Europeans.

However, before we apply too readily such words as freedom and democracy to the Vietnamese village, we ought to pause to consider the original occidental usage of those terms. Within our own framework of ideas, the purpose of words like 'democratic' or 'autonomy' is one of contradistinction. That is, they imply the existence of the opposite concepts, 'autocratic' and 'centralization'. These other concepts imply in turn the notions of authority and sovereign power. But as we have seen, the Vietnamese tradition knew little of such notions; for its law was not based on authority and will, but on the recognition of universal harmony. In other words, the Vietnamese village was neither democratic nor autocratic, neither autonomous nor dictatorially controlled. The distinctions were irrelevant, even alien to the traditional system. Thus even in the fifteenth century, when the *xa* seems to have been subject to the traditional maximum of supervision from above, it would be wrong to assume that the nature of the supervision was precisely the same as what the Westerner means when he uses the word 'control'. The emperor made demands, and it was for the villagers to carry them out. But his guarantee that they would do so rested more on their sense of obligation than on an authoritarian system of coercion. Conversely when the villagers, who looked to the imperial officials as men who would guarantee their protection and good order, found that a local mandarin was corrupt or made unfair exactions, they could not appeal against him to the law: their only defence was either open revolt, or to leave the village and return when the official had gone.

This contrast between Vietnamese and Western European systems of local government has an important parallel in the sphere of political theory. In all parts of the world, the basic object of rural government may be said to be the same: to provide security. But on the question *how* security can best be guaranteed to ordinary people in their villages, there have been many different replies in human history: each cultural tradition has produced its own ideas. In the modern West men believed that the foundation of government was good law: a good system of administration and justice, in which officials were held more or less to the path of virtue by the rule of law. Thomas Hobbes, contemplating the turmoil of civil war in England, advocated as a solution a particular system of government: absolute monarchy. Other thinkers have tended to the view that what ought to be absolute is not monarchy but the law itself. Out of this tradition grew the Western theory of constitutional, democratic government. But in Viet-Nam, as in China, the traditional demand was not for good laws so much as for good men. 'With the right men', says the *Doctrine of the Mean*, 'the growth of good government is as rapid as the growth of vegetation in the right soil.' Rules were necessary of course; but if government seemed lacking in effectiveness the first thought was not to change the laws but to change the men. Law was deemed less important than virtue.

The formal regulations concerning the *xa* tell us only a little of what we need to know about rural society in Viet-Nam. Beneath the formal surface of administration there lay the reality of village politics. The formal organization as it is recorded in the imperial decrees hardly allowed for the possibility of conflict within the village. Open differences of opinion, and the provision of rules for settling them by debate or voting, were alien to the concept of social harmony. In any case, any system of formal opposition within an institutional framework would have involved loss of face for those Vietnamese belonging to the party that was overruled in any situation. Whatever the reality, decisions within the village council must at least have the appearance of a consensus.

That conflicts occurred in practice need not be doubted, but, since the regulations and decrees do not tell us about them, it is only rarely that the outsider has a chance to observe them. A valuable glimpse of the realities of village politics in Viet-Nam —in this case in Cochinchina—is afforded by an incident which occurred in Tân-An province in the years 1895–6, and which the French officials referred to as 'l'affaire de Môc-Hoa'. It is covered in great detail by a series of reports still preserved in the National Archives in Saigon.[5]

During the autumn of 1895, for reasons which are not recorded, a conflict arose between the leading notables of the village of Tuyên-Thanh and another group or faction within the village.

There may have been in the background a long-standing feud between members of two clans for control of the village, for the chief notables all belonged to the Vo family and their opponents to a family called Nguyên. Or possibly it was a case of a newly rising clan seeking to take over from an established one. Within the village itself the Vo were virtually the ruling clique, and since the custom of the village was that new notables should be elected by outgoing notables the group in office was in a position to perpetuate its control over affairs indefinitely. Their opponents on the other hand had influential friends at the level of the canton and of the province. The leading figure in the Nguyên group, Nguyên Van Nghi, held the office of deputy-chief in the canton of Môc-Hoa, within which the village lay; and he was on friendly terms both with the canton-chief, Lê Van Thu, and with a man called Hoc who had an influential post within the office of the French administrator of Tân-An province. Nghi, Thu and Hoc were in fact all Catholics, and on good terms with the French missionary priest at Tân-An. It may well be that Thu was the most important figure in the situation, for he had acquired great influence in many villages of the canton, and the crisis at Tuyên-Thanh may possibly have arisen partly from a conflict between the canton-chief and the Vo clique.

In December 1895, Thu and Nghi—with the aid of Hoc—were in a strong enough position to persuade the administrator of Tân-An to dismiss the ten Vo notables of Tuyên-Thanh and to hold a new election. They were also able to secure election in their place for several members of the Nguyên clan, and to enable the newly elected men to take over the highest offices on the council. The Vo leaders were thus ousted, and the new clique was free to pursue a policy of promoting Catholicism in the village. Nghi was said to have promised a place on the council of notables to anyone who was converted to the Christian faith. But the Vo were not so easily disposed of. The following February (1896) Vo Van Vang and his supporters presented a complaint against Nguyên Van Nghi and his friends to the Governor of Cochin-china at Saigon. An inquiry was ordered and the Vo party succeeded in gaining the sympathy of the French official in charge of it, Navelle. In May, Navelle's report to the governor recommended the dismissal of Thu and Nghi from their offices in the canton, and the annulment of the recent election of new notables at Tuyên-Thanh. The Nguyên group were now placed on the defensive and had to find some way of discrediting their rivals in French eyes. On the night of the 11th June a fire in the village seriously damaged the house of a Catholic catechist, Antoine Quy, and the Vo were immediately blamed. About the same time the Catholic group organized the writing of a number of letters to the French authorities from various villages in Môc-Hoa canton, defending the virtues of Thu and Nghi. They began to hope that the advantage gained by the Vo might be reversed once more.

But to no avail. In late July or August, when the case of the fire was heard at a provincial court, the Vo were able to show that the house of Antoine Quy had been burnt down by the Nguyên party themselves in an attempt to incriminate their rivals. As for the letters supporting Thu and Nghi, the French officials declined to take them seriously. Towards the end of August a new election of notables took place at Tuyên-Thanh, in accordance with the old rules, and the Vo regained their ascendancy. Between then and the end of the year the ousted Nguyên group made as much trouble as they could for the Vo notables, with a series of petitions and complaints. But by this time the provincial authorities had made up their minds that the Vo were in the right and the new complaints against them were dismissed. The final fling of the Catholic group was a request—fully supported by the ecclesiastical authorities—for partition of the village. But that too was turned down.

To see this case as merely an example of tension between Catholics and Buddhists would be to miss the point. (Nor, for that matter, was it simply an instance of tension between the missionaries and anti-clerical officials amongst the French.) The central feature of the affair was the conflict between two rival factions, perhaps clans, for control over the village or even over the whole canton. It is not difficult to imagine comparable situations arising where all the people involved, including the provincial and central government officials, were Vietnamese. Indeed if the typical Vietnamese village was one which embraced more than one clan, such inter-clan feuding may well have been a very common feature of politics at this level. The existence of a great many secret associations would also contribute to conflicts of this kind. Nor need one assume the existence of a colonial government as a prerequisite for conflicts between canton or district officials and the notables of villages. A great deal of political manoeuvring must have gone on beneath the surface of formal village harmony.

However, the Môc-Hoa affair did involve Frenchmen, and it illustrates an important aspect of the relationship between Vietnamese villagers and their colonial masters under French rule. It so happens that in this case the details of the situation were brought to light by an administrative inquiry, but such a revelation was by no means inevitable. The initial success of the Nguyên party in securing the removal of the Vo notables depended on their connection with Hoc, the secretary and adviser to the French administrator at Tân-An. Hoc seems to have had considerable influence over decisions of this kind, and in other circumstances an official in his position might well have been able to hoodwink his superior so completely that no Frenchman would ever have realized the true course of events. In dealing with a country of many thousands of villages the French were always faced with the problem of knowing what went on amongst their Vietnamese subjects, for without that knowledge they were powerless to enforce their own regulations effectively. They had a police system, of course, and they could also sometimes (though hardly in a case like that at Môc-Hoa) obtain intelligence from missionary priests. But ultimately they were dependent on native informants or officials of one kind or another, and much could be concealed from them if the need arose. The French were not unaware of the problem, and became increasingly concerned at the difficulty of finding adequate personnel to manage village affairs. In a report of 1922 the Governor of Cochinchina complained that the notables of villages were 'for the most part very inferior to their task not only because of their barely elementary education, but even more because they bring to their work a routine spirit, hostile to every new idea'.[6] The fact was, the report continued, that fewer and fewer people wanted to become notables, so that good candidates rarely presented themselves for the office.

This need not mean that struggles for village election of the Môc-Hoa kind no longer occurred. What troubled the French was that they could not find notables with the degree of French education necessary for full co-operation between village and higher authorities. They should not have been so surprised at the difficulty. Only a small minority of children, even in Cochinchina, received a worthwhile education in French, and not unnaturally they aspired to something more than village work: for example to appointments in government departments at Saigon or Hanoi. Nor was this in itself a new development. Before the French came, it had been usual for the best educated people to seek imperial office, and for villages to be run by the less well-educated. What was new in the situation was the degree of reliance which a government of foreigners, whose command of the Vietnamese language was limited, placed on native notables for a service which the latter were probably very reluctant to perform. If the notables identified themselves with the French, they were liable to lose the confidence of the village; if they identified with the mass of the population and showed signs of being anti-French, they were liable to be removed. Not surprisingly many were content simply to pursue their own interests and to use their position for personal or family gain.

French fears were not unjustified. As we have seen there was a long tradition of secret religious and political activity in Viet-Nam in which the classic method had been for the leaders of opposition to the government to undermine the control of the centre over local communities. The French may have been right in thinking that all the ordinary peasants wanted was to be left in peace. But if they could not themselves guarantee that peace, the way was left open for the growth of secret anti-government associations to assert their own power in the villages. The kind of thing that could happen is well illustrated by events in Cochin-china during the years from 1905 to 1916, when a considerable number of what the French called 'les sociétés dites secrètes' flourished in a great many of the villages of the region.[7]

Sometimes they were no more than criminal gangs, terrorizing the countryside and living a life of robbery and violence. A well-documented example was the case of Mai Van Kiêm and about forty or fifty of his associates, who held sway over the villages round Trang-Bang (in the province of Tây-Ninh) for about eighteen months before their arrest in February 1916. Their first recorded act of violence was in September 1914 when they attacked a local man who dared to oppose them, and then set fire to his house. One man was imprisoned for three months after this incident, but the main culprits went unpunished: no one would give evidence against them and the local notables were too frightened to act. On another occasion, a few months later, a Vietnamese district official made an inquiry into Kiêm's activities, but the evidence was so distorted as to make it appear that he and his friends were the victims of a rival gang. When four notables were robbed one night, they were so intimidated that the court had no choice but to acquit the accused and set them free. It was not until the general crisis of February 1916 that the French authorities finally discovered the true situation and brought Kiêm's band to justice.

By that stage the French were far less concerned about mere criminals than about the political societies which had seemed suddenly to spring up in various parts of Cochinchina. In 1913 they forestalled a plot for open revolt in Saigon and Cholon, and possibly in some rural areas too, by arresting just in time a man called Phan Phat Sanh who dreamt of becoming emperor as 'Xich-Long' or 'Red Dragon'. Of Chinese descent, he had been associated at first with the overseas Chinese secret societies whose aim was to restore the Ming dynasty in China. But his own ambition appears to have been to use the secret society network of southern Viet-Nam to establish a throne for himself. To this end he had spent two years building up a following in Saigon and the province of Cho-Lon, and had found a retreat for himself at a monastery in the Cambodian border-province of Kampot. Whatever supernatural powers he claimed for himself, they failed him at the last. But he had followers, and his own organization was crude by comparison with that created by his leading supporters during the two or three years which followed his arrest. In February 1916 they planned to seize Saigon prison as the signal for a general Cochinchinese rising. The French again foiled the rebels before things got out of hand, but were alarmed when they discovered subsequently the extent and complexity of the network of secret societies involved.

Amongst the most notorious of the secret society organizers was a man known variously as Cao Van Long, Bây Do, and Ma-Vang. His career will serve to illustrate the nature of this network. Born in the province of Bên-Tre, he seems to have donned the

priestly robe about 1910, and to have made his home thereafter
at a temple or pagoda on a remote hillside in the province of
Châu-Dôc. His retirement was not however that of a hermit. He
spent much of his time wandering through the provinces of the
Mekong Delta organizing and encouraging silent opposition to
the French. As he went, he distributed magic charms bearing the
secret name of his temple, which were supposed to protect the
recipient against all kinds of attack. His robe was thus more than
a disguise, it was an essential element in his power over the rural
population. When in 1917 he was arrested and sentenced to life
detention, the Governor of Cochinchina commented:

> Thus ended the legend which had made a demi-god of this
> wretched apostle. His conviction will go far to destroying the
> prestige enjoyed by all such false bonzes and sorcerers amongst a
> naïve and credulous population.[8]

His optimism proved unjustified. A decade or so later new and
more serious troubles were being prepared in Cochinchina and
elsewhere in Viet-Nam. If at that time there was less superstition
amongst the populace, it was small comfort to the French to see
the 'false bonzes' replaced by revolutionary and socialist politicians.

The pattern of conflict in the Môc-Hoa affair was between two
factions of similar kind and similar social status. No doubt this
kind of conflict was found later, even perhaps in the most recent
period of Vietnamese rural strife. But with the political societies
the conflict was between the villages and higher levels of
administration, with the notables often taking the side of the secret
societies or politicians. Or sometimes, in 1916, there was conflict
within the village itself: between the notables and the rest of the
population, or rather between the notables and the secret society
leaders. In Bên-Tre province for example, an outbreak of violence
near Mo-Cây early in February 1916 included attacks not only on
Chinese shops but also on a village *dinh*, where many of the local
archives were taken out and burnt. This kind of incident was still
more common in the disturbances of 1930–31, especially in the
provinces of Nghê-An and Ha-Tinh. As socialistic and Marxist
ideas began to spread through the countryside the notables
tended more and more to identify themselves with the French
desire for preservation of the social order.

It is another serious limitation of the formal records concerning the history and administration of the *xa* that they say very little about the realities of social structure in the traditional village. Only in the French period do we find the opportunity to analyse Vietnamese social structure at all systematically, and by then it had already begun to change under the Western impact. Even then, the subject is not an easy one to study in detail. Some writers have drawn attention to the growing contrast between patterns of landownership in Tongking-Annam and in Cochinchina; but this was not necessarily the most important fact about Vietnamese agrarian society under colonial rule. That the agrarian statistics collected about 1930 demonstrate such a contrast is not in doubt. In Tongking and Annam the majority of the peasants were owner-occupiers: fewer than $1\frac{1}{2}$ per cent of the owners of rice land in Tongking (and 10 per cent in Annam) leased out land to tenants. In Cochinchina the figure was 36 per cent: much of the land had been still uncultivated when the French arrived and had been brought into use under the French system of large-scale concessions, with the result that by 1930 there were many places where the majority of the cultivators were tenant-farmers. As much as 45 per cent of the land in Cochinchina belonged to owners of fifty hectares or more, and some of these were very large landlords. Yet to argue that this made agrarian conflict more likely in Cochinchina than elsewhere is to ignore the fact that the most important elements in peasant discontent were poverty, credit, and heavy taxation. And the poorest peasants in Indochina were very often those who owned their own small parcels of land but simply could not obtain a living from them adequate to meet such crises as a bad harvest or a sudden rise in taxes. The most hated men in such a society were often not the landlords but the moneylenders and the officials who had to collect taxes.[9]

The political movements of twentieth-century Viet-Nam saw in the grievances of the peasantry their greatest opportunity to mobilize the rural masses against the French. In the towns, politicians who were bold enough to oppose the French could be watched, their newspapers censored, and if necessary their freedom of movement curtailed. But in the villages, the French had to overcome the basic problem of control. The nationalists could spread propaganda more widely, and could escape arrest for long periods; they could even organize revolt. They found it difficult to co-ordinate their activities, and this explains why for many decades the French colonial officials could afford to treat their movements as of no fundamental importance. But the French never really solved the problem of local government in Indochina, and the time would come after 1945 when a political movement would be strong enough to raise a whole army by undermining the official chain of authority from Hanoi and Saigon down to the humble village, and by creating a rebel chain of command in its place.

PART TWO

France after the war proclaimed to the world the principles of law and democracy upon which her victories were founded. Should she not ask herself if her methods of colonization correspond to her ideals?

Alexandre Varenne, December 1925.

IV

The Nation

UNLIKE some Asian peoples in the twentieth century, the Vietnamese did not have to invent a wholly new word for 'nation'. They had always thought of their country as the *quôc* (Chinese *kuo*), a word which can be translated as kingdom, country or nation. (Or sometimes they preferred the purely Vietnamese word *nuoc* which had almost exactly the same meaning.) But precisely because they did have a word of their own, one has to ask whether when they used it in its more modern sense it carried all the shades of meaning that the term 'nation' had for the Westerners from whom it had been borrowed. What *quôc* had meant in the past can only be understood by looking at the relations which traditional Viet-Nam had had with its neighbours, and especially with China.

After ten centuries of Chinese rule (*c.* 110 B.C.–A.D. *c.* 902) the Vietnamese were able in the tenth and eleventh centuries to establish an independent *quôc* of their own. In 1077, and again in the 1280s, they defeated Chinese attempts to incorporate Viet-Nam into the Sung and the Yüan empires respectively. In 1407 a third Chinese invasion was at first more successful; but after twenty years of rule as a Chinese province the Vietnamese once more found in Lê Loi a leader capable of driving out the Ming armies. One further attempt by imperial China to reconquer Viet-Nam occurred in the years 1788–9, but it too ended in defeat at the hands of the emperor Quang-Trung. Yet in spite of all these struggles Viet-Nam was not wholly independent of China in the sense of having what the Westerner would call national sovereignty. Its rulers regularly sent tribute to the court of Peking, and in return received Chinese diplomas of investiture and seals of gold and jade.

In this they were not alone. China also received tribute from many neighbouring kingdoms: from Korea, Burma, Siam, Mongolia and the lamas of Tibet: in fact almost all the countries on the fringes of the Chinese world at one time or another sent tribute in this way.[1] For the Chinese refused to carry on relations with any other state on a level of equality. As Son of Heaven, the emperor of the Middle Kingdom (the *Trung-Quôc*, in Vietnamese) performed sacrifices to Heaven which placed him on a higher plane than any other earthly ruler; and since China was also, in her periods of unity at least, stronger than any of her neighbours, this claim to superiority commanded respect.

Even in order to trade with China the kings of Siam and Viet-Nam had to offer tribute, and it may well be that many of the missions which they sent there had an economic rather than a political motive. At the same time, we must not suppose that in sending their tribute these lesser monarchs were recognizing any active obligation towards China, nor acknowledging a Chinese right to interfere in their internal affairs. The East Asian tributary system must not be mistaken for some kind of oriental feudalism on a grand scale. It is true that there were occasions in the early fifteenth century when a Ming emperor sought to arbitrate *between* tributary states, and there was an occasion in 1540 when another emperor of that dynasty threatened intervention in a conflict between two rival claimants to the throne of Viet-Nam. But on the whole China's superiority, or one might even use the word suzerainty, was passive rather than active. As such, it was accepted by lesser states as part of the natural order of the world.

In their own countries the rulers of Viet-Nam and Siam tended to imitate China in this respect, and to demand a like tribute from their own lesser neighbours. Thus Viet-Nam at different periods claimed tribute from the Lao principalities of Vieng-Chan and Chieng-Khuang, and from the king of Cambodia, as well as from the chieftains of hill-tribes entirely within the Vietnamese sphere. By the nineteenth century Viet-Nam and Siam were approaching the point where their simultaneous claims to tribute from Cambodia and from the Lao princes would bring them into serious and continuing conflict. Indeed there was a short war between them in 1835–6. The French settled the issue by establishing their own protectorates over Cambodia in 1865 and over Laos in 1893.

In both these cases the French used the Vietnamese claim to tribute as the basis of a policy which ended in concessions by the Siamese. This use of the tributary system by Europeans was however uncharacteristic. The general effect of the Western intrusion into East Asia was to destroy the system. As far as South East Asia was concerned, the flow of tribute to China was interrupted by the period of internal civil war which followed on the Taiping rebellion (1853–64), an event which would probably have caused disruption in any period. By the time the war ended, the Europeans had demonstrated their power to such an extent that China no longer seemed powerful enough to justify her claims to superiority. Moreover from 1842 onwards successive European victories over China drew an increasing proportion of her trade out of the tributary system into the Treaty Ports. In 1863 Siam virtually rejected a Chinese request for tribute, and in fact sent no more missions after that.[2] The Vietnamese, having experienced a direct European attack, may well have felt they had more reason to stay close to China, and continued to send tribute as late as 1883. But the practice was brought to an end two years later, after a war in which the French defeated China on precisely this issue: by the Treaty of Tientsin, the Chinese surrendered all claims of this nature to France. In the next two or three decades China painfully adjusted herself to the occidental theory of international relations, accepting her place as just one among many nations. Viet-Nam was prevented from making a similar adjustment; as far as international relations were concerned she was merely a part of France. Nevertheless in the longer term the French intrusion opened the way for the *quôc* to develop into something like a sovereign nation.

If the external situation of the Vietnamese *quôc* differed from that of the Western nation-state, the difference was even more true of its internal structure. On the eve of the French conquest Viet-Nam was a very much less coherent and unified state than might at first sight be supposed. The area of the present Viet-Nam had been ruled from Huê by a single monarch only since 1802. Before that the history of the country had been a long and complicated story of territorial expansion and frequent internal division.

The area which the Chinese had ruled down to about A.D. 900 did not stretch further south than the seventeenth parallel, and in some periods not even so far as that. The greater part of what is now Central Viet-Nam belonged then, and for some centuries more, to the Hinduized kingdom of Champa; whilst the area still further to the south (Cochinchina) belonged to the Khmers. During the five centuries between 1000 and 1500 the independent Vietnamese kingdom of Dai-Viêt gradually absorbed territory on its southern border until by the sixteenth century there was only a very small Cham state left, centred on the district round Phan-Rang. At this point, the expansion was interrupted by a series of events of perhaps even greater significance. In the first quarter of the sixteenth century there emerged a number of powerful clans at the court of the Lê dynasty, just at a time when the imperial clan itself failed to produce a successor capable of holding his kingdom together. One of these clans, the Mac, judged itself strong enough to overthrow the dynasty altogether in 1527. But its power was regionally limited, and although it had great power in the northern part of Tongking it had a much weaker following in the areas further south. This was its undoing, for a few years later the two most powerful clans of Thanh-Hoa province—the Trinh and the Nguyên—combined to take control of those areas and to proclaim the restoration of the Lê dynasty. The sixty years which followed were a period of continual conflict between the two imperial claimants, ending in 1592 with the recovery of Hanoi by the supporters of the Lê. The emperor was not however restored in the fullest sense of the word. He still had responsibility for the ritual functions of the Confucian monarch, but real power now lay with the Trinh and the Nguyên. Had either one of these clans been all-powerful, the dynasty would almost certainly have been deposed. As it was, any attempt to seize the throne would have merely renewed the civil war without either side having much hope of final success. Before there could be a change of dynasty, one clan would have to eliminate its rival by means of court intrigue. If both clans had been forced to remain in the same capital for another generation it is not unlikely that the Trinh would have done just that. But the Nguyên had another alternative. In 1600 the chief of that clan (Nguyên Hoang) escaped from Hanoi and established himself in the conquered territories of the far south, where the family had been virtually hereditary governors for several decades.[3]

This was a decisive turning-point in Vietnamese history, for it meant that during the next century and three-quarters there were

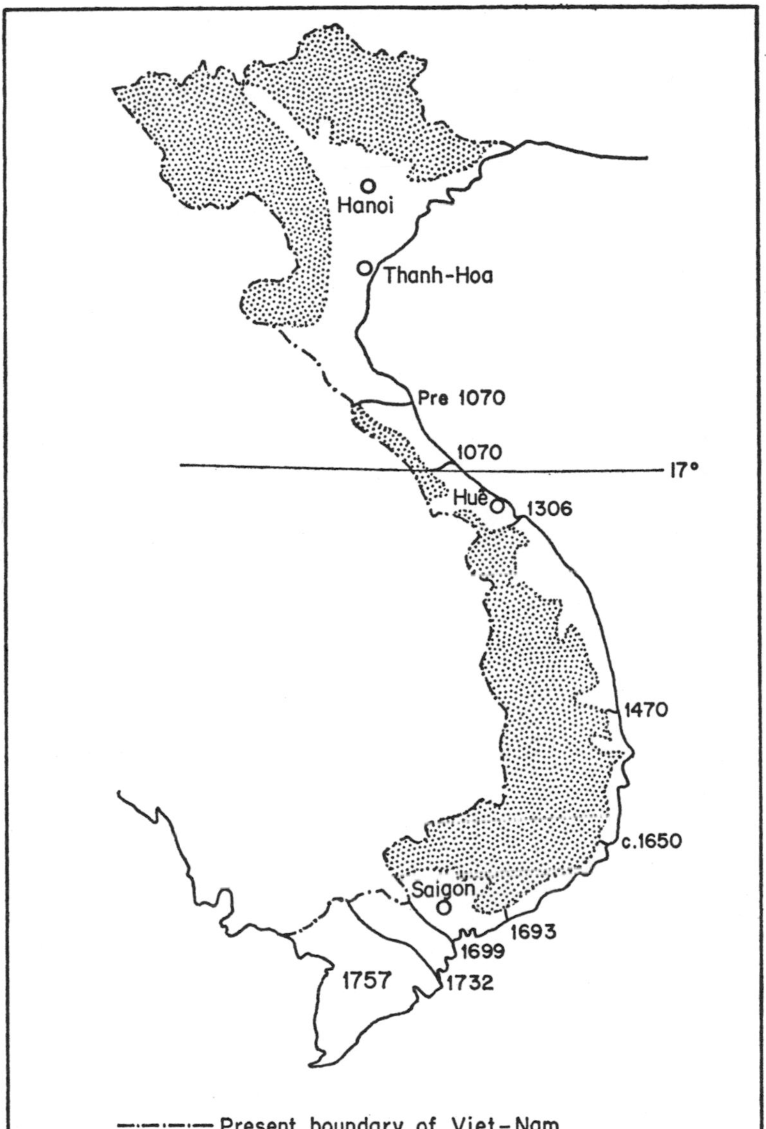

Hanoi
Thanh-Hoa
Pre 1070
1070
17°
Huê
1306
1470
c.1650
Saigon
1693
1699
1732
1757
Present boundary of Viet-Nam
Limits of Vietnamese settlement (c.1950)
'Montagnard' areas
Dates are those of annexation of territory by the Vietnamese

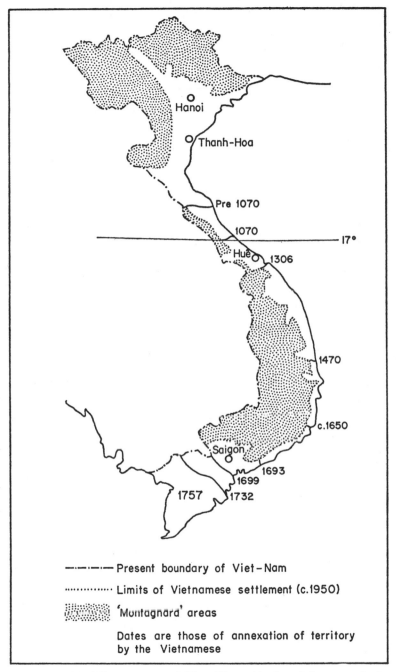

Map I: The Expansion of Viet-Nam (11th–18th centuries)

virtually two separate kingdoms, both formally recognizing the Lê dynasty but otherwise independent. Between 1620 and 1680 the Trinh made repeated attempts to recover control of the southern provinces, but in vain. Meanwhile the Nguyên resumed the southward territorial expansion of the Vietnamese. Towards the end of the seventeenth century they defeated the last Cham king and drove him into the hills. Already by then they were exerting influence from time to time over the kings of Cambodia, and in the century or so after 1658 they forced the Khmers to surrender most of the area which was later to become the 'six provinces' of Cochinchina. Gradually the conquered region was settled by Vietnamese migrants; it also became the home of Ming refugees, fleeing from the Manchu conquest of South China, who in the latter part of the seventeenth century settled at places like Biên-Hoa, My-Tho and Ha-Tiên. This Chinese element, as well as the assimilation by the Vietnamese of some of the Khmer inhabitants of the region, helps to explain some of the social and cultural contrasts between Cochinchina and other parts of Viet-Nam. The fact that it was the last area to be drawn into Viet-Nam and settled by migrants from the north is the reason why it is also far less densely populated than the rest of the country and is capable of producing a rice surplus.

The division of Viet-Nam into two kingdoms lasted for several generations; it came to an end when the more southerly one was itself overtaken by rebellion and a period of disunity. In 1773 a group of rebels under the name of Tây-Son, 'the men from the western hills', became increasingly powerful in the provinces of Qui-Nhon, Quang-Ngai and Quang-Nam, and even threatened the Nguyên capital at Huê. The Trinh ruler in Hanoi, seizing this unlooked-for opportunity, sent his own forces south in the following year, and it was to them that Huê finally fell. The Nguyên family fled or were killed, and in 1777 their dominions were virtually partitioned between the Trinh and the leaders of the Tây-Son. The latter were not content however with this territory, or even with the addition to it of Cochinchina. When the Trinh suffered an internal crisis of their own in 1786 the Tây-Son intervened in Tongking as well, and by 1789 they were in control of practically the whole of Tongking and Annam. The Lê dynasty was finally deposed, and the country was divided between the two brothers who had led the Tây-Son armies to victory. But in

Cochinchina, the sole survivor of the Nguyên clan refused to admit defeat and in 1788 succeeded in establishing himself at Saigon. Once again the Nguyên found themselves established in the most southerly region of an expanding Viet-Nam. But this time they went much further than defending their position. Between 1793 and 1802 the young Nguyên Anh conquered first Huê and then Hanoi, bringing to an end the Tây-Son dynasty and uniting for the first time under a single regime the whole of modern Viet-Nam. He took the imperial reign-title Gia-Long and secured recognition from the Chinese.

Given a long period of stability in its relations with other countries, and a succession of strong rulers, this newly created unity might have led in time to the growth of a much more centralized state in Viet-Nam than had ever existed there before. Under Gia-Long himself, the northern and southern regions of the new empire were left with considerable freedom from interference from Huê. But his son Minh-Mang (1820-41) was more ambitious. He insisted on having greater control over both Tongking and Cochinchina, and when those areas rebelled against him in the 1830s he reasserted his authority with great vigour. The Cochinchinese rebellion of 1833-5 was a serious affair, and for a time a Siamese army invaded in the hope of destroying Minh-Mang's influence in the region; but in time the invaders were driven out and the area was pacified, leaving the way open for the Vietnamese to assert their control also over Cambodia. After the whole country had been pacified, Minh-Mang undertook a reform of local government, and in 1836 ordered a complete revision of the village tax-rolls throughout Viet-Nam.[4]

When Minh-Mang died however, in 1841, he was succeeded by lesser men who proved unable to carry on and extend this work. Control of Cambodia was lost under Thiêu-Tri (1841-7), and under Tu-Duc (1847-83) the country became embroiled in the expansion of the West. A Franco-Spanish attack in 1858 led eventually to the loss of three, and then six, provinces to France; by 1867 the latter country was in possession not only of all Cochinchina but also of Cambodia, and the geographical balance of Gia-Long's empire was destroyed.[5] Moreover in the North and Centre there followed a series of rebellions, which made it the more difficult for Tu-Duc to govern effectively the areas of his empire which remained. The debate at his court about how to deal with the French took place against a background of endemic internal disorder. It is relevant perhaps to compare Viet-Nam at this time with Japan, where an essential preliminary to successful technological response to the West was a period in which (immediately after the Meiji restoration) the government established strong central control over its empire. In Viet-Nam, only a new and successful pacification of Annam and Tongking by the court at Huê could have saved those parts of the country from the same fate as that of Cochinchina. But by 1881, when the French decided to annex the rest of Viet-Nam, nothing effective had been done. It was left to the French to restore order throughout their new 'protectorate'.

In time the Vietnamese began to ask themselves what was this 'France' which had so much power in the world? What was its driving force? Was it something peculiar to the French, or to Europeans generally, as a race? Or was it based on methods of organization and science which any race could learn? Could Viet-Nam perhaps become in time a nation powerful enough to drive out the French? Put succinctly these questions may appear in retrospect more logical and articulate than they appeared to Vietnamese at the time. But they reflect the direction of the thought of men like Phan Bôi Châu or Phan Châu Trinh. Slowly, hesitantly they were groping for some new approach to political life, and for a new sense of identity which would enable them once more to act effectively in the world.

The philosophy of social Darwinism which was abroad in Asia and in Europe alike at this period focused the attention of a great many politicians and thinkers on the question of race. The Vietnamese began to think of themselves not merely as a *quôc*, the people of one country ruled by one monarch, but also as a racially distinct 'people'—a *dân-tôc*. The racial distinction between themselves and the French was obvious enough. But they also became increasingly conscious of the racial difference between themselves and the Chinese. In this they were aided by the introduction of the Western study of archaeology. By the 1920s scholars of the Commission Archéologique de l'Indochine and of the École Française d'Extrême-Orient were beginning to piece together information about the ancient civilization which they associated with the bronze drums from Dông-Son, a site in Thanh-

Hoa province, and which had flourished in Viet-Nam before the coming of the Chinese.[6] The debate amongst Vietnamese scholars as to the relative importance of Chinese and 'Indonesian' elements in their culture still continues and will only be settled by painstaking research. But the political implications of the scholars' discoveries were felt long ago. A small but significant detail in a conversation between Nguyên Ai Quôc (the young Hô Chi Minh) and a Russian writer in Moscow in 1923 will serve to illustrate the point. The Vietnamese, whose nom de plume at that time meant literally 'Nguyên (who) loves his country', described himself—without any reference to Chinese affinities—as belonging to 'an ancient Malay race'.[7]

Another factor which helped the Vietnamese to distinguish between themselves and the Chinese during the early decades of this century was the reform of their language. Although they had long used classical Chinese as their formal court language, the Vietnamese had never allowed their own vernacular to die out completely. It was written down, in its own distinctive characters (chu-nôm), from the thirteenth century onwards; and as the language of poetry and fiction it seems to have had a role not unlike that of pai-hua, the popular language of China itself. The significant change which occurred under French rule was the Romanization of this vernacular, with the eventual consequence that the Vietnamese would come to regard Chinese as a language whose sound might be familiar but whose script was quite foreign to them. The method of writing Vietnamese phonetically in Roman script had first been invented in the seventeenth century by a group of Catholic missionaries who found chu-nôm too difficult for the translation of Christian texts. In 1651 Alexandre de Rhodes published in Rome the first Vietnamese-Latin dictionary, using the new script.[8] But down to the nineteenth century it was employed only for devotional literature and catechisms.

It was when the French took over Cochinchina in the 1860s that the new script began to be used as a language of administration. From about 1900 it was increasingly used in Tongking and Annam, and the trend was further promoted by the decision after 1916 to abandon the traditional examination system whose medium had been Chinese. But if the French hoped that the Romanization of Vietnamese would be a step towards the acceptance of their own civilization and the decline of Vietnamese culture, they were proved wrong. The Vietnamese had not lost touch completely with China, and they began to see in the spread of the Romanized script a parallel to the reform and modernization of language in China which was being undertaken under the leadership of such scholars as the American-educated Hu Shih. The new script of Vietnamese came to be known as *quôc-ngu* ('national speech') which paralleled the Chinese *kuo-yü*.

From about 1913 a number of periodicals were founded in Hanoi, which used the new script and sought to persuade the traditional scholars to abandon Chinese in favour of it. One of the most important of them was *Nam-Phong Tap-Chi*, founded by Pham Quynh and given the blessing of the French authorities, because they saw in it a means towards promoting a 'Franco-Annamite' culture. But out of it there developed in fact a Vietnamese literary 'renaissance' with younger writers seeking to imitate the forms of Western literature, but developing within those forms a content which reflected their own national aspirations. Something which the French had hoped would help to Westernize their colonial subjects became by the 1930s an element in their increasing sense of national identity. Novels, stories and poems in *quôc-ngu* became a focus of passive opposition to French rule.[9]

The sense of nationality will not in itself create a nation however. To borrow a phrase of Salvador de Madariaga, 'a nation is a psychological fact.' But also it must be an institutional fact, and it is not easy to develop national institutions where they did not exist before. The central problem of the Vietnamese in the twentieth century—and a theme which will be found through many of the chapters of this essay—has been that of translating their aspirations towards nationhood into a permanent institutional reality.

Merely to remove the French would not amount to a solution of this problem. The Confucian monarchy had, as we have seen, been fossilized as a result of French 'protection'. Of the traditional framework, it was the lesser institutions such as the clan, the family, the secret association, that survived into the twentieth century with the greatest vigour. To a remarkable extent, nationalism became focused on small associations with only a local following, rather than on the monarchy. There was, it is true, a movement for Constitutional monarchy during the period before about 1916; but it was overtaken in the following decade by more radical reformers, such as the Cochinchinese Constitutionalists, or by out-and-out revolutionaries. The latter operated in much the same manner as the old secret societies, and mutual suspicion between different groups of nationalists and revolutionaries made effective opposition to the French extremely difficult. This fragmentation of nationalism has been one of the most important factors in the unfolding of the Vietnamese tragedy.

In the circumstances, it was not inevitable that the whole of Viet-Nam would be drawn into a single national framework of institutions. The French divided the country into three parts: Cochinchina, which was a colony, and Annam and Tongking, which were protectorates. The two protectorates kept stronger links with one another than either had with Cochinchina, although there persisted within them a great deal of regional loyalty and suspicion of men from other provinces than one's own. Cochinchina, which was ruled for longer by the French and was more deeply influenced by Western culture and education, remained an area apart. Might it not, had circumstances favoured it, have become a nation quite separate from the rest of Viet-Nam? It has, after all, never in its history been ruled directly and completely from Hanoi.[10] There was even, for a while in 1945-46, a movement afoot in certain French circles to grant Cochinchina separate independence, but it came to naught. This possibility of two nations in Viet-Nam rather than one must be borne in mind when we come to look in more detail at events after 1946.

Yet in fact there has never been a Cochinchinese nationalism in the sense that the people (or for that matter the elite) of Cochinchina have felt themselves to belong to a Cochinchinese nationality. Vietnamese of all regions have tended to think of Viet-Nam as a single nation. What has very often divided them has been the difference between their respective views of how a single Viet-Nam ought to develop. For Northerners have tended to think of Hanoi as the only possible capital, and have regarded people of other regions as inferior; people from the centre have seen Huê as the natural focus for the Vietnamese nation; whilst the Cochinchinese have often looked no further than Saigon, which during the colonial period was both larger and economically more important than Hanoi. This is not the same kind of regionalism as that with which we are familiar in thinking about Western countries; it does not in itself amount to separatism. But it has nonetheless been a major obstacle to the development of a single national framework, or even a single national movement demanding independence.

V

Religion

RELIGION had often entered into politics in traditional Viet-Nam and secret sects had played their part from time to time in rebellions against the emperor. In the twentieth century, when the Confucian system was ceasing to command respect as a basis for political activity and when some other framework was needed for the expansion of nationalist feeling, it is hardly surprising that religious sects once again became prominent in politics. The tendency was strengthened by the fact that Asia generally was experiencing something of a religious revival in the late nineteenth and early twentieth centuries. It was a natural response to the challenge of the Europeans, and especially the Christian missions, that Asians should begin to re-examine their own religious tradition. Encouraged by the growth of interest in their religions in Europe itself, many of them came to the conclusion that in matters other than material technology, the East had often been at least the equal of the West.

In some parts of Asia, this religious revival has contributed a great deal to the growing sense of national identity, and has even sometimes provided an institutional framework for nationalism. In Viet-Nam too this has been the case to some extent. But given the country's tradition of sectarian religion, it was not to be expected that any single religious body would prove capable of uniting the whole country behind a single set of beliefs. The Vietnamese religious revival was consequently diverse, but none the less important for that.

The one religion which had attempted to become anything like an orthodoxy in traditional Viet-Nam was Confucianism. But it had been the monarchy that had made of Confucianism something more than a mere sect religion, and with the declining prestige of the monarchy under French 'protection' the possibility of that religion continuing to be both an established orthodoxy and a focus for national revival was considerably reduced. There was, it is true, a Confucian revival in certain quarters. Professor Levenson has shown how Chinese conservatives in the first two decades of the twentieth century tried to make of Confucianism a kind of state religion, even within the Republic. That movement found reflection in Viet-Nam, notably in the writings of Trân Trong Kim whose *Nho-Giao* ('Confucianism') appeared between 1920 and 1930. But when a prominent younger journalist called Phan Khôi criticized Kim's ideas in a newspaper of 1931, he evoked an echo of response throughout the country.[1] In so far as Confucian ideas survived amongst the generation of Vietnamese which reached maturity after 1920, it did so only as a set of ethical values, a way of living, and not as a movement capable of holding together an organized mass following. Nor, with the eclipse of the monarchy, was there great scope for Viet-Nam to develop the kind of religion that Japanese *Shinto* became in the twentieth century: a national cult held together by the rituals of the imperial court. The important elements in the Vietnamese religious revival therefore were Buddhism and Taoism, and the sects which sought to unite both religions (and even Christianity) into a single doctrine of the One.

Since the Vietnamese religious revival was one of sects rather than of a single orthodox 'Church', it is no cause for surprise to discover that it was as much influenced by limitations of region as were the nationalist political movements of the period before 1945. In Cochinchina, two religious movements dominate the scene: the *Cao-Dai* religion, and *Hoa-Hao* Buddhism. The former is the older movement, and may indeed have lost some of its early supporters to the latter. Caodaism could still claim at least half a million adepts in 1966; and the *Hoa-Hao* sect in the same year had about 550,000 members, mainly in the west of Cochinchina.[2]

To regard Caodaism as a kind of reformed Taoism may possibly give a better indication of the character of the religion than a description of it as reformed Buddhism; but neither term does anything like justice to its complexity. It belongs to the tradition, by no means new in China, of trying to draw together the three religions of Confucianism, Buddhism and Taoism into a religion of the One, or of the Way. An innovation of Caodaism is that it includes also Christianity, and claims to be heir to all the religions of the world. (The fact that Islam has played hardly any part in Vietnamese history is no doubt the explanation for its very peripheral part in Caodaism.) The new religion was officially established in the year 1926, but its roots go deeper than that, and in part its origins may go back to the sects or secret societies which organized the anti-French movement of 1916 in many parts of Cochinchina. Perhaps it should be traced even further back, to the sects of the *Dao-Lanh* religion which participated in the opposition to French rule in the 1870s. But we must return in a moment to the political role of the Caodaists, for to concentrate upon it to the exclusion of other aspects would be to forget the essentially religious character of the movement, which is to a large extent genuine.

The name *Cao-Dai* is that given by the religion to the Supreme Being, or God, whom it worships. It means literally 'high tower' (or 'high palace'), and is found originally as a symbol of the Supreme Being in a number of Taoist and Chinese Buddhist scriptures. It was also, though the fact may be of no relevance, used by early Protestant missionaries to translate 'Jehovah' when rendering the Bible into Chinese. In Caodaist temples, the *Cao-Dai* is represented not as a tower but as an eye: to this extent one can say that the Caodaist God is personal. But the symbol is still much less personal than that of Christ on the Cross.

The formal title of the religion is not Caodaism, however: that was merely a convenient French appellation. It is known in its own official records as the *Dai-Dao Tam-Ky Phô-Dô*, and the meanings of the three elements in this title tell us a good deal about its fundamental character. *Dai-Dao* means the 'Great Way': that is, the Way of Heaven, the Way of the *Tao Teh Ching* which governs the order of the universe and to which men must strive to conform. *Phô-Dô* means in effect 'salvation': literally, the crossing of the infinite, in the sense of being helped across by some greater Being. *Tam-Ky* means simply the 'Three Periods'. The *Cao-Dai* religion is therefore the 'Great Way of the Three Epochs of Salvation'. It is partly an apocalyptic religion, for it believes that the third epoch is shortly to begin and that it will be the epoch of great peace. But it is also a religion of purification, for it urges on all men that they should purify themselves in preparation for this third epoch. The Buddhist concept of *karma* enters into it as well. Thus it is more than a merely devotional religion, and makes greater demands on its adepts than the chanting of sutras: they must believe, and they must live upright lives.

The idea of three epochs allows for the introduction of all other religions into the Caodaist doctrine: for all are the result of attempts by God during the course of the two previous epochs to save mankind from materialism. The third epoch differs from all others because in that epoch all the religions of the earth will be united. In many of its features Caodaism is not unlike the *Tao-Yuan* religion which grew up in northern China during the 1920s, and which aimed to unite all five of the religions of China: Confucianism, Taoism, Buddhism, Islam and Christianity. G. Goulet, writing in 1926, traced religions of this kind back to a much earlier sect in which the 'three religions' were united, for whose existence he found evidence in a Chinese text dated 1613.[3]

There is no necessity to explain Caodaism in terms of direct influence from outside during the 1920s. The fundamental urge to create a religion of the One lay deeply rooted in the Sino-Vietnamese tradition. But its revival at this particular time probably was due in large part to the new spirit that was abroad in East Asia following the European holocaust of the first world war. The death and destruction which the West brought upon itself after 1914 led Asians to question the superiority of Western values that they had previously taken for granted. They turned to spiritual values in reaction against the previously unchallenged materialism of their conquerors. Caodaism was the religious movement in which Vietnamese participated most fully in the universalist aspect of the Asian religious revival. Yet at the same time, even it had a nationalistic overtone, for the Caodaists emphasized with some pride that it was their country in which the Supreme Being had chosen to manifest himself to mankind anew.

The Caodaists were very conscious that their doctrines depended upon divine revelation. It is in their method of communication with the divine that they have found the greatest difficulty in persuading Westerners to take their religion seriously. For that method is frankly spiritualist. The most important adepts of the religion are the spirit mediums who speak or write messages from spirits at special seances. The Westerner, influenced by the Christian tradition if not himself a believer, finds it difficult to appreciate that in Viet-Nam this represents more than an activity of cranks; but traditional Vietnamese religion has always been spiritualistic, and Caodaism has made no major innovation in this respect.[4] Through the medium—using either the planchette or the beaked basket—the Caodaists communicate with a whole host of spirits, of whom the *Cao-Dai* is the greatest but not different in essence from the others. Many sacred Caodaist texts are derived not from the supreme being but from other spirits, including those of great poets and heroes of the past. One of the most important of these is the spirit of Li T'ai-po (Ly Thai Bach), an eighth-century Chinese poet famous for his habits as a tippler and for his skill in Taoist meditation. Another spirit who has played a part in the growth of the religion is that of the fourth-century general Quan-Công (or Quan Thanh-Dê), the Chinese God of War. It is on a comparable level that the Caodaists venerate the spirits of several Western heroes, notably Victor Hugo, and Jeanne d'Arc. Into their hierarchy of spirits the Caodaists have fitted all the great spiritual leaders of mankind: Confucius, Lao-Tzu, the Buddha, Moses, and Christ. To say that they venerate these spirits as 'saints' is to risk imposing too Western an interpretation on oriental reality. For the Vietnamese, the power of the protecting spirit is as much a part of spiritual reality as is belief in divine incarnation for the Christian.

The popularity of the new religion in the years after 1926 was immediate and considerable. Its involvement in politics was therefore almost inevitable. It is impossible not to see in the suddenness of Caodaist expansion a reinvigoration of the secret societies and sects which had been active a decade earlier. The continuity was not direct, and there is nothing to indicate any personal continuity of leadership; the men of 1916 were too discredited to try again. But the network of temples and relationships still remained. The Caodaists were not trying to create something utterly unfamiliar to the Cochinchinese peasantry. The new leadership was better educated than that of ten years before, most of the prominent Caodaists being former officials of the government who had been taught at French schools. It was also more specifically religious, for the Caodaist was not just a local *thây-phap* selling magical charms: he had a system of belief which could satisfy the growing number of country notables educated in local primary schools. Some of the leading people in the religion were indeed much more interested in religion than politics, notably the founder of Caodaism, Ngô Van Chiêu, and the head of the Bên-Tre Caodaists, Nguyên Ngoc Tuong.

Nevertheless for the politically minded there was an obvious opportunity to mobilize ordinary people and eventually to use the organization for political ends. The first important move towards such organization seems to have been the creation of three principal centres: at Cân-Tho or Bac-Liêu, at My-Tho, and at Tây-Ninh. The third of these has attracted the most attention, partly because it was the most articulate, partly because its leadership later co-operated with the French. The first Caodaist temple at Tây-Ninh was established in 1926, but since then it has been replaced by a much more lavish structure whose ornamentation has been described as gawdy by many Western tourists, but which manages to symbolize most of the features of a highly symbolic religion. In 1930 the highest dignitary of the religion, Lê Van Trung, invited adepts from all areas of Cochinchina to go to Tây-Ninh and settle there on a substantial acreage of land bought for the purpose. He may well have had in mind a Vietnamese imitation of Tagore's Santiniketan, or of the Gandhian *ashram*. But he was also thinking in terms of a state within a state. The Caodaist hierarchy was not only religious in character: it included a bureaucratic hierarchy also, within which Trung himself was a high minister. There was even some attempt to differentiate between legislative and executive power, but we have no means of knowing how effective it was in practice.

For a time, around 1930, it may have seemed possible that the whole movement could be directed from the one centre of Tây-Ninh. But as so often happens with Vietnamese organizations unity proved difficult to maintain. By 1932 rifts appeared in the leadership on issues that were sometimes personal, sometimes political, and sometimes religious. The relationship between the Western Caodaists (of My-Tho, Bac-Liêu and Cân-Tho) and those of Tây-Ninh had never been very close: the former groups now broke away and formed a number of branches on their own. A little later the Tây-Ninh group itself split up, and Nguyên Ngoc Tuong established his own 'holy see' at Bên-Tre, leaving Pham Công Tac to succeed to the authority (though not the title) of Lê Van Trung at Tây-Ninh. By about 1935 there seem to have been about ten different sects or branches of the religion, each with its own leaders and sometimes its own peculiarities of belief. The seriousness of the schisms should not however be exaggerated. For this was not a religion dependent on an apostolic succession and a conviction that there could be only one law-giving authority within it. A unifying authority was far less necessary to hold a religion like Caodaism together than it was in medieval Christendom. Although attempts to reunite the faithful in the late 1930s, and again in 1946, were not very successful, the adepts of all branches probably continued to feel a sense of belonging to the same religion.

Some of the Caodaists probably joined the *Hoa-Hao* sect when it emerged in western Cochinchina in 1939.[5] *Hoa-Hao* Buddhism differs from Caodaism in that it does not claim to unite all religions into one, and in that it venerates the person of its founder, Huynh Phu So. His career, except that he was never a Christian, shows remarkable parallels with that of the founder of the Tai-Ping religion in South China in the 1840s. His spiritual education took place at a temple in the hills near the Cambodian border. Then in 1939, according to one account, in the midst of a great storm, he 'revealed' the principles of a new 'Buddhism of Great Peace'. He gathered around him a number of disciples, and his beliefs quickly spread. The religion which he revealed and preached is extremely puritanical, and is opposed to elaborate ritual of all kinds. It has a kind of spiritual centre in the village of Hoa-Hao (Châu-Dôc province), but it has no great temples comparable to those of Tây-Ninh or Bên-Tre.

During the 1930s, both the *Cao-Dai* and the *Hoa-Hao* sects became involved in the policies of the Japanese towards Indo-china. It is said that Pham Công Tac was from the first a follower of the prince Cuong-Dê, whom the monarchist reform movement had chosen as its imperial candidate in 1904, and who had lived since 1911 in Japan. (He died there in 1951.) Certainly by the later 1930s Tac was in contact with Japan, and was prepared to collaborate with the Japanese. When the Japanese army occupied Cochinchina in 1942, by agreement with the French, the latter were afraid that the *Kempetai* would use the Caodaists as part of a base for a non-French government in southern Viet-Nam. Consequently they arrested a number of the leaders of the sect, and deported Pham Công Tac to Madagascar. The Japanese also tried to use Huynh Phu So and his sect as part of their plan, but seem to have decided that he was either not sufficiently well-disposed towards them, or that he was not capable enough as a politician to help them.[6]

This breach between the sects and the French authorities was healed after the Japanese surrender in 1945. The French were faced with the problem of recovering control of their former colony and of defeating the Communist-led *Viêt-Minh*; at that period, the religious leaders had to decide whether to come to terms with the French or to throw in their lot with the *Viêt-Minh*. The *Hoa-Hao* sect seems to have been generally hostile to Communism, and in 1946 its leader Huynh Phu So incurred the odium of the *Viêt-Minh* by trying to form a political organization of his own. For this he was murdered the following year (April 1947), whereupon his followers came to an agreement with the French which allowed them to administer the provinces where they were strongest, and virtually to maintain a private army. The Caodaists at Tây-Ninh also came to an agreement of this kind with the French, on the understanding that Pham Công Tac was allowed to return to Viet-Nam and resume his direction of the religion. Not all the Caodaists however supported the French: other sects within the movement joined forces with the *Viêt-Minh*. Information on this point is scarce, but it would seem that the group led by Cao Triêu Phat in Bac-Liêu province was pro-*Viêt-Minh* at least down to 1949.[7] Another Caodaist group later withdrew from Tây-Ninh, and indeed from the war, and posed for a time as a 'third force': this was the group of Trinh Minh Thê, who found a curious immortality in the pages of Graham Greene's novel, *The Quiet American*. These differences of policy between different groups are a reminder of the fact that although it is convenient to use such blanket terms as Caodaist or *Hoa-Hao* Buddhist, these movements in reality consisted of federations of smaller associations: the situation of 1945–54 in Cochinchina was considerably more like that of 1913–16 than some observers would allow.

The traditional pattern of sectarian opposition to government had not for the most part included any tendency for a successful rebel sect to make any ideological innovations. On taking power it would take over the whole Confucian system of administration and all its values, though it might have the strength to make things work better for a time. In the absence of (or rather decline of) the Confucian system in the twentieth century one might have expected the 'political' sects of that period to work out some new set of political ideals. But although the Caodaists made important religious innovations, they did not develop any new political theory which might have been the basis of a non-monarchical state. Some were Westernizers, but none produced a set of political ideas that was specifically Caodaist.

The sects so far described had their roots in Cochinchina, and apart from the communities of Caodaists at Da-Nang and Hanoi they did not make a great deal of headway outside that region. When we turn to the other principal element in the Vietnamese revival of religion, the Buddhists, we are dealing with a movement which had many followers in all three regions although it was perhaps strongest in Central Viet-Nam.

The Buddhists of the various Buddhist Associations that have flourished in Viet-Nam since about 1930 were conscious of belonging to the Buddhist revival in Asia as a whole: therefore they must be seen against the wider background of that revival, which has embraced both the Theravada and the Mahayana branches of the religion. In the Theravada world, the first modern movement for the reform of Buddhism occurred in Thailand in the 1840s, when Prince Mongkut created the Dhammayutika Order in Bangkok. Its influence outside Siam however was curtailed later in the century by the Europeans' annexation of Burma and Cambodia; Ceylon, the other traditional centre of Theravada religion, had been a British colony since 1798. The Buddhist revival which began to take place in those other countries towards the end of the nineteenth century was of a different kind, for it made Buddhism the focus of anti-colonial nationalism. In both Burma and Ceylon, in the 1890s, there grew up a movement for Buddhist schools and colleges, in imitation of—but also in competition with—the Christian missions. In Burma that was followed about 1916 by a more political move on the part of some younger Buddhists to make an issue out of the British habit of wearing shoes inside pagodas and monasteries. By the early 1920s this produced an even bigger movement, in which '*pongyi* politicians' used their influence amongst the populace to stir up anti-British feeling. From that time onwards Buddhism was an established part of Burmese nationalism, and it continued to be so after independence was achieved. It derived much of its force from the memory that before British rule the Theravada *Sangha* in

Burma had been virtually a State Religion under royal patronage; and in 1961 Buddhism was once again elevated to be the country's State Religion.[8] In Ceylon the relationship between Buddhism and nationalism developed more slowly, but by the 1950s the religion was a major factor in politics there too, though not 'established' by the state. The Theravada countries saw a great intensification of Buddhist activity in the 1950s. The Sixth Buddhist Council was opened in Burma in 1954 (the Fifth having been held at Mandalay by King Mindon in 1871). And Ceylon led the celebrations for the 2,500th anniversary of the Buddha's attainment of Nirvana, in the Buddha Jayanti year of 1956.

The most important country in the twentieth-century revival of Mahayana Buddhism has been Japan. There too the first appearance of new vigour came about the turn of the century: Japanese Buddhism however did not become a focus for nationalism, since that was the almost explicit function of Shintoism. There were indeed occasions when Shintoism and Buddhism came into conflict. But since the end of the Pacific War there has been no more Shintoism, and Buddhism has played an important part in the nation's adjustment to defeat. The diversity of the religious revival in Japan has been considerable. At least four groups of Japanese Buddhists can be identified by even the most superficial observer, and a full exploration would show that within them there are many subdistinctions.[9] First, the *Zen* Buddhists, who seek sudden enlightenment through meditation under the direction of a master: they do not attach great importance to any of the scriptures. Second, the *Shingon* sect, whose beliefs include that of sudden enlightenment but are also to some extent tantric in character: their most sacred text is the Diamond Sutra. Third, the *Jodo* and *Shin* sects, which are Amidist: their Buddhism is devotional, based on the Amitayus Sutra, and they hope for salvation in the 'True Pure Land', the paradise of the former Buddha Amitabha. Fourth, the sects of *Tendai* and *Nichiren*, which are also devotional but whose path to salvation lies through the veneration of the Sakyamuni Buddha (Gautama) and the chanting of the Lotus Sutra. It is the fourth group which has been most active politically. One of its offshoots is the *Soka Gakkai* sect which honours especially the founder of the Nichiren sect. That movement claims about three million adherents, and as a political party has a number of representatives in the Japanese Diet.

In China, Buddhism was virtually eclipsed by the Communist take-over in 1949, but it had seen something of a revival in the first three decades after the first Revolution of 1911.[10] Shortly after the overthrow of the monarchy there was a debate on the question whether Buddhism should become the new State Religion, and although the idea was rejected the debate itself helped to produce increasing interest in the religion. During the 1920s, when many Chinese were becoming disillusioned with the Western superiority which they had formerly taken for granted, there grew up a Buddhist educational movement, leading to the foundation of a Chinese Buddhist Society in 1929. Seven years later it had nearly five hundred branches. The revival spread to the overseas Chinese communities in South East Asia, and in 1933 the Lotus Society was founded in Singapore, the forerunner of the Singapore Buddhist Federation created in 1950. In the Nanyang the trend was not halted by the Communist take-over as it was on the mainland, and in Singapore especially it continued to progress during the 1950s and 1960s.

After the second world war the gulf between Theravada and Mahayana Buddhism (the Lesser and the Greater Vehicles) began to be bridged. The World Fellowship of Buddhists, created in 1950, held its first congress in Ceylon and its second in Tokyo. However it is still necessary to make the distinction between the two Vehicles, and to remember that despite some interaction their twentieth-century revivals were separate movements. The most important difference between the two kinds of Buddhism has always been that of diversity of belief and organization. Theravada Buddhism has a tendency towards orthodoxy (albeit not always fulfilled) which finds expression in the *Sangha* organization, whereas the Buddhism of the Greater Vehicle is much more diverse and its characteristic institution is the sect. Thus in Thai Buddhism there are only two Buddhist orders, not widely different in belief; whereas Japan has a much larger number of sects, each with its own distinctive beliefs and practices. It is important to appreciate that Viet-Nam belongs (apart from its minority of Cambodians and a small number of Vietnamese who have imitated them) to the Mahayana tradition; and it is a mistake to suppose that its religious revival in recent decades has amounted to the introduction of Theravada Buddhism.

As in so many other respects, Viet-Nam was influenced by

China in its Buddhist revival; it was also deeply influenced by Japan. Vietnamese Buddhism began to follow the example set in these neighbouring countries when, during the years 1929-34, Buddhist Associations were created in various parts of the country, notably Saigon, Tra-Vinh, Huê and Hanoi.[11] Some of the associations were made up of monks (*tang-gia*), others of laymen who lived with their families but enjoyed a special religious status (*cu-si*). As time went on, some associations flourished, others declined. But in these early days none of them aspired to become anything like a nation-wide *Sangha*, and none of them acquired political prominence.

Twentieth-century Buddhism in Viet-Nam is almost entirely devotional, and of the four Japanese groups noticed above it is the third and fourth which have direct parallels in Saigon and Huê: the Amidists and the Lotus school. The distinction between them is less sharply drawn here than in Japan, but it is possible nevertheless to identify certain pagodas as practising predominantly one or the other doctrine. The Lotus school is particularly strong in Central Viet-Nam. Zen Buddhism, which once existed in Viet-Nam, seems to have died out; as for the Buddhism of the Diamond Sutra, it is possibly still practised, but its pagodas are less prominent in national life than those of the Amidist and Lotus schools. One of the most important literary contributions to the Buddhist revival was an article written in 1932 by Trân Van Giap, a member of the École Française d'Extrême-Orient, on the development of Buddhism in Viet-Nam from the sixth to the thirteenth centuries.[12] That period was indeed the 'Golden Age' of Vietnamese Buddhism, to which present-day monks and *cu-si* look back for inspiration. (It was also, the reader will recall, the period of Viet-Nam's first emergence as an independent kingdom, and it saw some of the greatest victories of Vietnamese heroes over Chinese armies.) From the fifteenth century, as Confucianism became more formalized, Buddhism declined in importance as far as the court was concerned, with the result that less was said about it in the chronicles. But it would be a mistake to suppose that the religion declined to the point of virtual disappearance between then and the twentieth century. The revival of the 1930s was not entirely without roots in the past, even though it was to a remarkable extent a movement of the towns.

The history of Buddhism during the Japanese occupation of Viet-Nam (1942–45) is still unwritten. The Japanese presence may well have strengthened the revival, but any gains it may have made then were lost in the chaos that followed the Japanese defeat. It was not until 1948 that the Buddhist Associations began to recover from the conflicts of the post-war years. But by 1951 they were able to go further than they had ever gone before: at a Congress in Huê they succeeded in creating a single Buddhist organization for all three regions of the country, and declared their affiliation to the World Fellowship of Buddhists. The creation of that Fellowship in the previous year was no doubt one of the sources of inspiration for the Vietnamese Buddhists. But the emergence of the new organization at a time when the Communists were said to be infiltrating most organized movements in the country has led to doubts in some minds about the relationship between the *Viêt-Minh* and the Buddhist National Congress at Huê. The doubts still persisted in the early 1960s when the Buddhist campaigns against Ngô Dinh Diêm and his successors were under way.

Whatever may be the truth on that question, there can be no doubt that during those campaigns a certain section of Vietnamese Buddhists revealed a militancy that was partly religious and partly nationalistic. These were the Buddhists who organized street demonstrations, and burned themselves alive in order to emphasize their demands or their opposition to the government. Their activities are to some extent comparable to those of the Japanese *Soka Gakkai*, and on closer examination it turns out that they were in fact Buddhists of the Lotus school, rather than Amidists. Their greatest strength lay in Central Viet-Nam, and it is interesting that almost all the monks who burned themselves in the summer and autumn of 1963 were natives of that region, including Thich Quang Duc. Unlike the Caodaists and the *Hoa-Hao* Buddhists, the Lotus school concentrated their activities in the towns; they did not try to raise rebellion in the countryside. Nor did they—by contrast with the Amidists—succeed in winning much support for their activities in the Cochinchinese Delta. In 1963 they succeeded in making an alliance with the Amidists of the South, but it did not last long after the fall of Diêm.

The militant Buddhists became, for a time, an important factor in the political situation. But in their opposition to the war of the 1960s, and in their criticism of the governments in Saigon whose policy was to pursue the war, they did not enunciate any particular programme for political development. They did not put forward any set of ideas that was comprehensively and distinctively Buddhist. Perhaps one must conclude that Buddhism is such an essentially personal religion, concerned with the inner life of the individual rather than with the external life of society, that no such programme is possible. It is a basis for civilized moral values, for the virtue of the monk and the *cu-si*, but not for institutional reform. If so, then it is futile to look to Buddhism as such to provide a new political framework for the development of the nation.

A third major group in the Vietnamese religious revival were the Catholics: although their beliefs derive originally from the West, they have become the foundation of religious life for over two million Vietnamese. (Of the 2,290,000 Catholics in Viet-Nam in 1966, as many as 830,000 were still living in the North.) The first converts to Christianity in Viet-Nam were made by Jesuit missionaries in the first half of the seventeenth century who, having discovered that the country was a fertile field for their efforts, put into it much of the energy which in other circumstances might have gone into Japan. Later on, the place of the Jesuits was taken by the priests of the Société des Missions Etrangères, whose headquarters was in Paris. By 1682 there were said to be 200,000 Vietnamese Christians; and despite persecution the Church in Viet-Nam managed to survive at about that strength until the nineteenth century. Under French rule of course the missionaries were able to operate far more securely, and it was at that period that the greatest number of conversions was made.[13]

To the Vietnamese Confucian rulers the Catholics appeared as no more and no less than a new kind of sect, which had to be kept under some kind of control or it would become politically dangerous. Nor was that view wholly unjustified, if we consider Bishop Pigneau de Behaine's role in the politics of Cochinchina between 1785 and his death in 1799, or Father Marchand's participation in the rebellion of Saigon in 1833–35. But in their own minds of course the Catholics were very much more than a Taoist sect. Their more sophisticated organization certainly set them apart from other religious groups; so too, and on a more fundamental level, did their absolutist conception of the world as divided into Christians, who enjoy grace, and pagans or infidels, who do not.

Politically this absolutist view has the importance that it has made the Catholics rigorous opponents of Communism in all forms, on grounds of doctrine and not merely of comfort. The fact that over 800,000 Catholics remain in the Communist-controlled North Viet-Nam suggests that they do not easily give way in such matters. The presence of twice that number in South Viet-Nam is even more important as a factor in the continuing struggle against Communism south of the seventeenth parallel. But when it comes to the question of positive political ideals, it may well be asked whether in the long run the Catholics have as a Church contributed any more to Viet-Nam's modernization than other religious groups. The most essential feature of Catholic political theory is that power should be divided between Church and State, because the authority on which these institutions are based has been divided by God. Under French rule it was possible, at least for the missionaries and for pro-French priests, to enjoy some form of recognition of spiritual authority, and to live in the hope that one day Viet-Nam would be completely converted to their faith. But in the context of an independent Viet-Nam such a position is less easily maintained. For a while, during the war years of 1946–54, it was possible for some Catholic clergy to hold out against the *Viêt-Minh* and at the same time to be virtually independent of the French. Thus the Bishop of Phat-Diêm, Lê Huu Tu, was able for a time to defend his bishopric on a basis not unlike that of the Caodaists at Tây-Ninh. But such circumstances could not last forever, and in the end he had to flee to Saigon. The Catholics in an independent Viet-Nam are bound to face up to the fact that they are a minority of the population, and therefore cannot impose an absolutist doctrine of divine authority. The most they can hope for is toleration.

To sum up therefore, one can say that although the Vietnamese religious revival has had a considerable impact on politics, the character of the religions concerned—Caodaism, *Hoa-Hao* Buddhism, Amidist and Lotus School Buddhism, and Catholicism—has not been such as to lead to the growth of any new political theory out of the religious revival. And what Viet-Nam needed to replace its old Confucian orthodoxy was a political theory. Nor has any single one of the religions succeeded in uniting the whole country behind its own faith. In this respect religion has played a very different role in the modern development of Viet-Nam from that which it played in certain other Asian countries, notably those of the Islamic world. In that, perhaps Viet-Nam has been fortunate: for its sufferings in the twentieth century have not included communal violence between religious groups. Although some journalists tended to characterize the movement against Ngô Dinh Diêm as a struggle between Buddhists and Catholics, it was in fact much more complicated. Viet-Nam has never (since the persecutions of the reign of Minh-Mang) seen religious violence comparable to that which occurred, for example, in British India at the time of partition.

VI

Constitutionalism

BETWEEN Viet-Nam and China there was a long-standing cultural affinity which makes it natural to compare the ideas and institutions of the two countries, both traditionally and in the modern world. But when in the nineteenth century Viet-Nam became the one country of the Chinese cultural world to be conquered and actually ruled by Europeans, their experiences began to some extent to diverge. Viet-Nam came to have something in common with other areas of Asia which she did not share with China, for example with British India.

India is the most striking example of an Asian country which borrowed ideas from its conquerors in order to overthrow them, and in so doing achieved a fusion of Eastern and Western thought. Having been brought under British rule by stages during the century and more before 1857, India had a much fuller experience of Western culture than China, and a longer period in which to work out a *rapprochement* between its own tradition and that of the West. Viet-Nam's period of European rule was much shorter, but its relationship with France was similar in kind to that of India with Britain, and the French had if anything a deeper cultural impact on most of their colonies than did the British. A comparison between India and Indochina during the colonial period might therefore be expected to contribute towards our understanding of the modern development of Viet-Nam.

The political solution to their problems which the Indians adopted had as its pivot the conception of government by constitional means. It might conveniently be termed, though the word was one more likely to be used in French than in British possess-ions, constitutionalism. In the latter part of the nineteenth century constitutional government was widely regarded as an integral factor in Western success throughout the world. In countries like Japan and Russia those people who demanded the modernization of government and law usually envisaged a constitution as a necessary part of the process. Japan formulated a constitution in 1890, which worked successfully until the rise of military power after 1930. The Chinese too looked upon the idea as one which they would adopt as soon as a reforming or revolutionary regime could be installed: Liang Ch'i-ch'ao, an admirer of England, and Sun Yat-sen, who was more impressed by France and the United States, both agreed on this.

But newly created constitutions were not always successful in practice. In Russia the parliamentary system that was hesitatingly set up in 1905 proved too fragile a plant to survive. In China, after the overthrow of the monarchy in 1911, a constitution was inaugurated but was never allowed to become the effective focus of government and legislation. Power passed to the generals, who refused to accept rule by an elected assembly or a civilian president. It is the more remarkable therefore that in India constitutionalism took deep root. The National Congress, which was already holding its first meetings in the decade that saw the French conquest of Annam and Tongking, was a movement imbued with respect for English principles and conduct. Even when its objectives became more extreme, including total independence for India, it did not abandon completely the principles of the rule of law and of representative government which had been learnt from the British. After 1920 it preferred non-violent passive resistance to action entirely within the law, but even in that there survived something of Gandhi's early respect for the British idea of fair-play. When independence was finally obtained, albeit in a climate of religious tension, the constitution adopted by the Republic of India reproduced the essential features of British parliamentary democracy.

Turning to Viet-Nam, one is led to wonder why French colonial rule there did not produce results similar to those of British rule in India. Why should Viet-Nam, despite its experience of colonial domination, have remained much more like China than India? Why was it that when the country eventually achieved independence in 1954, it came only after a long and bitter conflict in which constitutionalism was virtually squeezed out by the extremes of colonialism and revolution? Part of the answer lies in the nature of French policy; but we must also give some attention to the actual development of a constitutional movement in Viet-Nam, which most writers on Vietnamese history in the twentieth century have tended to ignore.[1]

French colonial policy has to be seen in terms of the intellectual debate about the merits of 'assimilation' and 'association' which developed during the 1880s and which was still not really settled when France lost control of Indochina. It must be seen too in terms of the problems (and administrative inertia) involved in the actual running of a colonial territory. As far as Viet-Nam was concerned, complete assimilation was never a practical possibility. As early as 1885 Paul Bert was proposing an administrative policy which, in its frank use of village traditions, would amount to a kind of 'association'. Bert died before he had been governor in Tongking for as long as a year, but his ideas survived him and became the basis of a more systematic theory of association. By 1900 writers like Chailley-Bert (son-in-law of the former governor) and Joseph Harmand were advocating a colonial policy based on the association of rulers and ruled in an enterprise which would be to the advantage of both.[2] This new theory owed something to the growing French admiration for British and Dutch colonial methods, and in particular to their practice of 'indirect rule'. It recognized, too, that in a country like Viet-Nam the people were not mere savages before French conquest, but had a culture of their own which they might wish to keep. Thus the assimilationist idea that the natives should be transformed into Frenchmen with the maximum possible speed gave way, in the minds of the associationists, to a greater respect for native institutions and traditions.

The new philosophy fitted in well with the growing concern amongst both colonial officials and politicians at home, that the colonies should be made to pay their way. In 1884 Jules Ferry had justified his policies in Tongking and elsewhere by the argument that 'for all the great nations of modern Europe, once their industrial power is formed, there is posed the immense and formidable problem: the question of the market . . . all the great industrial nations came in turn to the colonial policy'.[3] By 1900 the debate on whether colonies ought to be acquired or not had given way to one about how they could best be exploited, or their 'mise en valeur'. The original economic aims of colonization, which were commercial more than anything else, were supplemented by the additional desire to make colonies profitable in themselves by investing capital there. It was in this context that the associationists looked forward optimistically to a future in which the colonies would develop economically, on the basis of Western capital and native labour, both sides benefiting from the result. Cultural assimilation, and the 'civilizing of the natives', began to seem less important than the reaping of economic gain. The most important problem to which the new attitude gave rise did not become apparent until a rather later period (after about 1917), when the Vietnamese themselves began to ask whether association had any political implications.

'Assimilation' and 'association' did not coincide with any precise division of thought amongst the Vietnamese themselves. One might think, on first acquaintance with the two theories, that the colonized people would themselves prefer association. But in practice the latter theory had a variety of different interpretations. Sometimes it was thoroughly conservative in its implications: Lyautey for example, one of the most famous associationists, was at heart a monarchist who believed in using traditional institutions as a means to better control over colonial peoples. In Viet-Nam such an approach meant the preservation intact of the Confucian system and all its traditions; and indeed to a remarkable extent this is what actually happened under the Résidents-Généraux in Tongking and Annam (especially Annam). But as we have seen, the more progressive Vietnamese politicians by the first decade of the twentieth century were dissatisfied with traditional Confucianism. They wanted either to modernize the monarchy, or to do away with it altogether.

It was the interpretation placed on 'association' by later, more progressive Governors-General (notably Albert Sarraut and Alexandre Varenne) that had some appeal for the Vietnamese elite. Sarraut and Varenne both alarmed the comfortable colons of Saigon and Hanoi by making speeches which raised the hopes of the more 'moderate' Vietnamese nationalists. (The quotation at the beginning of Part II is from one such speech by Varenne.) They dared to think in terms of political as well as of economic association. Their kind of association did not emphasize the value of traditional institutions: it concentrated on the development of education and economic growth. Sarraut, for example, founded the University of Hanoi in 1917—about the same time as he abolished the imperial examination system that had been allowed to survive in Annam and Tongking. Ironically, he promoted in the name of association a new phase of cultural assimilation. But he envisaged eventual Vietnamese independence; the assimilationists had never admitted the remotest possibility of an independent, or even 'associated', Vietnamese nation. The new theory of association both opened up that possibility and enabled moderate Vietnamese to regard a spirit of nationalism as not wholly incompatible with a Franco-Vietnamese cultural *rapprochement*.

Constitutionalism in Viet-Nam had two principal roots. One was this new concept of association, as interpreted by Sarraut and Varenne from about 1917 onwards. The other was the movement for constitutional monarchy which had grown up during the first decade of the twentieth century, under the influence of Liang Ch'i-ch'ao and his admiration for Japan.[4] As a Vietnamese movement, one may date the beginning of this early constitutionalism from the secret conference held by a group of younger scholars in the province of Quang-Nam in 1904. Among those present were two of the most famous of all Vietnamese nationalists, both of whom belonged to roughly the same generation as Liang Ch'i-ch'ao: Phan Bôi Châu, a native of Nghê-An province in northern Annam; and Phan Châu Trinh, whose home was in Quang-Nam. Phan Bôi Châu was later to desert the cause of constitutional monarchy, under the influence of Sun Yat-sen's programme for revolution. Phan Châu Trinh was more firmly constitutionalist, and more willing to learn from the French. His letter of 1908 to the Governor-General of Indochina marks the beginning of Vietnamese hopes that they might improve their lot by simply demanding reforms from the French.

The outcome of the meeting of 1904 was the creation of a new political society, the *Duy-Tân Hôi* ('Reform Association'), whose object was an independent Viet-Nam and a reformed monarchy. To that end the association selected as its 'pretender' to the throne a prince who claimed descent from the emperor Gia-Long (through the eldest son who had predeceased that monarch). The prince, Cuong-Dê, was smuggled out to Japan, and remained an exile until his death in 1951. The reformers appear to have had some part in almost all of the anti-French activities of the years 1904–8, which was the period when the colonial rulers first had to deal with opposition of a 'modern' kind. Three of these movements deserve mention.

The movement known as the *Dông-Kinh Nghia-Thuc*, which was centred mainly on Hanoi but had the support of people from Annam and Cochinchina, was educational in purpose, being organized to help young students to escape from the country and go to Japan. The French were able to put a stop to this by an agreement with the Japanese authorities in 1909. In the meantime, the colonial authorities launched a university of their own in Hanoi but closed it down within a year owing to student unrest. Secondly, at about the same period there was a group in Cochinchina led by Gilbert Trân Chanh Chiêu (a French citizen) which planned to develop a textile industry in the area; possibly it was influenced by the Indian *Swadeshi* movement. It sought French assistance to this end, but without any success, and in 1908 the authorities in Saigon suppressed the group on the grounds that it was using its industrial venture as a cover for political opposition. In 1908 too, there arose a peasant movement in Central Viet-Nam (especially in the province of Quang-Nam) against high taxation and heavy corvée labour. It involved little violence, and fairly soon subsided; but it seems to have had the support of the *Duy-Tân* association, even if it was not actually promoted by it. This was the first major peasant demonstration against the French in which specific grievances were raised in the hope of persuading the French to modify their policies. Neither Châu nor Trinh appreciated at this stage the wider possibilities of such a peasant movement, which were later to be exploited by the Communists. The reformers of this time were in fact groping in the dark, trying to find a way of opposing their colonial masters without bringing down upon themselves the kind of military suppression which had been used to quell the risings of Phan Dinh Phung and others in the period immediately after the conquest.

The trouble of 1908 did in fact lead to oppression. One leader, Trân Quy Cap, was executed immediately. Phan Châu Trinh himself was arrested and sentenced to life imprisonment on Poulo Condore; however in 1911 he was released and exiled to France, where he continued his campaign to win over French leaders to a more constructive policy in Indochina. Phan Bôi Châu escaped to Japan, and subsequently became a disciple of

Sun Yat-sen. The *Duy-Tân Hôi* however made one further attempt to impose its ideas on the French, in 1916. It launched a plan to abduct the young emperor—whose title was, somewhat surprisingly, Duy-Tân—and to raise a revolt in the provinces of Quang-Nam and Quang-Ngai. The emperor was in fact spirited away from his palace one night, but the French discovered him in a nearby temple two days later, before the revolt could begin. Duy-Tân himself was exiled to the island of Réunion, and the rebel leader Trân Cao Van was executed. That was virtually the end of the Reform Association, though there continued to exist in Quang-Nam a group of people ready to look to Japan as a model: it was their political heirs who twenty-five years later formed the pro-Japanese *Dai-Viêt* party in Central Viet-Nam.

The most important constitutionalist party which Viet-Nam produced under French rule, which was constitutionalist in its methods as well as in its aims, was that founded in Cochinchina about 1917. Its origins are to be found in the movement for French education known as the Société d'Enseignement Mutuel, originally created by Frenchmen before 1900. By the second decade of the twentieth century that society had a great many French-educated Vietnamese members, especially in Cochinchina, and there was a considerable sense of camaraderie amongst Cochinchinese who had attended the Collège Chasseloup-Laubat in Saigon. In 1917 a group of them formed the Parti Constitutionaliste and established a newspaper, *La Tribune Indigène*.[5] They were able to act somewhat more openly than political groups in Annam and Tongking, since some of them were French citizens and it was permissible for a Frenchman to publish a political newspaper in the French language. Besides their interest in education, they had two principal motives. One was to persuade the French to grant more freedom to Vietnamese in the colony; the other to create an *esprit de corps* amongst the Vietnamese themselves in the hope of reducing the hold which the overseas Chinese had over the Cochinchinese economy. Their first venture into organized activity was in fact economic, not political: an attempted boycott of the Chinese in 1919. It was not very successful, but it enabled the organizers to gain valuable political experience.

The most important individual in this group was Bui Quang Chiêu, a native of Bên-Tre province, who had been born in the same year as Liang Ch'i-ch'ao (1873). He received a French education, and then went to Paris to study agronomy—an aim which, incidentally, Sun Yat-sen expressed at about the same time but was never allowed to fulfil. On his return in 1897 Chiêu entered the government service of Indochina and for thirty years or so devoted his working life to the promotion of sericulture. At the age of forty he was a recognized expert on his subject, and by the time he retired he was a deputy director of the agricultural services for the whole of Indochina. But he was not content merely to serve in a colony where only a tiny minority of his compatriots were allowed the kind of opportunity which he himself had had. He was a founder member of the Parti Constitutionaliste, and within a few years he emerged as its leader, along with Nguyên Phan Long. His political philosophy, and that of the party generally, is indicated by the articles which appeared in the *Tribune Indigène* between 1917 and 1924, and in its successor the *Tribune Indochinoise* after 1926. A summary of the Constitutionalists' demands written towards the end of 1924 concentrated on four points: educational expansion, including the creation of a real university at Hanoi; reform of the judiciary, and the appointment of native *juges de paix*; changes in the naturalization laws, to enable more people to acquire French citizenship; and the creation of a really representative council or parliament based on a wide franchise. Ironically, all but the last of these points could have been put forward by a French idealist who really believed in assimilation. But it was the last point which counted, for what Chiêu wanted in the end was a Viet-Nam run on modern lines by Vietnamese.

The fact about the Constitutionalist Party which most distinguishes it from all other groups in Viet-Nam at this (and later) periods is its emphasis on representative institutions. The French, as we have seen, were slow to introduce their own constitutional principles into the government of their colonies, and many educated Vietnamese learnt of the virtues of democracy from the writings of Rousseau and Montesquieu long before they had any chance of voting in an election themselves. Nevertheless the French did make some attempt to introduce representational institutions in Viet-Nam, though they never allowed them any genuine legislative power. Advisory councils at the provincial level, elected on a narrow franchise, were created in Cochinchina in 1889 and in the other regions in 1913. Municipal councils were also established, again with limited electorates, in Saigon and Hanoi. But only in Cochinchina was there an elected council for a whole region of the Union. When it was created in 1880 the Conseil Colonial of Cochinchina had ten French members and six Vietnamese, and the latter were elected by a mere few hundred people. Thanks partly to the efforts of the Constitutionalists the number of Vietnamese members was increased to ten in 1922 and the native electorate allowed to expand from a mere 1,500 to over 20,000. But this was still a small number of voters in a population of six million, and not surprisingly Chiêu and his colleagues saw it as merely a small step in the right direction.[6]

It was the Conseil Colonial which gave the Constitutionalists of Cochinchina their opportunity to learn about representative opposition. Nguyên Phan Long became vice-president of the council in 1922 and used his position to press for a genuinely 'Franco-Annamite' approach to policy. In November and December of the following year he led a campaign against the proposal of the French to create a virtual monopoly over the port of Saigon and to grant it to a French concern. The campaign failed; only seven of the ten Vietnamese members voted against it, and even if all of them had done so they would not have amounted to a majority for there were now fourteen French members. Even so, the Constitutionalists succeeded in rallying a good deal of opinion in Saigon behind their cause, and they began to see more clearly the possibilities for organized protest against the government. In 1926 they reached the height of their influence. In the early months of that year, Chiêu visited France and publicized the ideas and demands of his party there. Then in October, at the elections for the Conseil Colonial, the list of candidates of the Parti Constitutionaliste swept the board. It was at this stage that Chiêu himself was elected to the Conseil, and immediately he became vice-president.

Their success did not last however. Had the French at this point decided that by encouraging the Constitutionalists they would stave off the rise of a more extreme opposition, had they chosen to grant Cochinchina some kind of constitution, it is just possible that Chiêu could have gone on to build up a party comparable to the Indian Congress Party, smaller in scale but capable of uniting into a single movement the majority of the colony's moderate politicians. But the French saw no danger of extremism at this period, and showed no inclination to give even a small amount of real responsibility for decisions to the elected councillors. Moreover they refused to allow the Constitutionalist movement to spread to the other regions: in the summer of 1926 Pham Quynh proposed the formation of a Constitutionalist Party in Tongking, but the Governor-General was not willing to grant it the legal recognition which Chiêu's party by now enjoyed in Cochinchina. Nor were any steps taken to introduce the principle of election into the advisory councils of Tongking and Annam. Unaware of the historical significance of the moment, the French allowed an opportunity to slip by which would never return.

Frustrated by its lack of real progress, the Constitutionalist Party began to break up. By 1930 it had split into about three factions, and although between them they still controlled most of the native scats in the Conseil Colonial, they had lost much of their buoyancy of a few years before. In the colony at large they had to watch the political initiative pass to more extreme leaders, forerunners or allies of the Communists. 1930 was the year in which Cochinchina once again experienced the upheaval of a rural revolt based on secret societies. It seemed to a great many young Vietnamese that to spread propaganda and discontent in the villages was the only way to get what they wanted. True, in the 1930s there were Marxists like Ta Thu Thâu, who would gain election to the municipal council of Saigon and stand in elections for the Conseil Colonial. But never again would a single party enjoy the confidence or the electoral cohesion achieved by the Constitutionalists in 1926. Bui Quang Chiêu himself, moreover, was drawn away from his homeland for most of the period between 1933 and 1941, in order to serve as Vietnamese representative at the Ministry of Colonies in Paris. By the time he returned home, to a country about to be occupied by Japanese forces, the time for a constitutional movement had passed. In that very year, 1941, the *Viêt-Minh* Front was established by a small band of Communists in the Chinese province of Kwangsi.

The Parti Constitutionaliste differed from other Vietnamese political groups in this period (except possibly the Communists) in being remarkably cosmopolitan. It was not merely that the

French education on which they placed so much emphasis opened up for them a vast new range of cultural experience. They were also conscious of belonging to a generation in which the whole of Asia seemed to be waking up. Whilst many of their fellow Vietnamese had their eyes exclusively on China and Japan, the Constitutionalists also looked towards India, and were greatly impressed by the example of Gandhi and Rabindranath Tagore. In 1929, Bui Quang Chiêu and his friend Duong Van Giao visited India and made a pilgrimage to Tagore's experimental school at Santiniketan. Later the same year, they persuaded Tagore to call briefly at Saigon during one of his Far Eastern tours. In his speech of welcome on that occasion, Chiêu expressed an idealism which he felt that he and his followers shared with their visitor:

> Far from being hostile to the civilization of the West, our illustrious guest from Santiniketan wishes with all the vigour of a poet to reconcile the civilizations of East and West, in order to bring to the world the beauty and goodness which they can generate together.[7]

The Cochinchinese leader was perhaps ready to embrace in his own philosophy a larger element of occidental civilization than were Gandhi and Tagore, and his main source of Western values was France rather than England; but he believed his spirit to be the same as theirs.

The reconciliation of civilizations was a function of education, and one of the most persistent demands of the Constitutionalists was for the expansion of schools by the French. In their eyes one of Sarraut's most valuable contributions to Vietnamese development was his creation of the University of Hanoi in 1917, followed a little later by the final abolition of the traditional system of imperial examinations at Huê. But the standards of the new university were never so high as those of French metropolitan universities, and the Constitutionalists would not rest content until there was a proper higher educational system established in Cochinchina. Even more urgently they called for the expansion of primary and technical education. Something was done, but not enough. Impatiently, in the 1920s both Bui Quang Chiêu and Nguyên Phan Long founded their own private schools in Saigon during the 1920s. Meanwhile in Tongking a comparable movement for educational expansion was started by Pham Quynh.

Unfortunately, despite their claim to be 'civilizing' Asia, the French were too afraid of the political consequences of education to embark upon a thoroughgoing expansion of schools and colleges. Most unfortunate of all was their failure to educate the rural population, which tended to produce a cultural gulf (even within family groups) between the French-educated elite of Saigon and the people of the villages. A similar gulf existed of course in India; but in Viet-Nam, as in China, its consequences were much more serious because there the cities had never dominated the countryside to the extent they did in India and other parts of Asia. The most educated Vietnamese were therefore bound sooner or later to loose their leadership of the rest of society, unless they themselves could succeed in educating it before it was too late.

The generation of Asians which included Rabindranath Tagore, Liang Ch'i-ch'ao and Sun Yat-sen, and also Bui Quang Chiêu and Phan Châu Trinh, brought about what some have called an Asian Renaissance. A more appropriate term might perhaps be an 'Asian Enlightenment'. It combined recognition of the power of reason with the desire for human progress, in much the same way as had the Enlightenment of eighteenth-century Europe, and in so doing it generated a comparable optimism and sense of universal values. But if the European Enlightenment was doomed to the disillusionment of revolutionary violence in the decades after 1789, the Asian Enlightenment likewise ended all too often not in the triumph of intellect but in the violence and bloodshed of civil war. In Viet-Nam the tragedy was especially great, and the war exceptionally long and bitter. It destroyed, for a generation at least, the possibility that an enlightened elite would lead the country smoothly to independence and further progress. The fate of Bui Quang Chiêu is a symbol of the tragedy, for he was a personal victim of its violence: in late September 1945, he was taken from his home by the Communists and killed.

VII

Revolution

'IF the colonials are obstinate in refusing to the Annamites elementary liberties, the latter will not be able to disown the violence of the masses and the action of the *émigrés*.' The warning was given in 1925 by a young Cochinchinese, Nguyên An Ninh, who a few years earlier had joined the increasing number of Vietnamese students in Paris, and had then returned home to plunge into nationalist politics (such as they were) in Saigon.[1] It appeared towards the end of a pamphlet in which he expressed hopes for Franco-Annamite understanding and co-operation, setting forth many of the same demands as the Parti Constitutionaliste.

But Ninh was nearly thirty years younger than Bui Quang Chiêu, and considerably less patient in his attitude towards the French. Born in the province of Cho-Lon about 1900, he came of a family which had supported the reform movement of 1907–8 and he had inherited his father's distrust of the colonial regime. In Europe he became even more acutely aware of the contrast between the standards of liberty and equality which the French upheld in their own country, and their disregard of such standards in Indochina. If the 'principles of eighty-nine' were valid in Paris or Marseilles, then why not in Saigon? He returned home imbued with the ideals of socialism and liberty, but very quickly reached the conclusion that the French would never make any real concessions to the Cochinchinese subjects unless they were forced to do so. Late in 1926, or possibly earlier, Nguyên An Ninh began to form a sort of secret society, calling it the 'Hope of Youth' Party; he recruited to it people in the countryside as well as in Saigon, and as was inevitable sooner or later, it attracted the attention of the Sûreté. Quite what he intended to do with the party at this stage never became clear, for in the latter part of 1928 he was arrested and imprisoned for several years. His followers, as we shall see, were taken over by the Communists;

and he himself by the time of his release from prison sometime before 1936 was converted to Communism in some form. In that year we find him acting in association with the Trotskyist group of Ta Thu Thâu which ran the newspaper *La Lutte*. But in 1937, after his attempt to create a new secret movement and to organize an All-Indochina Congress (which would have been a left-wing front rather than a copy of the Indian Congress), he was once more imprisoned by the French. He died on the island of Poulo Condore in 1943.

This was a career typical of the more impatient members of his generation: a generation, moreover, which included several of the present leaders of the Democratic Republic of Viet-Nam. It was in the mid-1920s that such people began to turn away from constitutional and Franco-Annamite ideas, and towards the concept of revolution. Some, like Nguyên An Ninh, looked to French history and the revolutionary tradition of their colonial rulers. Others, probably the majority, looked towards China where in 1925 the *Kuo-Min-Tang* and the Communists began what amounted to a second revolution, centred upon Canton. In this they were following the lead of an older man, Phan Bôi Châu, who had begun to think of revolution about 1907 when he first came into contact with Sun Yat-sen.

Phan Bôi Châu had himself tried to imitate the methods of Sun Yat-sen's early career: terrorism in the towns and subversion in the army. Sun's importance in Vietnamese eyes was no doubt increased by his brief sojourn in Indochina in 1907-8, between his expulsion from Japan and his deportation by the French to Singapore; for during that time he launched at least two attacks into Yunnan and Kwangsi from the territory of Tongking. About the same time, as the more moderate Vietnamese nationalists were organizing the movement to encourage students to go to Japan, Phan Bôi Châu began to plot an armed rebellion of his own in Tongking. The success of the first Chinese revolution in 1911 gave him added confidence, and in the following year (at Canton) he founded the *Viêt-Nam Phuc-Quôc Hôi* ('Viet-Nam Association to Restore the Nation' sometimes called the 'Vietnamese Independence Association'). It flourished for several years, finding recruits in Tongking and Annam as well as amongst Vietnamese communities in Kwangsi, Yunnan and Siam. But Phan Bôi Châu does not appear to have succeeded in creating a network of rural secret societies such as grew up in Cochinchina at about the same time (1913–16). He persuaded the veteran leader Hoang Hoa Tham to set up a remote stronghold in upper Tongking, which held out until Tham himself was killed in 1913. But beyond that the activities of the Association did not go far beyond the throwing of bombs from time to time in Hanoi and other urban centres, and the plotting of some kind of mutiny in the army. When the latter finally occurred at Thai-Nguyên in 1917, it was quickly suppressed.[2] For the next eight years or so after that event, the Association did hardly anything.

Nevertheless its principal achievement was to create a link between Vietnamese nationalism and Sun Yat-sen, which was to prove of the greatest importance in the 1920s. By the time of his death early in 1925 Sun had been converted to the Leninist conception of how a revolutionary party should be organized. It was in the wake of the Soviet mission to Canton, led by Michael Borodin, that there arrived on the scene late in 1924 the Vietnamese Marxist Nguyên Ai Quôc. Whilst Borodin was directing the revolution of the *Kuo-Min-Tang*-Communist alliance, his Vietnamese colleague was left to create a comparable revolutionary machine in Indochina.

'Nguyên the Patriot', at this time a man of about thirty, was a native of the same province as Phan Bôi Châu: Nghê-An (in North Annam).[3] The son of a minor official who had retired about the time of the 1908 revolt, he had been educated first in Chinese characters and the Classics, and then sent to Huê to study French. Before the age of twenty he had gone to sea as a deck-hand, and after a period of wandering had settled in Paris. During the first world war he became a prominent figure in the Paris community of Vietnamese students and political exiles, and there is a story that in 1916 he and Phan Châu Trinh were imprisoned in the Santé at a time when the French government feared attempts by Germany to aid a Vietnamese rebellion. It was at this time that he took the pen-name 'Ai Quôc' by which he was best known until he adopted that of Hô Chi Minh in 1942. He became an ardent socialist as well as a nationalist, and in December 1920 he was amongst the founders of the French Communist Party at the Congress of Tours. Unlike Nguyên An Ninh, however, he showed no inclination to return to Viet-Nam to start a revolutionary movement amongst the peasantry:

he probably accepted the orthodox Marxist position at this time, that the revolution must depend on the proletariat. And in the context of the world as a whole there seemed more likelihood that the Soviet Revolution would spread to France than that there would be a real revolution in Viet-Nam. Yet he cannot have been wholly blind to the importance of the peasantry, for in 1923 he went to Moscow as a delegate to the first congress of the Peasant International. And from there he went on to Canton. His task now was to spread the Communist movement to Viet-Nam, and by the middle of 1925 he had organized the *Viêt-Nam Cach-Mang Thanh-Niên Hôi* (usually known by the abbreviated name of *Thanh-Niên*, the 'Viet-Nam Revolutionary Youth Association'). Recruiting first a number of younger followers of Phan Bôi Châu, it gradually spread its net wider, and by 1929 it was reckoned that the Association had about a thousand sympathizers or members in Indochina itself, of whom a fifth had made the journey to Canton in order to be trained at the Whampoa academy in revolutionary and military tactics.

The problem which Sun Yat-sen had found difficult, that of effective organization, was one which also faced the Vietnamese revolutionary groups. The Vietnamese had first to organize an opposition movement that would be capable of bringing them to power. Secrecy was essential, and it is hardly surprising that they adopted the traditional secret society and its sworn brotherhood as their first method of organization. For whereas the French would tolerate Constitutionalists, at least in Cochinchina, they were determined to root out the advocates of revolution by all means at their disposal including the secret police. The swearing of oaths was to some extent a guarantee of loyalty in such circumstances, though it was not invariably effective and the Sûreté often knew a great deal about what was going on. One of the most valuable things the Vietnamese revolutionaries acquired from the Soviet example was the cell system which enabled a secret party to function without all the members knowing one anothers' identity.

The need for secrecy blended with an important element in the traditional Vietnamese character: inherent caution and a preference for inaction. In 1909 the Governor-General of Indochina summed up the Vietnamese personality as he had observed it:

> The Annamite is of an observant and prudent disposition; he conceals and dissimulates his impressions; he knows how to wait; his temperament does not make him act except after careful deliberation; which is to say that he never excites himself without a motive, and that any demonstration of opinion of a serious nature is always the fruit of long and silent preparation.[4]

Often the caution was so great that action never followed preparation at all. One is reminded of the Vietnamese would-be terrorist who in 1912 went all the way from Kwangsi to Nam-Dinh, with a bomb which he planned to throw at the Governor-General at a feast to honour laureates of the examination, and then failed to throw it and took it all the way back to Kwangsi. Such caution accounted for the natural reluctance of revolutionaries to confide in one another, and was an additional factor tending to make revolutionary associations small societies rather than (at this stage) mass parties. A small group could never on its own hope to achieve a country-wide revolution. Federations and alliances of small associations were essential, and they were often formed at moments when the tide of revolution seemed to be rising to its height. When times were hard, disagreements would develop and the alliances would break up, although the differences were very often not so deep as to prevent any further collaboration at a later date. Being small moreover, political associations tended to be limited geographically, drawing most of their members from a particular region or province. This did not mean that in any one region there would be only one society: before it could dominate even a single province, a group had to compete with its rivals and somehow eliminate them. But it meant that if there was to be an effective revolution there would have to be not only co-operation between small groups, but also co-ordination between regions.

When it was founded in 1925 therefore, the *Thanh-Niên Hôi* was just one amongst many organizations, and there was no inexorable logic which would ensure its eventual domination of the scene: no reason why it, rather than the party of Nguyên An Ninh for example, should lead the Vietnamese revolution. It owed its eventual success partly to the organizational methods it learnt from Moscow, but very largely to the skill and ingenuity of Nguyên Ai Quôc. Its first problem was to get some sort of footing in Viet-Nam itself, and then to expand so that it covered all regions of the country. Its method was either to make alliances with existing groups or to undermine them by absorbing their membership. Often it would do both. The method is somewhat reminiscent of the 'take-over bid' in the competition between rival firms in Western countries.

Insight into how the method worked on the ground is provided by the story of the relationship between the *Thanh-Niên* Association and the *Cach-Mang Dang* between 1926 and 1929, as it was subsequently told to the Sûreté by a former member of the latter organization.[5] The *Cach-Mang Dang* ('Revolutionary Party') had been founded in 1925 by a group of former adherents of the *Phuc-Quôc* movement, and its principal centre of strength lay in Nghê-An and the neighbouring province of Ha-Tinh. In time it established branches in Thanh-Hoa and at Huê, as well as at Hanoi, and it entered into an alliance with a party called the *Tân-Viêt Dang* in southern Annam. Its programme was republican and revolutionary, but not Marxist. Because of its strength in the home province of Nguyên Ai Quôc (and of other founders of the *Thanh-Niên*) it was a natural target for a 'take-over bid' by the latter association. In fact it was the *Cach-Mang Dang* which made the first move, in 1926, by sending some of its own members to Canton to open relations with the new organization there. They became converts to the *Thanh-Niên* cause, and when they returned home they suggested to their former leaders an alliance between the two parties. In the next two years a series of conferences between representatives of the two sides was held, but no agreement was possible because the leaders of the *Cach-Mang Dang* refused to virtually submerge their own party in the other, and to accept the discipline of the leaders in Canton. But as time went on the ground was cut from under their feet, one after another their followers being secretly lured away by the *Thanh-Niên Hôi*. By the middle of 1928 the *Cach-Mang Dang* had lost almost all its members in northern Annam, and the remnant moved to Huê where the society was reorganized as the *Tân-Viêt Cach-Mang Dang* under the leadership of Dao Duy Anh. The first round had gone to the Communists, but the society still had a body of members in southern Annam. But the rivalry continued, and when the

Tân-Viêt leaders were arrested in July 1929 the *Thanh-Niên* seized its opportunity to make further gains. By the end of 1929 they were the most important movement in Central Viet-Nam, although they probably did not have complete discipline over all their new members.

Characteristically however the *Thanh-Niên* Association itself split into two rival branches at a congress in Hong Kong in May 1929, on the issue whether to adopt an overtly Communist title and programme. The two sides were in competition with one another for the rest of the year, and the breach was not healed until February 1930, when Nguyên Ai Quôc (who had had to leave Canton in 1927) was called on to return and created a unified Indochina Communist Party. It is from that time that the present *Lao-Dông* party in Hanoi dates its foundation.

In Cochinchina and Tongking the Communists were less immediately successful, though they had established cells in Hanoi, Haiphong and Saigon by 1928. In Cochinchina, real progress probably began for them with the imprisonment of Nguyên An Ninh towards the end of 1928, for the Communists seem to have won over many of his followers, or at least made an effective alliance with them. It was probably a little later that they also began to win a following in the area round Cao-Lanh on the Mekong. But large areas of the South were not affected by Communism at this period. Many areas of Cochinchina remained under the influence of various branches of Caodaism, whilst many village notables who might elsewhere have been won over to revolution continued to support the Constitutionalists.

In Tongking, the most important political party down to 1930 was one whose programme and methods were closest of all to those of Sun Yat-sen and the early *Kuo-Min-Tang*. It called itself the *Quôc-Dân Dang* ('National People's Party'), and its main links with the Chinese seem to have been through Kwangsi or Yunnan. Founded in 1927, it followed Chiang Kai-shek's example of refusing to co-operate with the Communists, so that although the *Thanh-Niên* may have infiltrated its membership there was no question of a merger. Its members were mainly officials, school-teachers and soldiers, and its main strength seems to have been in the country to the north and east of Hanoi. But there is little evidence that it sought a large peasant membership, or tried to mobilize the countryside against the French. Its

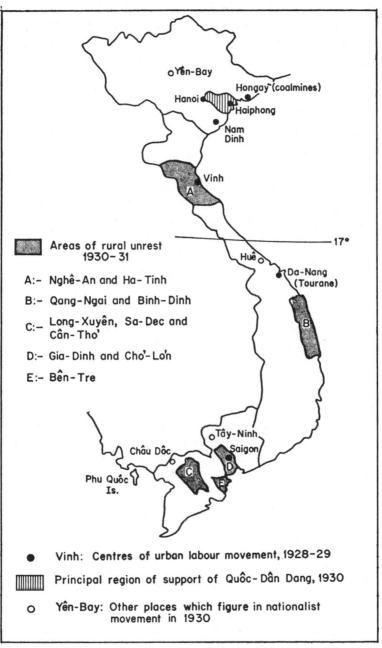

Map II: Political Unrest in Viet-Nam *c.* 1930

methods were still those of the bomb-plot and the military revolt. The rebellion which it tried to stage in Tongking in February 1930 and which failed to get under way because of faulty coordination was to have been a mutiny of native soldiers backed up by acts of terrorism in Hanoi. It is usually referred to as the Yên-Bay mutiny because that was the only place where any fighting took place, but had it not misfired it could have been a much more serious affair.[6] It was not until after the failure of this plot, and the execution of its leader Nguyèn Thai Hoc in 1930, that the Communists had any hope of dominating the revolutionary movement of Tongking.

The Communists and their allies staged their own revolt later in 1930, in various parts of Annam and Cochinchina. Its inspiration was drawn not from the old methods of Sun Yat-sen but from the example of the Chinese Communists, who had raised rural rebellions in Kiangsi and Hunan in 1927 and three years later were still administering a large area of those provinces under a system of Soviets. Whatever his ideas on the peasantry in the early 1920s, by 1930 Nguyên Ai Quôc was leading a movement which depended for a great deal of its support on a rural membership. A statistical summary of Communist support in Tongking and Annam, made by Quôc himself in April 1931, shows that whereas the party itself had 1,828 full members, its associated organizations numbered a membership of 35,770. Moreover many of the full members lived in rural areas. The most remarkable fact about the summary was that of these totals, 1,332 of the party cadres and over 33,000 of the organized peasants were in the two provinces of Nghê-An and Ha-Tinh.[7]

Not surprisingly it was in those two provinces that the revolt reached its greatest intensity, and it was later said that for a time the peasants had succeeded in establishing a Soviet there. After a series of relatively peaceful demonstrations in different places between the 1st May and the 1st August 1930, the revolt began in earnest about the beginning of September with attacks on the official headquarters of four sub-prefectures in southern Nghê-An and northern Ha-Tinh. Violence continued during the remainder of the year, and the French used not only troops but also aeroplanes to quell repeated disturbances. There were more attacks on administrative offices and police-posts, and a railway station was occupied and sacked; but attempts to march on the provincial towns of Vinh and Ha-Tinh were halted by the police or troops before they could become serious threats. About the middle of December the situation calmed down, but further disturbances broke out the following March and lasted till August (1931). Meanwhile from November onwards there was trouble of a similar nature in Quang-Ngai, the province which seems to have been the original centre of the *Tân-Viêt Dang* (by 1930 an affiliate of the Communists), and also the only other province where Quôc's survey noted a substantial peasant association. The fact of organization appears to be the main reason why these three provinces rose whilst others remained quiet. The suggestion of a contemporary journalist that Thanh-Hoa, whose calm stood out in sharp contrast to the turbulence of Nghê-An, was quiet because its peasantry was materially better off would seem to be only a subsidiary factor in the explanation.

In Cochinchina too the trouble was probably greatest in the provinces where the Communists had found most recruits. In Long-Xuyen and Sa-Dec, on the Mekong, and in Cholon and Gia-Dinh provinces close to Saigon, the most serious trouble occurred between May and October 1930. It was directed initially against heavy taxation, but in many places it became more specifically Communist as time went on. In the province of Bên-Tre, where evidence of Communism was most conspicuous, the unrest reached its climax a little later, in February and March 1931. The lack of co-ordination in timing, between the different areas of Annam and Cochinchina, cannot however be adduced as evidence in itself that they were not all part of a single revolt. It is highly likely that there was a lack of co-ordination within the Communist movement itself, an inevitable consequence of the character of an organization consisting of many small groups strung together. Those who believe that the whole revolt was organized in detail from Hong Kong by Nguyên Ai Quôc find some support in the fact that it did not long outlast the arrest of the Communist leader in June 1931.

'The violence of the masses and the action of the *émigrés*' were complementary phenomena, and without a peasantry willing to be organized by leaders from outside there could have been no revolt. The French authorities never lost control of the situation, in that none of the threatened administrative centres was actually occupied by rebels. Nevertheless the persistence of the peasant organizations was remarkable, and from beginning to end the disturbed state of the country lasted for over a year. In this the Communist revolt was of a character very different from the Yên-Bay mutiny, and in the long run its implications were much more serious. Unlike Mao Tse-tung's followers in Hunan and Kiangsi the Vietnamese peasants were not organized as an army and were not particularly well armed. But their very endurance gave an indication of what might be possible if the whole rural population were mobilized on the side of an armed independence movement. The lesson was not lost on their leaders.

The regional limitation of the Communist-led rebellion of 1930–31 shows that despite its successes of the previous two or three years, the Indochina Communist Party was still not a truly nation-wide organization drawing support from all parts of Viet-Nam. It was not until 1945–46 that they were finally able to gain effective ascendancy within the revolutionary movement, and to control a front organization capable of uniting behind them a large enough section of the people to wage a successful war against the French. Even then they did not draw every nationalist group into their orbit, and as late as 1954 they still had not dominated the whole of southern Viet-Nam.

The difference in this respect between Cochinchina and the North and Centre of Viet-Nam deserves to be borne in mind in any assessment of the eventual division of the country into two halves. We have seen that administratively Cochinchina's experience of French rule differed considerably from that of the protectorates of Annam and Tongking; and that in consequence French cultural influence was much deeper than elsewhere in Viet-Nam. Economically too there was a marked contrast between the areas: Cochinchina had enough land to export large quantities of rice, and the port of Cholon became a major centre of the trade. It attracted a large number of Chinese immigrants, and this affected the general character of Cochinchinese society. Secret sects and societies flourished to a much greater extent there than in the North, and out of them there eventually grew the new Cochinchinese sect-religions of Caodaism and *Hoa-Hao* Buddhism. The Communists thus had to contend in Cochinchina with both a more thoroughly French-educated elite (including Constitutionalists) and a number of religious movements which were not very receptive to atheistic Marxism.

But there was yet another reason for the weakness of Communism in the South, if by Communist we mean Stalinist: that is, the branch of the movement which gave its allegiance to the Third International in Moscow. Cochinchina was one of the two areas of Asia (the other was Ceylon) to produce a Trotskyist movement in the decade following Trotsky's expulsion from the Soviet Union. There were indeed two Trotskyist groups in Saigon in the 1930s: one led by Hô Huu Tuong, the other by Ta Thu Thâu (who before his departure for Paris in 1928 had been a teacher in the school run by Bui Quang Chiêu). In addition, it is probably fair to say that Nguyên An Ninh was at that period closer to the Communism of Trotsky than to that of Moscow. From 1933 to 1937 the Trotskyists and the Stalinists in Cochinchina (the latter led by Duong Bach Mai and Trân Van Giau) collaborated in a united front and in the production of a newspaper, *La Lutte*.[8] The influence of the Trotskyists steadily grew, and when the front broke up in 1937 it became clear that Ta Thu Thâu and his friends were by far the stronger component of the alliance. In the elections for the Conseil Colonial in 1937 the three Trotskyist candidates won their seats easily, in competition with both Constitutionalist and Stalinist opponents. It was the nearest any single organized group had come to dominating such an election since the success of the Constitutionalists in 1926. But with the coming of the second world war the Trotskyists, like the Stalinists, were subject to repression and the opportunity for further progress as a legal movement was lost. Nevertheless their presence and popularity severely restricted the growth of Stalinist Communism, and this had its effects in the years after 1945.

In order to understand how the alignments of the period between 1945 and 1954 developed, we must look very carefully at events during the years 1945 and 1946. The Japanese occupation of Indochina, which began in earnest in July 1941, was initially only a military occupation: responsibility for administration was left in the hands of Decoux, the French Governor. But in March 1945 the Japanese finally took full political control and established an 'independent' Vietnamese government under the leadership of the pro-Japanese Trân Trong Kim. It was supported by a number of groups which had been willing to work with the Japanese, including the *Dai-Việt* party which had been created in 1942.[9] But it proved too weak to survive the Japanese surrender later in the year, and when the Japanese lost the war it collapsed. It had been agreed at Potsdam that when the surrender took place, Indochina would be occupied by Chinese (*Kuo-Min-Tang*) forces in the north and by British troops in the south, the dividing line being at the sixteenth parallel. But neither army was given any political authority in Viet-Nam, and consequently the Japanese surrender produced a political vacuum. It was this which gave the *Việt-Minh* Front its opportunity.

The *Việt-Nam Độc-Lập Đồng-Minh* ('Viet-Nam Independence League', the full name of the *Việt-Minh*) had been created after a conference of the Indochinese Communist Party at a place called Chin-si just over the border of Kwangsi, in May 1941.[10] Its secretary was Nguyên Ai Quôc, who had been in Russia for much of the time since 1933, and its membership was predominantly Communist. But its programme was simply defined as the liberation of the people and the salvation of the nation. It aimed to become a union of patriots, working ultimately towards 'new democracy' under its own leadership, but hiding its real ideological nature until such time as independence had been won. South China was not however at that time a hospitable place for Communists, and the new movement could not expect a great deal in the way of support from the *Kuo-Min-Tang* authorities there. In fact, Nguyên Ai Quôc spent all of 1942 and the first month of 1943 in a Chinese prison. Whilst he was there, in October 1942, the Chinese strongman of Kwangsi (Chang Fa-kwei) took the initiative towards creating his own league of Vietnamese independence movements, the *Việt-Nam Cach-Mang Đồng-Minh Hội* ('Viet-Nam Revolutionary Alliance'). Although the *Việt-Minh* were allowed to participate in this alliance, the predominant group within it was the *Quôc-Dân Dang*: that is, the branches of that party which had survived the suppression of 1930 by living in Yunnan and Kwangsi. The other principal group which entered the alliance was the pro-Japanese *Phuc-Quôc* movement, also a party of men who had long been in exile. However, by a remarkable piece of diplomacy Nguyên Ai Quôc managed to convince Chang Fa-kwei of his willingness to join in this new organization, and was released from prison under the name of Hô Chi Minh. He became the most influential man in the new movement, which because it included the *Quôc-Dan Dang* was given whole-hearted support by the Chinese. Between the winter of 1943 and the spring of 1945 he was able to use this position to establish for his *Viêt-Minh* followers a base-area in the province of Cao-Bang. When the Japanese surrender came, he was ready to act. On 13th August 1945 the *Viêt-Minh* formed a 'National Liberation Committee' and decided on the plan to seize power in Hanoi. By the 20th they were in control of Hanoi, and had become virtually a provisional government. On the 25th they secured the abdication of the Emperor Bao-Dai. And on the 2nd September Hô Chi Minh read the 'Declaration of Independence of the Democratic Republic of Viet-Nam' in Hanoi.

The sense of independence was general throughout the country. But Communist power was by no means so universal. Viet-Nam was not the kind of country in which a coup in Hanoi could confer on a government or party immediate control over the whole nation. If the *Viêt-Minh* was eventually to gain political control over the newly independent republic, it had to work very hard to make itself the dominant party in every region and every province. It began by eliminating potential constitutional leaders: Bui Quang Chiêu, Pham Quynh, Ngô Dinh Khôi (elder brother of Diêm) and Ta Thu Thâu were all murdered by the Communists within a month or so of the 'August Revolution'. But the other revolutionary groups could not be so summarily dealt with; nor could the Cochinchinese sects.

In the first half of September Allied forces occupied key points in Viet-Nam as previously arranged: the Chinese in Hanoi, the British in Saigon. This gave the Communists yet another factor to contend with, for they knew well enough that both the occupying forces were vigorously anti-Communist and would not acquiesce in the creation of a Marxist-Leninist government in either of their occupation zones. In the South the occupation was to prove an insuperable obstacle, for when fighting broke out in Saigon towards the end of September the British rearmed the French troops in order to restore order. By early October the British were co-operating fully with the French in an operation which led to the latter recovering control over the greater part of Cochinchina by the end of the year.

In the North on the other hand Hô Chi Minh was able to play a clever game of bluff with the Chinese general Lu Han, by pretending to co-operate with the *Quôc-Dân Dang*. In November he dissolved the Communist Party altogether (that is, as an open organization), and the following month he agreed that seventy out of the 350 seats in the forthcoming elections for a national assembly should be reserved for the nationalists. By so doing, he was able to persuade the Chinese to allow the elections to be held in January 1946, and so to add to the *Viêt-Minh*-dominated provisional government an elected assembly in which the *Viêt-Minh* had a majority. Also during this period, the provisional government had to organize famine relief to cope with the consequences of the loss of most of the Tongking harvest of 1945. It was only in February 1946 that Hô Chi Minh was brought face to face with the problem against which these tactics proved unworkable: the government in Chungking made an agreement to hand back the northern half of Viet-Nam to France, in return for the termination of French extra-territorial privileges in China itself. In March, the *Viêt-Minh* had to accept a compromise with the French. A long series of negotiations continued, which eventually produced a supposedly more lasting compromise. But by the end of 1946 Hô Chi Minh was convinced that only war would give Viet-Nam real independence under a *Viêt-Minh* government, and after a serious clash in Hanoi on the 19th December the provisional government withdrew from the capital and began its protracted 'resistance' struggle. In the meantime, for much of that year Vo Nguyên Giap led *Viêt-Minh* forces in a campaign to eliminate the *Quôc-Dân Dang*, whose protection had been the presence of Chinese troops and which was left in a weak state when they withdrew. The *Quôc-Dân Dang* had allies, in the *Dai-Viêt* and other non-Communist revolutionary parties, but it was unable to stand up to the Communist attack. If one thinks back to the situation of 1925-9, one can perhaps see in the conflict of twenty years later the same kind of 'take-over bid' as before, but on a larger scale and with arms.

In the events of 1945-6 one can indeed identify the 'Vietnamese Revolution'. Its effect was to kill the possibility of a smooth evolution towards constitutional independence such as occurred in India. But beyond that, its outcome was still not predictable at the end of 1945. The Communist Party played a very prominent role in the events of that year, but its eventual domination of the situation was by no means a foregone conclusion. It was only with the French decision to reimpose some kind of colonial rule on its former possession that the pattern of conflict began to crystallize into that with which we are familiar today.

VIII

War and Partition

WAR and Communism have shaped the pattern of Vietnamese history since 1945: the first was indeed the opportunity of the second. If the French had not decided after the Pacific War to recover control of their former colony by force, it is by no means certain that the Communists would have emerged as the strongest contender for power in an independent Viet-Nam. It was only the war of 1946–54 that enabled them to establish their hold on the North, and part of the Centre, of Viet-Nam, and only with the renewal of the war after 1958 that they became a powerful force in the South.

The fragmentation of nationalism during its formative years made some kind of internal conflict inevitable after 1940. But down to that time none of the movements in opposition to the French was in possession of anything like a regular army, not even the Communists. It is instructive to compare the situation of the Vietnamese Communists at this date with that of the Chinese Communist Party. Mao Tse-tung's followers had begun to arm themselves as early as 1927, and had preserved a considerable measure of their armed strength by means of the Long March of 1934–5. During the years that followed, Mao ensured that his party became thoroughly militarized, and educated them in the theory of 'guerrilla strategy', which was used to great effect against the Japanese invaders. Moreover, during the decade after the Long March, the Chinese Communists were virtual rulers of an extensive Border Region with its capital at Yenan. By 1946 therefore they were well prepared to sweep across China and to drive out the *Kuo-Min-Tang* army by sheer force.

The Vietnamese Communists were very far from being able to imitate such victories in the years before 1946. At the time of the Long March most of their leaders were in prison or in exile, and it was only a French amnesty that enabled some of them to revive the party network in the late 1930s, and then to escape to Kwangsi when the colonial government again clamped down in 1940. It is true that by the beginning of 1947 both Hô Chi Minh and Truong Chinh (secretary-general of the Communist Party) were publishing articles on guerrilla strategy, but neither of them had the experience of a Mao or a Chu Teh behind him. Both were much better at politics than at war. By that time too (indeed as early as 1944) the chief military leader of the Vietnamese Communists, Vo Nguyên Giap, had established a 'base-area' in the province of Cao-Bang: but it was hardly comparable to the Yenan Border Region.

At the start of the war against the French the Communists were not even powerful enough to fight under their own banner. At most Party membership was around twenty thousand, possibly less. They therefore needed a patriotic front organization. Having formed the *Viêt-Minh* in 1941, which was itself not openly Communist, they created an even wider front movement in May 1946: the *Liên-Viêt Quôc-Dân Hôi* ('United Vietnamese National Association'). The Indochinese Communist Party was even formally dissolved in 1945, and it was not until 1951 that its leaders felt strong enough to bring it formally back to life, from its clandestine existence, under the name of *Dang Lao-Dông* ('Party of the Workers'). In the interval the Communist ambitions of the *Viêt-Minh* leaders were carefully concealed behind patriotic slogans. (This is not, of course, to deny that the Communists were to a very large extent patriots themselves, who espoused Communism as a tool of nationalism: the argument that one cannot be both nationalist and Communist is surely no longer tenable, for being a nationalist does not preclude a man from participating in an international movement.)

Under cover of these front organizations, the Communists made it impossible for any rival nationalist party to function in those areas where its own control was firm: in particular, Tongking and the northern provinces of Annam. By 1954 they had a firm grip on the rural population of those regions, and in some places had begun to consolidate it by means of the land reform campaign, to be described in a later chapter. Their methods were by this time somewhat more brutal than those of the twenties, when the *Thanh-Niên* association had demonstrated its mastery of the 'take-over bid'. They had learnt the truth—if that is the word—

of the principle which Mao Tse-tung had enunciated in an oft-quoted statement of 1938:

> Political power grows out of the barrel of a gun. Our principle is that the Party commands the gun, and the gun will never be used to command the Party. But it is also true that with guns at our disposal we can really build up the Party organization. . . . We can also rear cadres and create school, cultural and mass movements. Everything in Yenan has been built by means of the gun.[1]

As the war progressed, the Vietnamese Communists used their own command of the gun to strengthen their party.

When the French embarked upon the reconquest of northern Viet-Nam in 1946 they had little conception of the kind of war they would have to fight there. Previously they had faced only the problem of keeping a civilian population under control; and though they had never been totally successful even in that, they had been strong enough to prevent emergencies like that of 1930–1 from getting seriously out of hand. But now they had a dual problem: to recover and maintain control of the population in the villages, and at the same time to defeat a 'rebel' army. Whilst that army was small at the beginning, it was using the methods it had learnt from Mao to become stronger every year. The initial advantage of the Communists over other opposition groups in the field was that they alone had a technique for fighting the only kind of war that was likely to succeed against the military superiority of the French. Whilst they owed it in large part to the Chinese example, they were able to apply it successfully to the somewhat different circumstances of Viet-Nam; and they made their own formulations of the method in such works as Truong Chinh's *The Resistance will Win* (1947) and Vo Nguyên Giap's *People's War, People's Army* (1959–60).[2]

The two ideas which stand out in those essays are that the war must be a 'protracted war' and that it must be a 'people's war'. Truong Chinh wrote that 'the guiding principle in the strategy of our whole resistence must be to prolong the war'. The crucial phases of the protracted conflict were those in which the emphasis was on guerrilla strategy and 'mobile' war. In neither of these phases was there any definable battle front: actions were to be fought by the *Viêt-Minh* only when they had a local superiority of strength and were certain of victory: at other times they would fade away rather than engage superior numbers. To the French professional soldier, for whom virtue consisted in fighting to the last man, this may have seemed a policy of cowardice; but it accords very well with the traditional Vietnamese belief in Fate, and the notion that likelihood of success should be the criterion for any decision between action or inaction. As for the overall strategy of the war, its prolongation meant wearing down the colonial power, rather than making a frontal assault on it. The late Professor Fall suggested that it was General Giap who first appreciated that in a very long war the French parliament (and the French taxpayer) would ultimately be one of the best allies of the *Viêt-Minh*. As things turned out, it was never necessary to make a frontal assault on Hanoi at all: the city was won through negotiations, brought about when the French finally acknowledged that Fate was not on their side, and gave way.

The principal objective of the Communists during the first two phases of the war was not to capture or defend territory, but to win over the rural population. It was in this sense that their strategy was one of 'people's war'. Truong Chinh found a phrase which appealed to the Vietnamese poetic imagination in the Maoist slogan: 'The people are the water, our armies the fish.' The reality was sometimes rather more harsh. In order to mobilize the people in support of the struggle, it was necessary to educate them to hate both the French and the 'pro-French' Vietnamese: it might sometimes also be necessary to make ordinary villagers fear the rebels more than they feared the government, and this accounts for the brutality of which the Communists were sometimes guilty. By whatever means, they succeeded in ensuring that large numbers of people withheld their co-operation from the colonial authorities and took the risks involved in supplying and protecting the *Viêt-Minh* army. Thus the French administrative machine was undermined so that whoever might have formal responsibility for a particular area, the real power lay with the *Viêt-Minh*.

This concentration upon winning over the mass of the people was fundamentally Marxist in character, though Marx had not foreshadowed the method. But in many other respects the kind of revolutionary warfare devised by Mao Tse-tung had roots which were less ideological than cultural and historical. Dr Jerome Ch'en has remarked how much of Mao's thought derived from his study of Chinese history, and in particular of great rebellions like that of the Tai-Ping. A similar element of historical inspiration was evident in the military thinking of the *Viêt-Minh*, whose leaders looked to the example of Vietnamese heroes who defeated Chinese armies in the past: Trân Hung Dao, Lê Loi, and the Tây-Son emperor Quang-Trung.[3] On several occasions the Chinese captured Hanoi but subsequently failed to control the country as a whole in the face of guerrilla resistance. In this respect Vietnamese experience contrasts strikingly with that of other countries of the Indochinese Peninsula: in the wars between Burma and Siam for example the fall of the capital city usually meant the loss of the whole kingdom. Control of Hanoi was never the key to control over Viet-Nam, as the French found to their cost in the years after 1945.

Another military figure from the Vietnamese past whose reputation and skill may have influenced the Communist guerrillas was the seventeenth-century general Dao Duy Tu. It was Tu's reorganization of the southern army, and his construction of the fortifications of Dông-Hoi, that saved the Nguyên principality from annexation by the Trinh in the first of the wars between the two 'states' about 1630.[4] Those fortifications are situated in Quang-Binh province (northern Annam), which was the home of Vo Nguyên Giap: the twentieth-century general therefore would be sure to know the story of their creator and his campaigns. (The inspiration may be even more important for Giap, since unlike many of the other *Viêt-Minh* leaders he was a man of humble birth, and he may well have found encouragement in the career of a great general who had once been debarred from the civil examinations because his father was an actor.) The whole story of the Nguyên survival in the wars of the seventeenth century was a lesson for the Communist army, in that it was a striking example of soldiers defending their homes proving more effective in battle than an army fighting far from home in the interests of 'feudalist' commanders.

The French army, also fighting far away from home, was forced in the end to admit defeat. The colonial authorities found themselves caught in a vicious circle: they could not re-establish an effective rural administration unless they could defeat the

People's Army; but they could not win permanent military victory unless they had sufficient control over the countryside to prevent the peasantry from joining or supplying that army. The sad story of the French effort to escape from the closed circle has been ably chronicled by the late Professor Fall.[5] It was a story of repeated attempts to convert the war into a more conventional one, and to bring the *Viêt-Minh* forces to pitched battle. It ended in the bitter irony of Diên Biên Phu, where the one important set-piece battle was won by the Vietnamese. But it was not simply the loss of Diên Biên Phu that defeated the French, so much as the fact that their only method of dealing with the whole situation was one that required well-nigh inexhaustible supplies of men, materials and money. The French gave up because they could not afford to go on.

Their defeat was not however so overwhelming that they had to withdraw unconditionally. The *Viêt-Minh* was very strong in the North and in many parts of Central Viet-Nam. But in Cochinchina, and some parts of Annam, they had failed to eliminate all rival nationalist groups. In Cochinchina there were some provinces where the most powerful group was not the Communists (who were by this time the acknowledged leaders of the *Viêt-Minh*), but one of the politically active sects; and around Saigon the most powerful organization was the *Binh-Xuyên* secret society, which controlled both the police and the underworld of Saigon. The more openly the Communists revealed their rigid ideological approach to the future of Viet-Nam, the less chance they had of absorbing these groups; and in Cochinchina their command of the gun was not yet great enough to eliminate their rivals by force. This contrast between the North and the South of Viet-Nam was of the greatest importance in making possible the partition of the country at the seventeenth parallel.

Another factor making such a partition possible was the creation by the French of the Associated State of Viet-Nam in 1949, which was recognized as an independent state by the Western powers in 1951 (although its independence was very, very limited). In other circumstances, the creation of such a state might have been regarded as a major step forward to a genuinely associationist policy on the part of the French; as it was, it came too late to rally all the nationalist leaders behind a constitutionalist movement. Nevertheless, some Vietnamese leaders (especially Cochinchinese) were willing to co-operate, and Bao-Dai was persuaded to desert the *Viêt-Minh* and become head of the new state, on condition that in due course it would become completely independent. The actual arrangement of the partition of Viet-Nam was the work of the great powers at Geneva. But without the existence of both a substantial non-Communist element in the southern part of the country, and of the beginnings of a non-Communist state framework, no decision of the powers would have led to the kind of partition which in fact occurred. In view of the fragmentation of Vietnamese nationalism throughout the colonial period, the partition was not without a certain logic.

To speak of partition at all is to risk serious distortion of what actually happened in 1954. The events of that year did not bring into existence two distinct states or nations by any straightforward agreement to that effect. Nothing that happened at Geneva in the summer of 1954 affected the sovereignty of Viet-Nam: at least, not intentionally. The substantive element in the Geneva Agreement on Viet-Nam, that is the document signed by the military representatives of the French High Command and the *Viêt-Minh* Command, was purely military in scope. The partition into two zones which it laid down was a purely military one, as a means to enable the opposing armies to be re-grouped, and no foundation of authority was accorded to either of the two parties administering the respective zones. The only mention of political arrangements was a reference to the elections which would eventually decide on unification of the zones. As for the (unsigned) 'Declaration' of the Geneva powers, made on the day following the cease-fire, it too was at pains to insist that no final political settlement had been made: 'the military demarcation line is provisional and should not in any way be interpreted as constituting a political or territorial boundary'.[6] The nearest this Declaration came to any political pronouncement was in its statement that:

> So far as Viet-Nam is concerned, the settlement of political problems, effected on the basis of respect for the principles of independence, unity and territorial integrity, shall permit the

Vietnamese people to enjoy the fundamental freedoms, guaranteed by democratic institutions established as a result of free general elections by secret ballot.

The elections, were those that were to have been held by July 1956. Whatever might be said to have been the 'real' intention of the powers, the Geneva documents themselves include nothing that any international lawyer could interpret as a transfer of sovereignty, and certainly no statement that the sovereignty of Viet-Nam should be partitioned. The independence of Viet-Nam is enshrined in two other sets of documents, whose contents and effect are totally incompatible with one another. According to the Communists, that independence derives from the events and declarations of the 'August Revolution' of 1945: the abdication of Bao-Dai in favour of the Democratic Republic, and the declaration of independence which Hô Chi Minh read out in Hanoi on 2nd September.[7] If these two documents are accepted as valid, then everything the French did thereafter in relation to Viet-Nam was illegal, because France was no longer the sovereign authority.

This interpretation can be challenged, and if one is to argue that South Viet-Nam is in any sense a sovereign state, it must be disproved. The only possible alternative interpretation depends not on the Geneva Agreements but on the treaty initialled in Paris on 4th June 1954 between the government of France and a representative of the Associated State of Viet-Nam.[8] This interpretation assumes that there was in fact no interruption of French sovereignty between the signing of the treaties of 1883–5 and that of 1954, except for the granting of partial independence to the Associated State by the Élysée Agreement of 1949. It requires that one dismiss the events of August–September 1945 as illegal, and also the agreement of March 1946 between the *Viêt-Minh* and France on the grounds that it was invalidated by the subsequent outbreak of hostilities. (Cochinchina had in any case not been involved in the agreement of 1946, but had been allowed a nebulous 'autonomy' between that year and 1949.) It was on the basis of this second interpretation of the way Vietnamese independence came about that the Diêm regime refused to accept that Viet-Nam had been permanently divided, and also rejected the Geneva Declaration within a year of its being made.

Thus at the time when the Geneva Conference decided to

create two military zones in Viet-Nam, there already existed two governments, each claiming to be the sole sovereign authority in Viet-Nam. The real importance of the cease-fire agreement was that it created conditions in which both of them could continue to exist, one in Hanoi and the other in Saigon. The decision that elections should not be held for two years, moreover, gave both governments (even assuming they accepted the Declaration in full) a long breathing space in which to consolidate their hold on their respective zones. The decision to allow migration from one zone to the other within three hundred days of the cease-fire tended to reinforce this possibility. The fact that nearly a million non-Communists actually left Tongking for the South lent colour to the claim of the Saigon regime that it was the responsible government for all Vietnamese who were not actively Communist. Every day that passed from the time the fighting stopped would increase the likelihood that Viet-Nam would become virtually two states despite the insistence at Geneva on her theoretical unity. When July 1956 arrived, there were no elections.

PART THREE

The task is nothing less than to enrich the hopes and existence of more than a hundred million people. And there is much to be done. The vast Mekong River can provide food and water and power on a scale to dwarf even our own Tennessee Valley Authority. The wonders of modern medicine can be spread through villages where thousands die every year for lack of care. Schools can be established to train people in the skills that are needed to manage the process of development. And these objectives, and more, are within the reach of determined and co-operative effort.

President Lyndon B. Johnson,
April 1965.

IX

The Quest for Modernity

VIET-NAM in 1954 was very different from the country it had been, on the eve of French conquest, a hundred years before. When the French were defeated at Diên Biên Phu it seemed as if the wheel had turned full circle. France, despite her continued superiority in wealth and technology, had failed to recover control of territories which her armies had conquered with relative ease in the decades after 1860. The *Viêt-Minh*, without being able to equal French fire-power, appeared to have found a way of rendering the Western technical advantage of no account. Moreover their political philosophy was one which not only rejected the claims of Western civilization to be the highest point in human evolution, but asserted the counter-claim that by means of Marxist revolution an Asian country could actually supersede the West in the dialectical chain of historical development. In time, according to this same philosophy, Europe and America themselves would experience a comparable revolution—though that was not a matter of central concern for Vietnamese Marxists, whose primary interest was in the progress of their own country.

The French withdrawal in the face of such an enemy seemed like a permanent defeat for the West in Viet-Nam, as well as a disaster for those Vietnamese who still had faith in some form of Westernization. But precisely because there were such Vietnamese and because the United States at least was prepared to assist them, the Communist victory turned out to be incomplete. The Americans regarded Diên Biên Phu as a defeat for French colonialism, but not for Western civilization in general. They recognized that the success of the Vietnamese in defeating France owed much to one idea at least which Viet-Nam now shared with the West, that of the nation and its right to independence. They attributed the Communist nature of the victory to an accident of history which had given the leadership of the independence movement to the Communists; but now the struggle was over, they believed a great many Vietnamese would reject Communist ideology and would prefer continuing friendship with the West. The fact that many Vietnamese did prefer it, combined with American willingness to help them, led to the attempt to create in South Viet-Nam an independent pro-Western state.

Thus in the years after 1954 the two halves of Viet-Nam were able to choose two very different roads towards modernization. The international repercussions of the ensuing conflict between the two 'states' have tended to obscure the fact that the real issue, for the Vietnamese themselves, is whether one of these roads to modernity should prevail over the other. The ideal of economic development set forth in such statements as President Johnson's Baltimore speech of 1965 is one shared by both sides.[1] The issue is how the ideal is to be attained: what kind of policies should be adopted, and how the economic system ought to be related to other aspects of Vietnamese social development. For the great powers the broader international issues are perhaps the most important: but since our primary concern in this essay is with Viet-Nam itself, let us for the moment take Communist and American idealism at their face value, and consider the social and economic implications of the alternative lines of development.

Before the French conquest the economy of Viet-Nam was, by comparison with that of the industrial countries of the West, under-developed. It was not however completely *un*-developed; nor was it totally isolated from the wider economy of East Asia whose most developed regions were in China and Japan. Viet-Nam was exporting both raw and manufactured silk to Japan, for example, during the second half of the seventeenth century. We know this because for a while Dutch merchants participated in the trade, being the only Europeans at the time admitted to Japan.[2] The actual volume of Vietnamese exports at that period (or any other before the nineteenth century) cannot even be guessed, for the greater part of it was in the hands of Chinese merchants who have left no record of their activity. But the trade certainly had an impact on the Vietnamese economy, and by the mid-eighteenth century we find silver bars being used as currency where formerly only copper coins had been acceptable. Moreover the fact that the exports included manufactured silk indicates that this was more than merely commerce in primary products. In some provinces there was probably already a cottage textile industry.

Marxist historians writing in Hanoi in the 1950s have sought to identify something like a nascent capitalism in the economic developments of the Trinh-Nguyên period (the seventeenth and eighteenth centuries) and have even gone so far as to interpret the Tây-Son rebellion which brought that period to an end as a social revolution growing out of economic change. But in fact both Chinese and Vietnamese society were so different in character from the Western societies which produced the beginnings of industrial capitalism at a similar period, that it is misleading to describe anything in the East Asian countries before the nineteenth century by using the word capitalist. As far as Viet-Nam was concerned, industrial production must have been on a small scale, carried on by craftsmen working in cottages; the opportunities for profit, such as they were, lay not with the manufacturers but with the traders who were in most cases foreigners. The emperor taxed the trade, and his officials no doubt took their pickings, but this meant only an inflow of silver into those sections of society whose interest was in temples, wars and conspicuous consumption. Moreover, it was a section of society completely dominated by the imperial court. An Englishman who spent some time in Tongking in the later years of the seventeenth century, when both the English and the Dutch had factories at Hanoi, complained of the way in which the Vietnamese rulers oppressed the mercantile community. 'It is one of the policies of the Court', he observed, 'not to make the subjects rich.'[3] There were no Vietnamese independent of the Confucian hierarchy who ever had enough capital to invest in trade or industry on a large scale.

Even in China, where this was less true, nothing like an independent merchant class was able to establish itself and dominate the economy. There too the complete ascendancy of the Confucian court was never challenged by a 'bourgeoisie' in the literal sense of the word. At a time when European kings and princes were borrowing money from urban financiers—at interest—Chinese and Vietnamese monarchs were still in a position to demand what they wanted from their rich subjects, and to take it. Equally significant was the fact that money was never in itself a path to political advancement. Only landowners could enter the imperial examinations, or even buy their way to official titles, so that even the peasant who owned some land was nearer to the top of society than a merchant who had yet to purchase an estate.

Given the cultural and institutional framework of Viet-Nam on the eve of European conquest, which in spite of the Tây-Son 'revolution' was not greatly different from what it had been two centuries before, there was little chance of the country achieving any major economic development along new lines without the infusion of some new and challenging factor. It may be that eventually the mere pressure of population growth might have created such a challenge, without any foreign intrusion. But in actual fact, the Europeans arrived first, and they were the source of challenge. It was the French who took Viet-Nam its next step along the road of economic change.

Jules Ferry had justified the acquisition of colonies, before a reluctant public opinion, by arguing that they were an economic necessity. His successors were faced with the task of making them yield an actual economic gain, not necessarily to the government itself, but certainly to the French nation as a whole. In the early decades of the twentieth century the debate about forms of government gave way to a discussion of 'mise en valeur'. An important aspect of the work of Paul Doumer, as governor of Indochina from 1897 to 1902, was that he balanced the colonial budget and made the country a promising place for the investment of capital. He did not however solve the problem once and for all. His successors were less capable men than he in the financial field, and by 1910 there was once more an outcry in the French Assembly about the cost of administering colonies which ought to be able to pay their way. After the war of 1914–18 in Europe, Frenchmen had an even stronger motive for looking to the colonies to yield profits: the metropolitan economy needed every possible financial support for its own reconstruction.

Down to 1914, the principal results of the application of French capital in Indochina were in the fields of communications and mining.[4] Two small sections of railway were built in Cochinchina and in northern Tongking during the first years of the protectorate, but it was Doumer who inaugurated the first thoroughgoing programme of railway construction, with his plan for 1,700 kilometres of track. By 1914 the Yunnan and Kwangsi railways had been completed (including a large bridge over the Red

River named appropriately after Doumer himself), and long sections of the line that was to link Hanoi with Saigon were in operation. The system was further extended in the 1920s and 1930s, so that on the eve of the Pacific War Indochina had nearly 3,000 kilometres of railway. Meanwhile, the development of mining on a substantial scale had also begun in the early years of the twentieth century, with the opening up of new coal-mines in the Quang-Yên basin and the beginnings of zinc and tin extraction in northern Tongking.

In the two decades between the first and the second world wars, these lines of development continued. Mining and railways were further expanded; in addition, rubber production became an increasingly important element of the economy. Large areas of land to the north and east of Saigon were brought under this and other plantation crops, and the rise of the automobile industry in America and Europe created a rising demand for both rubber and tin.

These developments affected mainly the protectorates of Tongking and Annam, and the northern upland areas of Cochin-china. In the flat delta lands to the south of Saigon the most important change that took place under colonial rule was the expansion of the rice industry. The French undertook some important irrigation works which enabled an expansion of the cultivated area, and on the whole it was this rather than any major improvement of techniques that accounted for the growth in production. Most of the farmers and landowners were Viet-namese; but the opening up of the export market depended on the activity of Chinese immigrants to the area. Cholon became the focus of the trade, and it was the Chinese community there— and also the Indian moneylenders of Saigon—who took the lion's share of the profits.

Inevitably the general economic slump after 1929 was a setback to economic development, and it led many of the Chinese who had migrated to southern Indochina to return home. But the setback was only temporary. By the later 1930s the flow of trade, of capital, and also of Chinese, had resumed their previous levels. When Professor Charles Robequain published his study *L'Evolution Economique de l'Indochine Française* in 1939, he was able to record a long series of achievements over the previous six decades, and to express—as well as serious criticisms—a certain measure of optimism about the future of the country provided its immediate problems were overcome.

As Robequain well appreciated however, the French policy of 'mise en valeur' had not been designed to develop the Indo-chinese economy for its own sake. That indeed was his main criticism. The cultural idea of 'assimilation' had its economic counterpart in the doctrine of colonial protection and preference; and whilst the associationists had some success in revising 'assimila-tion' in the cultural and political fields, in economic matters it was usually the protectionist line that dominated policy. The first measure of French colonial preference was the act of 1892 which differentiated between French trade in Indochina and the trade of all other people there: the former being made free of the duties to be charged upon the latter. The policy reached new extremes in the 1930s with the result that by the time of the Pacific War France completely dominated trade with her Far Eastern possessions.

From the protectionist point of view it was equally important to limit colonial development to those fields which would com-plement production in the metropolitan country, and to prevent the growth of Indochinese industries that might eventually rival those of France itself. Apart from the establishment of textile factories at Nam-Dinh, the French did little to promote the modernization of manufacturing industries in Viet-Nam; they preferred to see the Vietnamese use manufactured goods imported from France. After 1930 they even allowed the traditional Viet-namese activities of sericulture and silk-spinning to decline. It was only with the coming of war, after 1941, that the rupture of sea transport between Indochina and France began to necessi-tate some improvement in the manufacturing capacity of the colony.[5] But even then the long-term interest of the Japanese, who for the time being replaced the French as the dominant power in relation to Viet-Nam, was to make Indochina part of their 'Co-Prosperity Sphere', not to industrialize it.

A further problem which troubled Robequain, and which the French had failed to approach from a Vietnamese point of view, was that of population. The density of population in Tongking and parts of Annam was already great by the end of the nineteenth century. By the 1930s there were districts where it was as high as 2,000 per square mile.[6] Yet in Cochinchina there was plenty

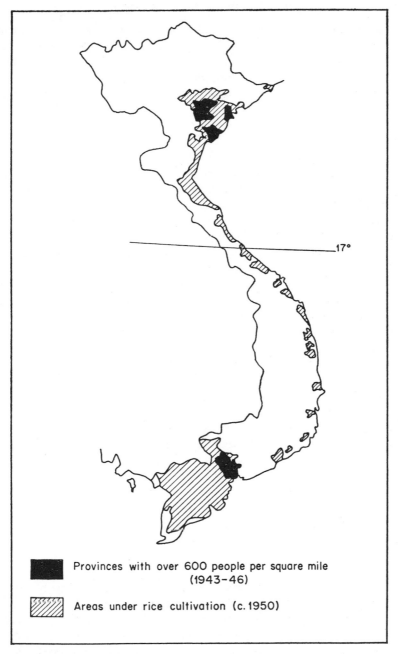

Map III: Population Density and Rice Land in Viet-Nam *c.* 1950

of land. French proposals for encouraging migration from North to South, though occasionally put forward, did not have much effect beyond ensuring that Tongkingese labour was made available for the cultivation of Cochinchina's plantations. A commission which reported on the population problem in 1936 criticized the ineffectiveness of previous action, and recommended a plan to move 50,000 families from Tongking to Cochinchina. But little was done towards implementing it before the arrival of the Japanese.

The unbalanced distribution of population remained in 1954. It must be taken into account when assessing the significance of the mass migration from North to South which occurred as a result of the Geneva partition of Viet-Nam into two zones. Whilst many of those who moved out of Tongking did so for political reasons, it should be remembered that their move was in the direction that was economically rational. Only political idealists under a tight discipline would have chosen at that time to move from the South into the over-populated North. Once the division had taken place, and no more migration was possible, the imbalance was even more serious; the solution proposed in 1936 was no longer relevant, until such time as the country might be unified again. Inevitably the population problem of the northern zone made the government in Hanoi covetous of Cochinchinese rice. The late Dr Nguyên Ngoc Bich, one of the most perceptive observers of the Vietnamese scene, suggested in 1962 that the most important single factor in the war of that time was the Hanoi regime's desperate need for more rice.[7] Conversely, when it came to industrial development the northern zone had the advantage, for the greatest part of the known mineral wealth of Viet-Nam is located there. Economically the division was quite without logic; but by 1954 Viet-Nam had entered a period when economic decisions were subordinate to those of politics and ideology.

An economic pattern which had been geared to the needs of metropolitan France was clearly inappropriate for an independent Viet-Nam. By the mid-twentieth century the world-wide insistence that modernization means industrialization made it inevitable that the Vietnamese would want to exploit their industrial as well as their primary resources. This demanded a new approach, and possibly an element of planning. Where should they look for inspiration? To the West? To the Communist countries? Or to other areas of Asia, not Communist but not yet industrialized either? Even after they had rejected European rule, the Vietnamese were still faced with the old question: could they learn anything from the West which would enable them to develop more rapidly or more successfully than if they turned their backs on their former masters? Once again there were opposing schools of thought, but this time the opposition became crystallized into a political conflict between two 'states'.

Both France, and to an even greater extent America, were already far along the road of industrialization when Viet-Nam became independent. To imitate them directly and immediately, to hope for a comparable achievement in a single generation, was out of the question. Moreover those countries had not only taken many generations to reach their existing level of investment and consumption; they had been able to do so without facing the contemporary Asian problem of a population growing faster than the rate of capital accumulation. The question arises, in relation to Viet-Nam and in relation to Asia generally, what does commitment to the 'Free World' (that is, to the West) imply when it comes to a model for economic modernization?

Professor Walt Rostow has paid special attention to this problem in his essay *The Stages of Economic Growth: a Non-Communist Manifesto*, published in 1959 a few years before he became prominent among Washington's 'hawks' as an advocate of the hard-line policy in Viet-Nam. His approach, like that of Marx, combines the methods of history and of economic analysis; and his first concern is to trace the stages by which Western countries (and also Japan) reached their present level of industrial achievement. As far as most of Asia is concerned, the important parts of the essay are those relating to what he calls the 'take-off': the point at which an agrarian society embarks firmly on the road to becoming an industrial one. In seeking to identify the social and political conditions necessary for any society to reach that point, Professor Rostow emphasises especially the character of the social group in whose hands wealth is concentrated. What is necessary above all is for spending capacity to be 'shifted into the hands of those who will spend it on roads and railroads, schools and factories, rather than on country houses and servants, personal ornaments and temples'. Putting the same point in another way, he argues the need for a new elite: 'it is essential that the members of this new elite regard modernization as a possible task, serving some end they judge to be ethically good or otherwise advantageous.'[8]

But who is to constitute that elite in Asia? Within the definition offered, they might be colonial administrators like Doumer and Varenne: but in the post-colonial world that kind of elite is no longer appropriate. Another group which might answer to the definition is the revolutionary political party, with sufficient power over both economy and society to plan their development according to Marxist-Leninist doctrines. But the whole point of Professor Rostow's work is to argue that an elite of that sort is both socially harmful and economically unnecessary. He dismissed Communism as 'a disease of the transition'. Taking into account his desire for economic growth 'on a political and social basis which keeps open the possibilities of progressive, democratic development', one is tempted to suppose that in practice the elite he has most in mind is that body of men imbued with the Weberian 'spirit of capitalism' who brought Europe, and later America, to their own point of 'take-off'. But what are the implications for Asia if, as Weber suggested, that spirit was an essentially occidental phenomenon? It was only in the West that such an elite grew spontaneously out of the traditional framework of society.

Perhaps what Professor Rostow really means is that the best hope for Asian economic progress is through the creation of an elite which has been educated in Western ways, and is capable of implementing policies based on Western economic theory. Certainly American policy in South Viet-Nam would make no sense without the existence of such an elite. It is unfortunate that neither Professor Rostow nor any of the Western economists who fundamentally agree with him (though not necessarily with all the details of his economics) has so far made a thorough study of the cultural implications of his theory.

Even supposing that a thoroughly Westernized elite can survive in Viet-Nam, the question of sources of capital still has to be answered. To pretend that a transfer of income from traditional landlords to a Westernized middle class is all that is necessary for sudden economic growth would be utterly unrealistic, especially when it is assumed that everything must happen within a political system based on law and democracy. In a country like Viet-Nam the function of the elite, within the terms of Professor Rostow's theory, is not simply to invest the capital accumulated within the country, but also to spend large sums of money granted by the Western powers in economic aid. When he speaks of the challenge of creating a partnership, he is speaking of a challenge as much to the West as to Asians themselves. In a Marxist-Leninist framework, the emphasis is on capital accumulation; in a Rostovian framework the emphasis must be on aid. Without aid, there is no point in Viet-Nam turning to the West for economic inspiration. And aid means, sooner or later, tying the Vietnamese economy to those of the West, and in particular that of the United States. What the West has to offer is not an explicit model for growth, but merely a set of principles and a world market. Those who would dismiss this as inadequate should ponder on the history of Western development itself. In the growth of European industry, the movement of capital from one country to another was an integral part of the process: even Britain owed finance capital to the Netherlands in the eighteenth century. And America's own industrialization would hardly have come about without large-scale capital investment from Europe. Americans are in effect inviting Asians to do what they have done themselves.

What is the alternative? In practice those Asians who reject Western aid find themselves turning in the end, if not in the beginning, to the models of Russia and China. For the Vietnamese to turn to China also lay in the logic of their history, though that need not mean that it was right for them to do so at this particular point in time. In fact the older generation of Vietnamese Communists learnt their Marxism from Russia or Europe, not from China. For many of them—despite the earlier translations of Adam Smith—contact with the writings of Marx and Lenin may well have been the first direct acquaintance with any theories about economic development. In Lenin's concept of imperialism moreover, they would find an economic view of the world which fitted in extremely well with their over-riding eagerness for independence.

By the time that the Vietnamese Communists began to gather

strength in the years after 1945, the leading thinkers of the world movement had already to a considerable extent disposed of the objection that the original theories of Marx did not apply to a pre-capitalist agrarian society. Whereas European Marxists have tended to emphasize the *effect* of new economic developments on political life, Communists in Asia have seized upon the interpretation of Marx (perhaps equally valid) that revolutions open the way to economic change. Their view is adequately summed up by Trân Van Giau in his introduction to the textbook on Vietnamese history which was prepared for use in the University of Hanoi:

> Only by passing through the class struggles of countless thousands of workers will it be possible to improve the old relationships of production, which have impeded the development of the forces of production a stage further.[9]

From this re-interpretation of Marx it is but a small step to the argument that a revolution in a predominantly agrarian society might in practice open the way directly to the creation of a socialist system of production. In a speech in the early 1960s for example, one of the leading theorists of the *Lao-Dông* party (its first-secretary, Lê Duân) proclaimed as much:

> The fundamental characteristic of the social revolution in our country is to advance towards socialism without going through the stage of capitalist development.[10]

There is an interesting resemblance between this objective and the ideas of Sun Yat-sen. Lê Duân's methods however were those which he had learnt from Chinese and Russian Communism. In that same speech he stressed the need for what he called socialist accumulation (of capital). Whilst admitting the value of 'the assistance of brother socialist countries,' he insisted— as have all Asian Marxist-Leninists—on the necessity of 'accumulation made in our own country'. This would inevitably mean sacrifices by the mass of the population. Though he paid lip-service to the need for a rising standard of living, Lê Duân spoke much more forcefully about the 'high sense of economy' that was required of the people. The real purpose of the speech was to justify the sacrifices implicit in the Communist method of economic growth: sacrifices based not on exhortation alone but also on discipline.

It was the methods of the Communists not their aims which antagonized the Western-educated elite of Viet-Nam. For these methods meant in practice the rejection of the West, as well as of traditional culture. In the long run it was impossible to divorce opposing views of economic development from much deeper questions concerning the whole development of society and its values. As it turned out, these deeper questions, and the political implications of opposing answers, came to occupy the forefront of men's thoughts. In comparing the development of the two halves of Viet-Nam in the period between 1954 and 1963, we must examine their political and social life as a whole.

X

Communism

THE division of Viet-Nam into two regions controlled by separate
and conflicting governments was not without historical precedent.
As we have seen, such a division occurred in the early seventeenth
century and lasted for about a century and a half. But that
earlier division was merely political. What was quite unprecedented
in the situation created by the Geneva armistice was the existence
of two competing governments opposed to one another on ideological as well as political grounds. A divided country in a world
separated ideologically into 'two camps', Viet-Nam became one
of the foci of international conflict. This most recent phase of its
history will not be intelligible to us unless we inquire more closely
into the significance for the country itself of ideological partition.

Ideology, as a factor in politics over-riding all others, is a
product of the Western insistence on the elimination of contradiction in philosophy and on the establishment of absolute good
in society. It first entered seriously into European politics at the
time of the Reformation, when kings and princes went to war on
issues of religion as well as in pursuit of power. It re-emerged,
with greater intensity, during the period following the French
Revolution. And it reached still greater heights in the many-
sided conflicts that resulted from the Russian Revolution and the
rise of German Nazism.

The quest for the absolute, either in philosophy or in politics,
was quite alien to the Vietnamese tradition; so too, therefore, was
the ideological basis of political conflict. The Confucian and
Taoist philosophies, in contrast to Christianity, were pervaded
by the notion that opposites not only can but must be reconciled:
indeed that the continuation of the universe depends on the
harmonious interplay of positive and negative forces. Even Mao
Tse-tung, in his essay *On Contradiction*, begins by defining 'the law of
contradiction' as the 'law of the unity of opposites in things'.[1]
Tradition dies hard.

In so far as educated Vietnamese began, after 1859, to be influenced by French civilization they came into contact for the first time with the attitudes of mind that were capable of producing ideological conflict. Some were converted to Catholicism and accepted the authority of the Pope, in an age when papal infallibility was just beginning to be defined. Catholicism apart however it is probably fair to say that the first major intrusion of ideology into Vietnamese political life came after 1920, with the discovery of Marxism-Leninism. In Communism the Vietnamese—or rather a small number of them—found for the first time a coherent political philosophy which declared itself totally incompatible with the old orthodoxy of Confucianism. Hitherto the traditional philosophy of government had never been completely rejected in Viet-Nam except by foreigners. Even the Cochinchinese Constitutionalists, who rejected or ignored the monarchy, did not oppose the ethics of the Confucian system. Bui Quang Chiêu would probably have described himself as still a Confucian.

But Communism was opposed to tradition in all its forms. It dismissed all established ideas and institutions as belonging to past stages of historical development whose values were about to be superseded. Just as in France or England democracy was 'bourgeois', so in China and Viet-Nam Confucianism was 'feudal'. The advent of this new iconoclasm meant that it was no longer possible to hold that *all* ideas could ultimately be reconciled with one another. Confucianism had persecuted the sect religions only in so far as they were political; beyond that, it had let them be. But this new sect religion was nothing if not political. The Communists had only one aim: power, on their own terms.

For those who espoused the new theory of society, it provided a sense of meaning and of purpose which seemed to be denied to those who remained outside. Confucianism had proved itself politically ineffective against the French, whilst the Westerners had—it seemed to them—failed to give the Vietnamese any coherent set of values (other than the hated colonial system) by which to replace it. Vietnamese Marxists have not, any more than the Chinese or for that matter the Russians, taken over every statement of the Marxist canon and made it an axiom of belief. Much that Marx wrote, especially in his analysis of capitalist societies, is irrelevant to Viet-Nam and is recognized by the Vietnamese Communists to be so. The importance of Marxism for them lies not in its details but in its spirit. What has appealed to them most about Marx's writings is that aspect which is summed up in his dictum (in the 'Theses on Feuerbach'): 'The philosophers have only interpreted the world in various ways. The point however is to change it.'[2] This was the antithesis of the traditional belief in Fate. The Vietnamese word for revolution is *cach-mang*, which literally means to 'change Fate'; but it can also mean to overthrow it. What Marx provided in his science of revolution was a positive alternative to the old acceptance of Fate, at least on the level of political systems. Truong Chinh once turned the whole philosophy of the *Kim Vân Kiêu* on its head by translating one of its lines to mean 'the will of man triumphs over Fate'. The Communists still apparently enjoy reading the sentimental story of Thuy Kiêu, but their formal interpretation of it differs completely from that originally intended: they see it primarily as a story of the tribulations suffered by a young girl because of the cruelty of a 'feudalist' mandarin.

On a philosophical level Marxism has provided its adepts with a set of beliefs and ideas which answer many of the questions most puzzling to twentieth-century Vietnamese. That is part of the reason for its success. But no philosophy can make much headway without influencing institutions. The really important factor in the rise of Communism in Viet-Nam as elsewhere has been the disciplined organization of 'the Party'.

The Vietnamese Communist organization which was founded in 1930 was in some respects very similar to the secret societies which had led rebellions in the past, both against Confucian emperors and against the French colonists. Its cell system and its method of organizing the peasantry in associations separate from the party itself were factors which enabled it to operate on a broader geographical basis than many earlier societies: but in that, its organization was merely an elaboration of old methods. What was new was the fact that long before it obtained power the party had a political philosophy, on the basis of which it intended to make sweeping changes in the system of administration and in society. No previous secret society that had successfully rebelled made radical changes in the framework of government and social relationships. But when the Communist Party came to power in North Viet-Nam, it was able not only to take the place of the Confucian hierarchy but to embark on a policy of social change.

The way in which the *Lao-Dông* party worked towards this social revolution, following its resurrection in 1951, is vividly revealed by the nature of the land reform campaign of 1953–6. The confiscation and redistribution of large estates had been an essential element in the Russian Revolution of 1917, and the preliminary to the eventual collectivization of land a decade or so later. In China too, land reform had been a part of Communist Party policy since the 1920s, and as the Communist armies gained control of all China between 1947 and 1950, a thorough programme of land reform was inaugurated. By 1952 the stage of confiscation was virtually complete in China, and during that year there were experiments with the next stage, co-operativiz-ation. Thus by 1953 the Vietnamese had two major precedents within the Marxist-Leninist world for the reform they were about to begin.

They had precedents too, though it is difficult to know if they were conscious of them, in the policy of certain traditional governments in Viet-Nam: for on several occasions in the past there had been imperial decrees limiting the amount of land that could be owned by any subject who was not either a prince or a high official. The background to such a decree in 1711 is well documented. A situation had arisen in which, as a result of bad harvests and high taxes, people were beginning to leave their own holdings and becoming tenants or labourers on large estates, as a result of which the government was losing its taxes. Reductions of tax had been announced on several occasions in order to entice them back to their homes, but then in 1711 it was ruled that no one could be allowed to create a large private estate. Some centuries earlier, in 1397, there had been a decree forbidding anyone outside the imperial clan to own more than 10 *mâu* of land (less than ten acres).[3] The original inspiration for such measures seems to go back to the land-equalization policies of T'ang China, and the notion of an ordered society in which every man had his fields. The Communists of course wanted to go much further than that, for they wished to abolish individual ownership altogether. But their first step was along the same lines as those traditional regimes: to prohibit or confiscate large estates. Therefore they had to face the same problem as those earlier governments: how to get their decrees enforced.

It was not the Communist method, following Soviet and Chinese precedents, to leave such matters merely to decrees. For the enforcement of decrees would depend on those who were already in control of village administration and who in all likelihood were the principal owners of land. The Communists aimed at a complete social revolution in the village, and to this end they sent Party cadres into every locality to ensure that land reform was enforced regardless of the wishes of the notables. Those people who were held to have too much land were 'tried' and condemned by public accusation meetings, losing both face and livelihood in the process. Some were still more harshly treated, being executed for their economic crimes. To some extent the realities of the campaign depended on politics rather than social structure: many of those killed were probably suspected anti-Communist politicians. But to the extent that the motive was simply to 'liquidate' a class of men whom the Communists believed undesirable, the method of village trials ought to have been quite effective.

So it would have been, perhaps, if it had been based on a thorough investigation of the patterns of ownership, and if the situation had been one in which there were a great many large estates whose owners could unmistakably be classified as landlords. But no such investigation seems to have taken place: consequently no allowance was made for the fact that in Tongking and Annam the amount of land in the hands of large landowners was very much smaller than in China. There were of course some landowners with substantial estates, but estates of over fifty hectares were much rarer in the North than in Cochinchina. The great majority of the population would appear, from the statistics of 1930 referred to earlier, to have been peasant-proprietors. Many were no doubt rich peasants, in Lenin's sense of the term: that is, they had enough land to need the labour of others to help them work it; but a rich peasant is not a landlord, even if he is anti-Communist. Mr Hoang Van Chi, in his highly critical study of the Communist revolution in North Viet-Nam,[4] pointed out that the method followed by the

Party in practice was not that of classifying the population on the basis of statistical information collected in Viet-Nam itself: it consisted of establishing quotas for different classes, based on information drawn from Chinese Communist programmes, and then filling them by identifying a given proportion of the inhabitants of each village as landlords, another proportion as rich peasants, and so on. Not surprisingly, many people found themselves being classified on a higher level than purely economic criteria warranted. Or they found themselves being classified as landlords because of their movable possessions. Many of those who suffered as a result were party members: no one was safe from the 'land reform battalions' when their activity was in full swing. That the suffering caused by their extremism is not merely a figment of the imagination of unsympathetic Western opponents of Communism is suggested by the subsequent admission of the party leadership that in the course of the campaign a great many mistakes had been made, and by the accounts of particular instances of injustice in the North Vietnamese press during the 'Hundred Flowers' period of apparent liberalism in 1956–7.

The course of the land reform can be divided into two parts. The first, inaugurated by the publication of the Agrarian Reform Law and Truong Chinh's speech to the *Lao-Dông* Party Congress of November 1953, came to an end with the Geneva Agreement, which permitted the exodus of hundreds of thousands of Northerners to the South between July 1954 and April 1955. The second, more extreme phase, began with an Agricultural Production Conference in Hanoi in November 1955, at which Truong Chinh was again the leading spokesman. In the next two months the pace of accusation and confiscation reached its peak, and by early in 1956 it was becoming clear to less fanatical members of the party leadership that the country could not stand such a pace of change for long. In April of that year Truong Chinh was relieved of his position as general secretary, and the following autumn his rival Vo Nguyên Giap was the principal spokesman at a central committee congress which admitted the 'errors' of the campaign and inaugurated a programme of 'rectification'. Many of those who had been imprisoned appear to have been released, and probably some of the more extreme decisions of the previous year were reversed.

Politically however the campaign had achieved results which

were irreversible, and which no one in the party's politburo can have seriously wanted to change. The terror had enabled the party to establish its power at the village level in most parts of the country, which was essential if it was to enjoy real control of rural areas. The firmness of this control in the villages helps to explain why the rising tide of discontent during the second half of 1956 did not get out of hand. During those months the new government gave free rein to the intellectuals, in accordance with its policy (borrowed from China) of allowing 'a Hundred Flowers' to bloom in apparent freedom. The culmination of this policy was a sudden clamp-down and a re-education programme; but the period of liberty would surely not have been permitted at all if the rural areas had not by then been under firm Communist control. On the one occasion when there was a serious rural revolt, in the pre-dominantly Catholic district of Quynh-Luu (Nghê-An province), it proved easy for the government to contain and to suppress it.[5]

Having established itself in power, the regime was free to embark upon a plan for economic development. Under the Three Year Plan of 1958–60, and in the early years of the Five Year Plan which began in 1961, some progress was made towards industrialization, though the form in which the statistics were presented made it difficult to estimate from outside how much was really achieved. But the food problem meant that agriculture continued to be the central concern of the North Vietnamese planners. In an area that was already overpopulated in 1954, population continued to grow; and food scarcity was endemic. In view of that scarcity, the government was naturally reluctant to resume the pace of agrarian change that had characterized the land reform period.

Western observers of the North Vietnamese scene have frequently asked whether Hanoi veers towards China or towards Russia in its policies of social and economic development. Whilst the question of the Hanoi government's relationship with the two competing Communist giants is clearly of the greatest importance in the sphere of diplomacy, as far as economics are concerned it is perhaps somewhat artificial. The Sino-Soviet conflict did not begin to raise issues of economic policy until the time of the 'Great Leap Forward' of 1958, when China began its experiment with 'people's communes'; but it was not until that same year that North Viet-Nam seriously began to create even 'low-level' co-operatives. Only in 1961 was it reported that 88 per cent. of peasant households had been brought into co-operatives of that kind, and 24 per cent into co-operatives of a more advanced type. Thus the agrarian programme of the Vietnamese Communists was so far behind that of China that there could have been no possibility of their imitating the 'people's communes' on a grand scale in 1958.[6] From such evidence as is available, it would seem that the stage of collectivization completed in China by 1957 was still incomplete in North Viet-Nam as late as 1963. In the succeeding years the war in the South reached proportions that compelled the Hanoi leaders to postpone further agrarian change. With the commencement of the American bombing of North Viet-Nam in 1965, it was probably as much as they could do to keep the existing structure from falling apart.

As a social philosophy, and a method of social organization, Communism has set out to replace Confucianism in Viet-Nam. But more than that, it has set out to replace *everything* in the Vietnamese tradition: its aim is not merely a political and economic but also a cultural revolution. That is, it wishes not merely to change society but also, whether they like it or not, the minds of individuals. Thus the campaign for land reform was not merely a movement to change the pattern of land-holding, or even to transform the rural balance of power. To the Vietnamese Marxist the term 'landlord' is not merely an economic category: it has many of the cultural overtones which have come in the West to be associated—and not only by Marxists—with the epithet 'bourgeois'. In the eyes of Truong Chinh, a landlord was not simply a man who had so many hectares of land or so many tenants and labourers on his estate. He was a certain kind of person, imbued with traditional values and representative of the 'feudalist' class whose way of life had dominated Viet-Nam for centuries. The aim of the revolution was to uproot that class, and to destroy its values. Since in purely Marxist terms the relationship between the 'feudal' way of looking at things and the feudal pattern of economic life was one of simple causality, all that was needed to destroy the traditional outlook in theory was to rearrange the pattern of ownership. But in reality the cultural tradition was not so exclusively dependent on economics, and was unlikely to be uprooted by purely economic change. Whatever might have been true in Europe, in Viet-Nam 'class' could not be measured precisely in terms of income and quantities of land. Its liquidation therefore required the additional element of terror.

For the Vietnamese the central questions about Communism do not revolve around such abstractions as economic analysis or the interpretation of history, nor even around the problem of rural social structure. They relate to the conflict between revolutionary and traditional values: between the claims of the party and the aspirations of the individual. The traditional Vietnamese view of the individual was very different from that of the modern West. There was no sense of a contradiction between the rights of the individual and the claims of society: such concepts did not exist in Confucianism or Taoism. But neither was there any political theory of absolutism, requiring that the individual subject his every desire to the demands of Confucian orthodoxy. If there was no antagonism between individual and society, the growth of harmony between them depended on the full development of both. Thus the ideal of the *chün-tzu* was one which could only apply to the individual, and it was held that if the life of the family and the nation were to be orderly, then the personal life must be cultivated. As well as his sense of harmony with the world, the Confucian-Taoist scholar had an ideal of personal detachment and inner certainty of himself.

French education brought the Vietnamese into contact with a new kind of individualism, but one which had considerable appeal for many of them. In Rousseau's *Contrat Social* they found a theory which reassured them that, even in modern society, a balance would be possible between the aspirations of individuals and the authority of the state: societies should be organized in such a way as to ensure for each individual the maximum of legitimate freedom. As for the more mundane effects of French culture on every-day life, it introduced the Vietnamese to new attitudes to personal freedom and responsibility. During the 1920s and 1930s there was a growing desire amongst young Vietnamese, especially in Saigon and Hanoi, to escape from customary obligations and above all from the discipline of the family. In literature this found reflection in something like a Vietnamese romantic movement.[7]

There had always been a romantic strain in Vietnamese poetry and novels, but love had been traditionally hedged about by

Fate, and the dominant mood was nostalgia rather than defiance of Heaven. In the twentieth century Fate was less completely supreme: or, at least, it did not always reinforce convention. The first Vietnamese novel in *quôc-ngu* prose, *Tô-Tam*, published in Hanoi in 1925, was the story of a young girl who fell in love with a fellow-student, only to face the inevitable dilemma when her parents arranged for her to marry someone else. She evaded the issue of filial piety by committing suicide. But ten years later the reading public was taken by storm by a much more ambitious novel, *Doan-Tuyêt*. In that novel too the story began with the love of two students, but in this case the girl chose to obey her parents and accept an arranged marriage, whilst her lover went off to become a radical politician. Later on however the ill-treatment and neglect of her husband led her to rebel and to leave him (an unthinkable thing in itself); and when he tried to prevent her going, she killed him. This set the scene for a trial in which the pleas of the defence achieved an acquittal, and the heroine was then permitted to flout orthodox conventions completely by becoming first a school-teacher and then a journalist. The author of this novel, Nhât Linh, was one of the most prominent of the new writers in Hanoi in the thirties, and leader of a literary group which called itself the *Tu-Luc Van-Doan*, the 'self-strengthening literary circle'.

The individual of the Taoist-Confucian was regarded by the Marxists as 'feudal', that of the Hanoi romantics and their public as 'bourgeois'. The Communists declared war on them both. Nhât Linh (whose original name was Nguyên Tuong Tam) was in fact an anti-Communist politician, associated with the *Quôc-Dân Dang* and then with the *Dai-Viêt* parties; he himself left Hanoi in 1954 and went to Saigon where he took his own life nine years later. But the individualism for which he stood as a writer was not the property of any particular party; it was a part of the climate of opinion with which the Communists had to contend if they were to revolutionize society along Marxist lines. It was an attitude of mind which many of those who fought for the *Viêt-Minh* in the period 1945–54 shared, for only the thoroughly indoctrinated members of the Party saw it as incompatible with socialism and independence. By 1954 however it was the fervent Marxist-Leninists who controlled the northern zone of Viet-Nam and the individualists found themselves under attack.

The Communists' counter-ideal also had its literary manifestations, one of the best examples (which has been translated
into English) being the novel which Huu Mai wrote in 1961,
recalling the heroism of Diên Biên Phu: *The Last Stronghold.*[8]
The most important hero of the story is a young officer called
Quach-Cuong, whose bravery is unsullied by fear and whose
ideological purity is unblemished by doubt—a fitting model for
emulation by the ordinary Vietnamese in peace and war. It is
not merely submission that the all-powerful party demands
from its followers, but strenuous effort directed towards the goals
selected by the party, in this case the capture of a key position
within the fortified complex of the French encampment. Other
characters, whose performance is equally praised by the author,
are shown having to struggle with their own fear, and overcoming
it only with great difficulty. Such is the political commissar of the
novel, Tuân, who takes time to accustom himself to the dangers of
the battlefield and to earn the trust which is placed in him by the
officers on account of his party position. Others grapple with
their fears less successfully, and some turn out to be hopeless
cowards. There is a tendency to see individualism as the cause
of cowardice, and to relate failure on the battlefield to class
origins in the bourgeoisie: significantly only officers are shown
as suffering from it. But it is interesting to find that the author
does not frown upon sentimentality in itself, or upon love, as
bourgeois failings. Even the Communist must make some con-
cession to the poetic sentiment of the Vietnamese, so long as it
does not interfere with politics.

Huu Mai's portrayal of the party and the people's army in
action is, however, somewhat idealized. The *Lao-Dông* leadership
has not limited its encouragement of the new virtues of self-
sacrifice and heroism to the publication of novels. It has made
more positive attacks on individualism by means of re-education,
or campaigns of 'rectification': in Sino-Vietnamese, *chinh-phong.*
The model for such campaigns was that conducted by Mao
Tse-tung in the Chinese Communist Party at Yenan in 1942; and
the Chinese have repeated the exercise on a number of occasions
since then, notably in 1957. 'Rectification' was one of Mao's
major contributions to the theory and practice of Communism,
and has had no precise parallel in the Soviet Union. One of
Mao's aims was to make his followers aware of their Chinese roots,

and to encourage pragmatism amongst them in borrowing from foreign theorists; the other was to 'remould' them, to make of them truly proletarian party members, capable of subjecting their own inclinations to the discipline of the party.

The first Vietnamese attempt at a full-scale rectification campaign came in 1953, on the eve of land reform.[9] It followed the principles which Mao had laid down in relation to the second of his aims, and was very clearly an attempt by the strongly pro-Chinese elements in the *Lao-Dông* party to bring their practice in line with that of China. A second rectification campaign followed in 1958, after a short period in 1956–7 when intellectual criticism of the party had been encouraged. It was at this stage that the *Lao Dông* leaders had their showdown with the intellectuals who had chosen to stay in the northern zone rather than flee to the South several years previously. To a large extent the issue turned on individualism in art and literature.

The leading spokesman amongst those intellectuals whose opposition to the regime was strongest was a seventy-year-old veteran of Vietnamese nationalism, Phan Khôi. A native of Quang-Nam, he had begun his political career as a follower of Phan Châu Trinh, and had never been deeply influenced by Marxism. But in 1954 he chose to stay in Hanoi. In September 1956 he was encouraged by the mood of apparent liberalism in Hanoi to begin publishing a review, *Nhân-Van,* in which he and his friends openly attacked the excesses of the party and its cadres. Three months later it was closed down, and in April 1958 he and his colleagues were arrested; Phan Khôi himself died in prison just before he was to be put on trial. The tone of *Nhân-Van* was not completely uncompromising towards the Communists and their ideals; had its writers felt great antipathy towards Marxism as a political theory they would not have stayed in the North. They did not even resent the exhortations of the party to intellectuals and artists to gear their works to the needs of the revolution: what they resented was the total lack of freedom to express their feelings as they wished. In particular they were disgusted by a system of censorship which entrusted to half educated party hacks the task of dictating to writers what they may write. 'Art is a private sphere,' wrote Phan Khôi, 'politics should not encroach on it'. And again:

It is true that arts and letters, being at the service of politics, must naturally be led by the latter. But may I ask one question? If the politicians want to reach their goal, why don't they use banner slogans, instructions and communiqués? Why the necessity of using arts and letters? [10]

The fundamental difference between the Vietnamese Communists and their opponents is that to the former these questions seem quite as unreasonable as to the latter they seem unanswerable. And this too is the difference between Communism and Confucianism as orthodoxies. It was possible to be both Confucian and Buddhist or Taoist without any outstanding inconsistency. If one is Communist, there is no room for any other belief, for all other ideologies are superseded.

XI

Non-Communism: The South

COMMUNISM was one possible solution to Viet-Nam's need for a new social framework to replace the traditional Confucian system. But for some Vietnamese—a large enough number for it to matter—the price of accepting this framework was too high. They wer? not prepared either to cut themselves off from every trace of traditional values, or to renounce all further relationship with the Western civilization which Marxists dismissed as 'bourgeois'. These people were well aware of the inadequacy of tradition on its own, and also of the failure of the French colonists to give their country the full benefits of the civilization of France itself. But they preferred giving the West another chance, under circumstances in which Viet-Nam was now politically independent, rather than accept the harsh discipline of Communism. It was to men of this stamp that responsibility for the government of South Viet-Nam fell in 1954.

It has often been said that the Communist leaders in Hanoi expected the South to dissolve into chaos long before the date fixed for the holding of elections (July 1956). But there was no guarantee that what emerged from the chaos would be a pliable pro-Communist regime ready to unify the northern and southern zones on Hanoi's terms. The migration of between thirty- and eighty-thousand 'hard-core' Communist troops to the North in 1954 left the party cadres who remained behind in no position to force their way to power in the immediate future. In the five years which followed the Geneva Agreement the most important conflicts south of the seventeenth parallel were between different groups of non-Communists, and it was some time before those conflicts gave the Communists an opportunity to resume their struggle for control of the country.

The groups in the South which seemed most likely to benefit from the partition were the Caodaists and the *Hoa-Hao* Buddhists, both of which had men under arms and controlled sizeable territories where the Communists still had no foothold. But the sects were weak in three important respects. First, they had no single leader capable of uniting them into an effective political force, which is not to say that such a man might not have emerged given time, but time indeed was short. Secondly, having depended on French subventions to pay their troops, they had no large supplies of ready money: again, in time they would be able to raise taxes from their respective provinces, but in the short term they might be thrown off balance by a government in Saigon that suddenly refused to continue French payments. Thirdly, and perhaps most importantly, the sects did not attract the sympathy of the Americans. Hardly any American at that time understood the nature of the appeal of these religions to the Cochinchinese peasantry, and they were not much impressed by the Caodaists' veneration of such apparently minor world figures as Victor Hugo. (The Caodaists themselves had made much more of such veneration in their French-language literature than they did in their own worship, in order to convince outsiders of their attachment to France.) The Americans dismissed the sects either as the equivalent of 'feudal warlords' or else as unreliable opponents of Communism, and the incompatibility of these two interpretations was not dwelt upon.

In the circumstances of June-July 1954 it was impossible for any man to take office as prime minister in Saigon without the approval of the Americans. The man chosen for the task was not a native of Cochinchina at all, but a man from Huê, Ngô Dinh Diêm. An ascetic Catholic, a fervent nationalist and anti-Communist, Diêm had all the qualities that official Americans of the McCarthy-Dulles era admired. His most important asset however was one which the Americans did not really appreciate until much later: the younger brother whom he made his Counsellor, and who was undoubtedly one of the most astute Vietnamese politicians of his generation. It was probably Ngô Dinh Nhu who created the situation of 1954 in which his elder brother was the most obvious candidate for the premiership, and it was probably he who worked out the tactics by which the Caodaists and the *Hoa-Hao* were out-manoeuvred in Cochinchina during the following year. The Americans might call the tune as far as finance was concerned, and their announcement that no one but Diêm would be given United States aid helped him a great deal. But they had far too little understanding of the subtleties of Vietnamese politics to exert decisive control over day-to-day events.

Following Diêm's appointment, the sect leaders demanded in September 1954 a place in his government; this they were given, for at that stage the prime minister's first priority was to prevent a military coup.[1] But the following February the end of the French subvention out of which the sects' armies had been paid gave him his cue for a more vigorous policy towards them, and towards the *Binh-Xuyên* secret society. In March these groups responded to Diêm's challenge by forming a 'spiritual union', with the object of ousting the government. Their ultimatum to Diêm and Nhu to resign was rejected, and during the course of the following six months the brothers succeeded in outwitting and checkmating their opponents in Saigon. By October, the Diêm government was strong enough to hold a referendum and obtained overwhelming support for a Republic: Bao-Dai was deposed as Head of State, and Diêm himself became President. The new Republic was inaugurated on 26th October 1955. In February of the next year, government troops occupied Tây-Ninh, forcing Pham Công Tac to flee to Cambodia where he died in 1958. The conflict between the new regime and its Cochinchinese subjects was by no means over, as we shall see. But Diêm and Nhu had won the first round, and were free for the time being to concentrate upon running the southern zone.

Ngô Dinh Diêm has been described as 'the last Confucian' but the ideas upon which his government was based (even though he did not always live up to them) were more complex than that.[2] He was not trying to revive the Confucian monarchical tradition; where he differed from the Communists was in taking Confucian ethics for granted. The brothers were indeed heirs to a dual tradition. Born in 1901 and 1910 respectively, they were the sons of a scholar-official at Huê who for a time was minister of rites under the emperor Thanh-Thai. But the family had been Catholic since the seventeenth century, and had suffered persecution on several occasions before the coming of the French. The brothers were brought up as Catholics; at the same time they could not but be influenced by the virtues and traditions of the Confucian court. Diêm, who did not go abroad until he was nearly fifty, was educated to become a scholar-official himself. For a few months in 1933 he served as Bao-Dai's minister of the interior, but resigned when it became clear that the emperor's attempt at modernization was not to be allowed to include any measure of independence. Nhu on the other hand was sent to study in France, at the École des Chartes, and during the 1940s became a keeper of the imperial archives at Huê. By 1945 both the brothers were active in political movements against the French, but as Catholics (if for no other reason) they refused to have any truck with the Communists. Any possibility of their joining the *Viêt-Minh* was destroyed when in August 1945 a group belonging to that organization burnt down the family house at Huê and murdered their eldest brother, Ngô Dinh Khôi.

Not surprisingly, the political philosophy of the Ngô brothers in power was one which embraced elements of both Catholicism and Confucianism. Known to the West as 'Personalism', that philosophy was their alternative to the Marxism-Leninism of Hô Chi Minh. Its Catholic element, together with its name, derived from the writings of the French philosopher Emmanuel Mounier, which Nhu first discovered as a student in Paris in the 1930s. Mounier differed from many Catholic political thinkers in taking the secularization of the State for granted. His principal concern was not with legalistic debate about the relative spheres of Church and State, but was an attempt to reconcile the thought of two men who were not Catholics at all: Marx and Kierke-gaard. What appealed to him about both writers was their rejection of the Hegelian 'absolute idea'. But he could not accept either the impersonal strain in Marxism or the remoteness from social realities of the Danish thinker. He wanted to combine Marx's insistence on the importance of material conditions with Kierkegaard's belief in the spirituality of the person. Towards the end of his life (he died in 1950) Mounier wrote:

> The choice is not between a blind impersonalism—an enormous cancer that proliferates until it kills—and the profound despair which prefers to be annihilated standing up. There are men who have begun to dispel these monstrous terrors by developing a richer notion of the personality of man, of his relations with his world and with his works.[3]

He counted amongst his forerunners Charles Peguy, Karl Jaspers, Martin Buber, and Nicholas Berdyaev.

It is unlikely that Nhu grasped all the nuances of the French and German existentialism which underlay Mounier's writings. But from a political standpoint he found in them two ideas which enabled him to oppose with greater assurance the Communism whose frightening aspect he and his family had first seen in 1930–1. One of them was the Frenchman's bitter antipathy towards the impersonal totalitarianism of the mass party, be it Fascist or Communist, which he saw as the Hegelian Idea institutionalized. The other was his emphasis upon the community as the protector of personal dignity, and in particular upon the family. The traditional Vietnamese family system had not afforded quite this kind of protection to its members, and Nhu cannot have been totally impervious to the new mood which—as one can see in the Hanoi novels of the 1930s—was challenging the dictatorial side of filial piety. But he believed that, whilst the clan should no longer deny its members any kind of individuality, the family should not be allowed to disintegrate completely. As well as stressing the family as an institution, Mounier called for greater equality between the sexes within it. One of the most 'Personalist' of all the actions of the Diêm-Nhu government after 1954 was Madame Nhu's unpopular family law which protected women from male exploitation by banning divorce.

This ideal view of the human person could of course be related to certain traditional ideals, and by making the connection Diêm no doubt hoped to render it more intelligible to his fellow-countrymen, perhaps also to himself. The 'New Life' movement of Chiang Kai-shek in the thirties (Chiang incidentally was also a Christian) had set an example along these lines, in its elevation of the four virtues of *li* (propriety), *yi* (justice), *lien* (integrity), and *ch'ih* (consciousness of honour). Diêm and Nhu chose as slogans for their own movement two different concepts, but ones whose meaning and spirit were very similar to those of the *Kuo-Min-Tang*: *tin*, meaning sincerity in the practice of virtue, and *thanh*, meaning a true awareness of one's duty and loyalty to others. They also placed great stress on the concept of *nhân* (Chinese *jen*, meaning humanity and love), which they combined with the word *vi* (person) to translate into Vietnamese Mounier's idea of the person. Neither Diêm nor Nhu, it would seem, had any great talent for writing, but a number of other people published books during the later fifties in order to explain the Personalist philosophy and to relate it to the more familiar teachings of Confucius. But Vietnamese Personalism was not an attempt to revive the institutions of Confucianism under a new guise, and one can describe Ngô Dinh Diêm as 'the last Confucian' in only a very limited sense.

Neither however was his regime the heir to the Constitutionalist movement of the period before 1945, even though it promulgated a Constitution in 1956. Like all others who have held power in Saigon since independence, Diêm and Nhu were very conscious of being revolutionaries. Personalism was their philosophy of revolution. Unfortunately, compared with Marxism, Mounier's thought was somewhat vague on the question of revolution. Formulated in and for a society which had experienced its revolution several generations earlier, French Personalism was weakest at the points where Diêm and Nhu most needed it to be strong. As far as Viet-Nam was concerned, it provided them with a sense of direction but not with a detailed plan for action and organization. They therefore had to work out their own specific application of its ideals. They went furthest towards doing so in the development of a land policy.

Diêm's ideas on the subject of land can be seen in some of his speeches, for example his New Year address of 1959 in which he enunciated the principle that every family should have at least a garden plot as its 'basic property', regardless of whether his primary occupation was farming. The principle was not utterly unreasonable in a country without any serious land scarcity. The Saigon government had in fact already begun to apply this principle soon after the partition, by settling on uncleared land many of the refugees who had fled from Tongking. It was one of the most successful aspects of Diêm's policy, and showed that given a spirit of enterprise American financial aid could be put to good use. But when it came to taking land away from families who already had too much, the government was less firm in its purpose. There were some areas in the southern zone which had been under sufficiently firm *Viêt-Minh* control for a policy of confiscation and redistribution to have been carried out before the partition. In those areas, the return of the landlords and their insistence upon collecting arrears of rent made a mockery of any official statements about 'basic property'. But in a society with an influential landowning group it was not easy for a government none too firmly entrenched in power to demand restraint in such matters. In October 1956 it passed an ordinance for the redistribution of land above the level of 100 hectares per family. But even when this measure was implemented, it was not enough to transform a landlord-tenant pattern into one in which peasant-proprietorship was the norm.

From about the middle of 1959, Diêm began a new kind of application of his idea: the creation of *agrovilles*, which would be semi-rural, semi-urban communities in which all families could enjoy the amenities of the town and yet still have their basic garden-property.[4] At the same time they would be more easily defended against Communist attack, and would therefore contribute to security. But to transform a society of villages and towns into a society of *agrovilles* was an ambitious idea at the best of times; in the situation of growing rural unrest which was already developing in Cochinchina by 1959, it was utterly impracticable. Nor was it a very popular plan in itself, for the physical creation of the new type of settlements involved something like a forced-labour system, and a naturally conservative peasantry did not appreciate the need for so much disciplined effort. In fact only twenty-three of these communities were ever brought into existence. The strategic hamlets, which were the preoccupation of Diêm's local government policy after 1961, involved some regrouping of the rural population, but for security reasons rather than in relation to ideas for social improvement.

If the Personalist philosophy provided some inspiration in the field of land policy, in that of economic planning it provided none. It was in no sense a philosophy of development, at least for an agrarian society trying to modernize itself, and in the economic field Diêm and Nhu could do more than accept American assumptions about the relationship between progress and free enterprise. A great deal of aid was in fact given, and some of it was put to good purpose, notably in the sphere of technical and educational development. But there was no overall plan for development, and the attempt to launch one in 1957 ended in failure. Even the degree of co-ordination achieved in India under the five-year plans of 1952–62 proved impossible in South Viet-Nam. The question of how much economic progress the country actually made during the Diêm years has been the subject of controversy, and it is impossible to measure it with any degree of accuracy. But it seems very probable that much of the apparently greater prosperity of the South by comparison with the Communist North was due less to long-term capital investment than to the availability of a large supply of consumer goods imported with American aid.[5]

By 1960 however economic development of any kind was beginning to suffer seriously from the growing problem of political control over rural areas. In an economy dependent to a large extent on the export of primary produce, notably rice and rubber, it was difficult to maintain the momentum of growth if the countryside which produced the export crops was not kept in a fair state of peace and security. If the government could not control the villages, then both economic and political modernization would be impossible.

The problem of control was the most important of all those facing the Saigon government after 1955. It was an analogous problem to that which the Communists faced in the North, and which the terror of land reform enabled them to solve. It was the same problem which had perpetually troubled the French, whose ultimate failure to deal with it had given the Communists their initial opportunity. The methods of a Communist land reform campaign were not open to the government in the South, pledged as it was to respect personal freedom and human dignity. But neither was it enough simply to take over—or to reconstruct —the French system of local government.

From 1956, South Viet-Nam had a Constitution whose theoretical source of authority or legality was a referendum in which 98 per cent of the electorate of the southern zone voted in favour of Diêm's proposal for a republic rather than a monarchy. Constitutionally, since the President and National Assembly were elected by the people, they represented the aspirations of the people. The very notion of 'control' is alien to democratic theory: it is the people who are supposed to control the government.

In Confucian theory too, the idea of control was condemned, for social harmony was believed to depend upon men's virtues. But there was a world of difference between the restraints of

Confucianism and those envisaged by Western democracy. The latter is founded upon two principles, both of which were foreign to the Vietnamese tradition: the rule of law, and representative government achieved through elections. The principle of law derived from the belief, traceable to the works of Aristotle and perhaps further back still, that good government depends on good laws. We saw in an earlier chapter how the Vietnamese tradition assumed the reverse, that virtue lies (if at all) in the person of the official and not in the laws or decrees he administers. The notion that laws might be so absolute that even rulers must obey them was directly opposed to such a tradition. So too was the practice of electing officials on the principle of popular representation, which originated in ancient Rome and was elaborated by the societies of medieval Western Europe. The feudal theory of government required that the monarch should consult his vassals before taking important decisions. As time went on procedures developed for the consultation not only of the feudal nobility but also of the bourgeoisie (in the literal sense of town-dwellers). Thus the foundations were laid for a Parliament in England and an Estates-General in France, out of which grew the modern conception of democracy.

Viet-Nam never had a feudal system in that sense of the word. When Marxists apply the term to traditional Viet-Nam they are using it in a more general sense, invented by Marx, to distinguish a pattern of economic relationships rather than a specific institutional system. The Confucian ruler selected his high officials for their virtue, judged by their performance in examinations; the wishes of the people did not enter into it. And although he made grants of land to them, he did not create hereditary fiefs whose future holders would have the right to become officials. He did not bestow upon anyone the right to advise merely by virtue of holding land. There was thus little scope for the development of feudal procedures of consultation in the natural course of events. In the villages perhaps, there was sometimes a genuine election of officials and a tradition of village meetings and discussion of affairs. But this never extended to levels above the district. The first Vietnamese experience of the procedure of electing local representatives to serve at the centre did not come until the French introduced the Conseil Colonial. But the colonial government did not allow this to develop into anything like true democracy, and constitutionalism was given little encouragement even after 1920.

It is hardly surprising therefore that the Constitution of 1956 did not supersede existing institutions and political habits. It was merely grafted on to the old framework of society, and inevitably for most Vietnamese it was less real than institutions with which they were more familiar. The realities of power still depended, as they had in the French period, on the ability of the government to keep the villages under control, or on that of an opposition movement to create a network of secret associations. Government forces were able to drive the Caodaists and *Hoa-Hao* Buddhists out of Saigon relatively easily, and to crush the *Binh-Xuyên* society in Cholon; they were even able to occupy Tây-Ninh and force the Caodaist Superior into exile. But these organizations still had roots in the countryside, and it was no easy matter to prevent their continued existence in the villages.

In order to cope more effectively with this problem of control, Diêm and Nhu developed their own political party into something like a mass organization. Its core, the *Cân-Lao Nhân-Vi Dang* ('Workers' Personalism Party'), was created by Nhu in or before 1954 in support of his brother. When they obtained power this party was expanded, and auxiliary movements were created. One of the most important of them was the *Liên-Doan Công-Chuc Cach-Mang Quôc-Gia* ('National League of Revolutionary Civil Servants') formed as early as 1954 and an important factor in the victory of Diêm over Bao-Dai the following year. In view of the Communist method of subversion by winning over civil servants, such an organization was probably a necessary defence for the new government. With the inauguration of the Republic a much wider organization was created, the *Phong-Trao Cach-Mang Quôc-Gia* ('Movement for National Revolution'). Then there were the more specialized associations, including a youth movement and also Madame Nhu's 'Women's Solidarity Movement' whose formal aim was to improve the lot of women in society. These various movements were active not only in Saigon but also in towns and villages throughout the country.[6] One of their functions was to rally support for the government in national elections; but also they were supposed to counter the spread of Communist and other subversive groups in rural areas. In the absence of archival evidence (which is unlikely to be forthcoming on this subject), it is impossible to measure their effectiveness except in terms of their ultimate failure to prevent the growth of the Liberation Front or even to protect Diêm against non-Communist enemies.

The *Cân-Lao* officials acquired a reputation for corruption and coercion which may or may not have been deserved. They were said to have directly imitated the methods which the Communists had applied so successfully in the North: successfully, that is, in the establishment of effective control from Hanoi. If that was true, then perhaps one should conclude that Diêm's organization was not ruthless enough. Certainly it was very much less ruthless than the Communists; perhaps where it was at fault was in departing from the ideals of Personalism somewhat haphazardly, to favour particular individuals or to harass particular opponents of the regime. However, the final verdict on what the party actually did is probably less important in the present context than the fact that its reputation was bad: it failed to win the confidence of the mass of the population, and the *sense* of injustice was allowed to grow.[7] As for the attempts of the Movement for National Revolution to educate the peasantry in Personalism, as the Communists indoctrinated the people on their side, it seems to be generally agreed that little progress was made. Perhaps Personalism was too subtle a philosophy for the people to grasp, by comparison with Marxism-Leninism; or perhaps it was badly taught.

A well-informed British observer, Mr Dennis Duncanson, has argued cogently that the problem of control could only be effectively solved, in a way compatible with Western ideals, when South Viet-Nam developed an efficient civil service. No such bureaucratic efficiency was achieved under Diêm, and corruption was therefore inevitable. There is much to be said in favour of this diagnosis of the South Vietnamese dilemma: Western democracy itself depends at least as much on fair and efficient government as on parliamentary representation. But the obstacles to its development in the conditions of Diêm's Viet-Nam were enormous. In the short term only sound political leadership could create conditions more favourable to it; and whilst Diêm often stressed his constitutional position as 'leader of the nation', the leadership he actually gave proved inadequate.

The eventual consequence of the government's failure to control the countryside of South Viet-Nam was the renewal of war. How this came about is a subject fraught with controversy. The official American explanation is that the new war stemmed from aggression on the part of the government of North Viet-Nam: that the Communists unleashed upon the South their special technique of 'revolutionary warfare' with the object of conquest.[8] The government of the United States has never been convinced, it would seem, that the Geneva Agreement was not a political settlement and that Viet-Nam has nevei been formally constituted as two sovereign states. However, if it is accepted that by virtue of the Franco-Vietnamese treaty of June 1954 the Saigon government has formal sovereignty, it is not necessary to invoke the fiction of dual sovereignty in order to justify United States policy towards the South. It would then become possible to admit that the renewal of the war there was due initially to internal political causes rather than to external military attack.

There were of course Communists involved. The origins of the *Viêt-Công* can be traced back to the operations of the *Viêt-Minh* in southern Annam and Cochinchina before 1954. In the former area there was probably complete continuity between one organization and the other, for provinces like Binh-Dinh and Quang-Ngai had been strongholds of Communism since 1930 or before. But in Cochinchina Communist strength had never been so great as in those provinces. We have seen that even in 1954 they were only one amongst a number of groups with grass-roots influence in the villages and with followers in possession of arms. In order to obtain better control of Cochinchina, they began about 1958 to create the movement which came to be known as the *Mat-Trân Dân-Tôc Giai-Phong Miên-Nam Viêt-Nam* (the 'National Front for the Liberation of the South of Viet-Nam'). Interestingly the word used for 'nation' here is not *quôc-gia* which means literally 'nation-family', but *dân-tôc* whose meaning is more akin to 'race' or 'people'.

The process by which this new organization was formed and gathered strength is, in the nature of the situation, not well documented. But enough has been said in earlier chapters of this essay to indicate that the process has to be seen in village terms as well as in terms of South Viet-Nam as a whole. Village politics are not easily penetrated by the outsider (even a Vietnamese outsider), and in circumstances of this kind hard information is scarce indeed. Probably in many villages there were factional conflicts of long standing, such as that which we saw at Môc-Hoa in the 1890s; village politics have probably not changed fundamentally since that time. If so, it would be possible for a budding political front to gather support by playing off the 'out' faction against that in power, regardless at this stage of any ideological considerations. Many villages too had branches of the religious sects whose leadership Diêm had so deliberately antagonized at the outset of his rule. Dr Hickey, in his study of the Cochinchinese village of Khanh-Hâu (Long-An province), shows that in one particular local community there were two branches of the *Cao-Dai* religion and also a reformed Buddhist group, all of them very active in the later 1950s.[9] It would be in keeping with Communist methods for them to infiltrate such religious groups and to try to use them for their own ends. In the case of one of the Caodaist sects, the *Tiên-Thiên* ('Former Heaven') sect, that seems to have been precisely what they did, with some success.

It is very likely that the Front increased its membership by means of the 'take-over bid' method which was described earlier with reference to the period after 1925. Now, that method was supplemented by the more violent one of assassination to eliminate people standing in the way of the Front, be they leaders of rival associations or over-zealous government officials. Power continued to grow out of the barrel of the gun. But not all those who joined the Front necessarily did so out of fear or terror: the Communists were able to play on many very real grievances, especially amongst the adepts of the religious sects. A considerable number of the latter were probably amongst the twenty thousand or more people imprisoned by the Diêm government in the years after 1955 who (it is now generally agreed) were certainly not all Communists.[10] In some areas too the peasants were aggrieved by the government's land-policy, and the demand that they should pay money for holdings which they had occupied freely during the war against the French. The Communists may too have exploited southern regionalism in the interests of a movement whose eventual aim was reunification with the North.

The regionalism which permeated Vietnamese politics in the

pre-French period, and which was an important factor in the frequency of revolts and unrest, is still an important factor in South Viet-Nam. The arrival on the scene of several hundred thousand Tongkingese in 1954–5 tended to reinforce it; so too did the fact that the Republic of Viet-Nam included both Saigon and Huê, neither of which was eager to recognize the superiority of the other as capital. Some Vietnamese, especially natives of Cochinchina, are inclined to the view that Ngô Dinh Diêm and his brother could never have succeeded in effectively controlling the provinces of the South (that is, Cochinchina) because he himself was a native of Huê. Not only that, but he very quickly alienated the most important potential leaders in the South by his attack on the sects. Some Cochinchinese it is true worked with Diêm, notably his vice-president Nguyên Ngoc Tho and two of his leading generals Duong Van Minh and Trân Van Dôn. But to a remarkable extent his top officials were men from the Centre, or else refugees from Tongking. The fact that so many leading officials were outsiders must surely have limited the government's ability to manipulate events in the Cochinchinese villages, quite apart from any question of political popularity.

But whatever its origins, by 1960 the Liberation Front was an effective force in the southern provinces of South Viet-Nam. Its development from that year until 1964 has been analysed in some detail by Mr Douglas Pike in a book based largely on captured documents.[11] From the information he gives, it is possible to deduce something of the original alliance of groups which formed it. Besides the Communists themselves who at this stage kept very much in the background, they included the Democratic Party, possibly a Communist Front but one with a very moderate programme; the *Tiên-Thiên* branch of the Caodaists; and a Cambodian Buddhist group. Many other less well-known associations may well have been drawn in, without having representation in the main committees of the Front, including perhaps some of the former *Binh-Xuyên* bandits. The formal leadership of both the *Hoa-Hao* Buddhists and the Tây-Ninh Caodaists appear to have held aloof from the Front and the Saigon government alike at this time. Conceivably the most potent non-Communist organization in Cochinchina, they were simply left on one side following their ouster from the capital by Diêm in 1955.

As time went on, the Communist cadres gradually emerged from the background to play an increasingly prominent part in the work of the Front they had surreptitiously created, which is what one would expect by analogy with the development of the *Viêt-Minh* Front between 1945 and 1951. But this time one must ask, which Communists? For at the centre of the controversy about the renewal of the war is the question of the relationship between the Liberation Front in the South and the government of the Democratic Republic in Hanoi. Mr Pike seems to offer a key to the answer by showing that in fact the relationship between the southern Communists and Hanoi changed a good deal over time.[12] Within the Front as a whole, the position of the Communists became stronger during the years after 1959 or 1960. An important step in the process was the foundation, towards the end of 1961, of the *Dang Nhân-Dân Cach-Mang Viêt-Nam* (the 'Viet-Nam People's Revolutionary Party'). But that party, though firmly Communist, seems to have been still very much a party of southern-born Communists. It was not until about 1963 that the Southerners within the Communist movement began to fall under the tight discipline of the Northerners who had previously advised and supported them. The trend continued during the next two years, as more and more cadres and troops from the Democratic Republic infiltrated into the South. By the end of 1965 the independent southern origins of the Liberation Front had ceased to be a major factor in the situation, for it was by then wholly dependent on northern troops for what chance it had of ever gaining control of South Viet-Nam.

This interpretation should not be taken as a denial of the assertion that infiltration of cadres from North to South began as early as 1959. But that infiltration, by comparison with what was to come in 1963 and later, was on a small scale; and many of those who infiltrated in the early phase were Southerners who had gone north in 1954, returning to join those of their comrades who had remained behind. Nor too, can one ignore the declared support of Hanoi for the Liberation Front. The Third Congress of the *Lao-Dông* party in Hanoi in September 1960 affirmed its support for the new movement in the South, and in December of that year the Liberation Front was placed on a more formal basis. But it must be remembered that the same Congress approved the Democratic Republic's first Five Year Plan, scheduled to begin in 1961, which suggests that the majority of the Hanoi leaders were at that time more concerned with internal economic development than with external adventures. They did not at this stage envisage full-scale war in the South.

Down to 1963, indeed, Mr Pike's evidence indicates that the strategy of the Communists in South Viet-Nam was geared to the objective of a 'general uprising' (*khoi-nghia*, literally to 'rise in support of justice'). The events of 1945, in which the Communists seized Hanoi and other major centres, had been a 'general uprising' of this kind; what they wanted now was to repeat that success. They were of course in possession of arms long before 1963, but their strategy was not yet one of full-scale guerrilla war. It was at some stage between about April and September 1963 that the Communists (and this decision probably was taken in Hanoi) came to the conclusion that the strategy of 'general uprising' was not enough. The balance of the Front's activities was therefore changed, making 'armed revolt' the new objective. In September two generals of the North Vietnamese Army held a military conference just across the Cambodian frontier to reorganize the forces of the Liberation Front; and in the following month a series of retraining courses in military tactics was held at various places in the Communist-controlled area of the South. The number of 'incidents' between *Viêt-Công* and government troops increased from 500 in September to 1,200 in October of that year.[13]

It may be of some significance that this decision coincided not only with the imposition of firmer Northern discipline over the People's Revolutionary Party, but also with a shift in the foreign policy of the Democratic Republic. The Hanoi leadership had previously steered a middle course in the Sino-Soviet dispute; but during 1963 it began to veer towards China and to take a harder line on the issue of 'peaceful coexistence'. Liu Shao-ch'i was welcomed to Hanoi in May, and in September the Democratic Republic sided with China in its refusal to sign the Test-Ban Treaty. Hanoi remained firmly committed to the Chinese side until after the fall of Khrushchev in Moscow, in October 1964.[14] By that time the change-over to military revolt was a *fait accompli*. Relating together all the changes of Hanoi policy which occurred during the summer and autumn of 1963 one is drawn to the conclusion that they represent a major turning-point in the development of the current Vietnamese war, and perhaps the point at which a many-sided political conflict began to be transformed into a straight military conflict between Hanoi (with outside support) and Washington.

XII

An American Solution?

BACK in the 1870s the young official Bui Viên had urged the emperor Tu-Duc to appeal to the United States for assistance against the threat of further French conquests. His hope went unfulfilled, but eighty years later the Americans eventually did begin to play a prominent role in Vietnamese affairs: not as protectors against another Western power, but in order to save Viet-Nam from Communist China. In the five years from 1951 to 1956 there was a gradual transformation of Viet-Nam's relationship with the West, as France gave way to the United States as the principal Western power in this part of South East Asia. This represented a major break in the continuity of Western influence in Indochina, and one whose importance should not be underrated.

If one looks at those parts of Asia where constitutional independence developed out of European rule—notably India, Ceylon and Malaysia—it is evident that the key role was played by a relatively small elite which drew its Western education and ideas from a single country, Britain. They were able to look to the same country both for cultural inspiration and for economic and political aid, for some considerable time after gaining independence. And when they sought aid and alliances elsewhere, they did so largely in order to avoid a situation where a single foreign power might gain too strong an influence over them while their independence was still young.

In the years after 1954 the French-educated elite of Saigon found themselves in a much more complicated position. If the Americans expected that the Vietnamese, hating their former colonial rulers, would immediately hasten to abandon everything French, they were disappointed. The long-standing cultural allegiance to France was not easily broken by the tide of political change. Many of the officials, and even cabinet ministers, of the Diêm administration were men who had served in the French

colonial bureaucracy and knew only French ideas and procedures of government.[1] The best schools in Saigon continued to be
French-controlled down to 1966, with French as the principal
language of instruction. Even the younger members of the elite did
not find it easy to accustom themselves to look towards America
for cultural and political inspiration. One might even say that
South Viet-Nam faced a whole new challenge from the West,
arising from the domination of its independence by a power
with whose culture it was unfamiliar.

It is difficult to imagine two peoples culturally further apart
than the Vietnamese (even those with a wide French education)
and the Americans: on the one hand the Vietnamese, exceedingly
polite in all their relations with their fellow-men, yet at the
same time proud of their ability to conceal their deepest feelings
and plans, and often remarkably inexplicit in making decisions
and in action; at the other extreme the Americans, who can be
equally polite but who are probably the most explicit of all
Western peoples and whose culture is founded upon respect for
efficiency and precision. In the cultural confrontation between
them, the explicit American was often no match for the more
subtle and inscrutable Vietnamese.

When it comes to the question of what the Americans themselves were trying to achieve in Viet-Nam in this period, the
answer is less easily discovered than might be supposed. Unlike the
French, the Americans have not theorized a great deal about their
relationships with Asians in Asia, and there is not much literature
comparable to that which appeared in France in the latter part
of the nineteenth century discussing the methods of imperial
expansion and colonial rule. We must look instead to the statements of politicians, which tend to be in very general terms. One
of the most important can be found in the letter which President
Eisenhower addressed to Ngô Dinh Diêm in October 1954. It
identified two objectives which between them cover most of
the things the Americans actually did in South Viet-Nam during
the next ten years. First, the purpose of American aid was:

> to assist the government of Viet-Nam in developing and main-
> taining a strong, viable state, capable of resisting attempted sub-
> version or aggression through military means.

But secondly, the President went on to speak of the need for reforms on the part of the authorities in Saigon, and expressed his hope for a Vietnamese government:

> so enlightened in purpose and effective in performance that it will be respected both at home and abroad.[2]

The former of these objectives was undoubtedly the more important. The Americans had no primary interest in conquering any part of Viet-Nam, or in exerting permanently an indirect control over its internal affairs. Their motive for being there was to 'contain' China: the significance of Viet-Nam in this respect was simply that it was decided to draw the line of containment half way along the Vietnamese coast. Nevertheless, once the line had been drawn, the Americans were committed to ensuring that the country immediately to the south of the seventeenth parallel was not only politically stable but also a fine example of the progress that was possible within the 'Free World'. What this really meant is implicit rather than explicit in President Eisenhower's letter: the key phrases being 'enlightened in purpose' and 'effective in performance'. Effectiveness depended a great deal on economic stability, and large amounts of money were poured into Viet-Nam towards this end. (The theory underlying American economic aid was discussed briefly in Chapter IX.) But what of 'enlightenment'? The State of Viet-Nam was apparently expected to allow freedom to its subjects and a measure of participation or representation in the government. In the minds of many Americans, the extent to which that expectation was fulfilled became the yardstick by which they measured the success of Vietnamese development. The hidden assumption on which much of American policy in Viet-Nam was based was that the Vietnamese, given proper opportunity would live up to the ideals of liberty and democracy that had been born in the European enlightenment of the eighteenth century, and had been written into the American Constitution following the War of Independence.

The French failure to bring enlightenment to Viet-Nam hung over everything the Americans did in Viet-Nam in the Diêm period. The Vietnamese desire for independence seemed entirely natural to the Americans: had not they themselves once had to struggle against a colonial power? With their own anti-colonial tradition they felt they had something to offer to an Asian nation which no ex-imperialist European could give: sympathy. As for the theories of 'assimilation' or 'association' which had pre-occupied the French, they were condemned out of hand. But this benevolence was allowed to conceal (even from the Americans themselves) that they had not thought out any fundamentally new approach to the problem of cultural relationships between the white and the yellow races. Their policies proceeded not from theories but from assumptions, about the nature of human progress in general. Unfortunately those assumptions did not derive from any serious study of Asia, but from their own limited historical experience. In other words, the Americans fell into the trap of supposing that Asians, for all their apparent differences from Westerners, are at heart simply *people* who have not yet attained the same level of progress as that achieved by the Americans themselves.

The assumption is well illustrated by a speech of Secretary of State Acheson in 1950, soon after the final Communist victory in China. He denied that the sole interest of the United States in Asia was to stop Communism:

> Our real interest is in those people as people. It is because Communism is hostile to that interest that we want to stop it. But it happens that the best way of doing both things is to do just exactly what the people of Asia want to do, which is to develop a soundness of administration of these new governments, and to develop their resources and technical skills so that they are not subject to penetration either through ignorance or because they believe these false promises (of the Communists), or because there is real distress in their areas.[3]

All too few Americans have challenged this assumption. Liberals and conservatives alike in the American political firmament have taken it for granted that their country is the new guardian of the values of the Enlightenment. Despite their rejection of formal theories about a Western 'mission civilisatrice', their view of human progress is often Americo-centric. As the most powerful nation on earth, the United States has taken upon itself the responsibility for leading mankind towards its manifest destiny. In 1961 President Kennedy found it necessary to warn his people:

> We must face the fact that the United States is neither omnipotent nor omniscient . . . that we cannot impose our will upon the other

ninety-four per cent of mankind . . . and therefore that there cannot
be an American solution to every world problem.[4]
But by then the United States had embarked upon a policy
which supposed that there was an American solution to the
problem of Viet-Nam. They did so with only a very limited
appreciation of the many problems that had arisen out of Viet-
Nam's complex historical relationship with the West.

Throughout the period from about 1904 to 1954, the Vietnamese had not been struggling merely for independence: they
knew that they could only sustain their independence, once it
was achieved, if they could also succeed in modernizing their
country and strengthening its economy. Like the Chinese, they
viewed the West not in terms of Europe's (or America's) own
idealism, but in terms of what they themselves needed in order
to develop a modern independent nation. Once they had their
independence, what they borrowed from the West was for them
to decide, not for any outsider.

Their attitude to the West during the decades of French rule
may be said to have had three variations. (To regard them as
three progressive phases would be to assume that only the third
was valid, which many Vietnamese are reluctant to do.) First,
there was what one might call the *t'i-yung* variation: in their
first contacts with the nineteenth-century West, the Vietnamese
had imagined that all they needed to do was to borrow Western
techniques, whilst keeping their institutional and ethical traditions
intact. In Viet-Nam, this variation was in fact never tried; but
in China it proved a failure. Second, there was the variation
which sought to combine institutional reform (or even revolution,
in the political sphere) with the maintenance of traditional
religion and ethics so long as they did not clash with the need
for political change. This was the variation expressed in the ideas
of Liang Ch'i-ch'ao. In China itself, under Chiang Kai-shek, it
too proved a failure; but in Japan it was extremely successful. The
third variation was that of the revolution which would destroy
tradition completely and replace it with a new social theory:
Marxism-Leninism. This revolution would not be confined to
changes in political and economic institutions, but would strike
at the root of traditional attitudes by reforming also men's minds.

This third variation, which was applied in China after 1949 and in North Viet-Nam after 1954, was abhorrent to the Americans. Since the first variation was no longer a serious possibility, they (and the non-Communist Vietnamese) were left with only one possibility: the second. Whatever emerged in South Viet-Nam would, to be successful, need to combine elements of tradition with vigorous institutional modernization. Diêm's philosophy of Personalism was an attempt, in some ways a very appropriate one, to achieve this combination of ancient and modern; had the Caodaists gained power instead of Diêm in 1954, it is possible that they too would have produced an equally appropriate combination of their own. But whatever philosophy of change was adopted, it was not likely to be one that would coincide exactly with American ideas about freedom under law.

The Americans were not very well equipped by their own historical development to understand the problems which tradition posed for the non-Communist Vietnamese. Their own modernization had been a gradual process, developing out of a colonial society on the East Coast, which had itself already escaped from many of the limitations of tradition that existed in Europe. What survived of the traditional attitude to human relationships, derived from feudal Europe, was swept away by the Civil War of the 1860s. But that was a revolution only for the states of the South: in the North, and even more in the great West, the Americans never faced the need to revolutionize their own society and throw off traditional restraints on modernization. Their own struggle for independence was thus not a struggle against tradition, and Americans have tended as a result to underestimate both the strength and the diversity of tradition in Asia. In this they are at a disadvantage by comparison with European countries, and also with Russia, all of which have had to face the problem of escape from tradition in one way or another. The disadvantage is liable to be aggravated by unconsciousness of the extent to which American institutions have themselves evolved from the European traditions they have left behind. The rule of law and the concept of representative government, for example, were not culturally neutral: they derived ultimately from tendencies in the Western feudal tradition which have been absent from the traditions of East Asia. For all these reasons, the American intrusion into Asia after 1945 was a move fraught with dangers for all concerned.

The Vietnamese non-Communists who sought United States aid after 1954 did not do so out of admiration for American culture, of which they knew little, but because they believed that the sheer power of America was their only protection against enemies in China and North Viet-Nam. Any discussion of the relationship between South Viet-Nam and the United States since 1954 must at some point be focused upon the question why that power failed. For fail it did, in the Diêm years, to the extent that the purpose of American policy was to avoid the war which by 1963 had begun to materialize: and this remains true whatever may be the outcome of the war itself.

No answer to the question can be more than tentative at present, for the final assessment of United States policy in Viet-Nam must depend upon source materials not likely to be made available to researchers for some time to come. But the evidence available suggests avenues along which an answer might be sought. One school of thought dwells on the military and security factors, and the failure of the Americans to develop adequate methods of coping with Maoist 'revolutionary warfare'. In the Eisenhower period the American generals responsible for training the army of the republic of Viet-Nam concentrated on preparing it to meet a frontal invasion from the North, comparable to that which had occurred in Korea. It was not until the time of President Kennedy that 'counter-insurgency' became the order of the day. In 1961 the President twice rejected advice to send ten thousand combat troops to Viet-Nam in favour of a policy of helping the Vietnamese themselves to develop measures that combined political and military techniques. It was in this context that the Diêm government inaugurated its programme of strategic hamlets in April 1962. The idea derived from British experience in Malaya, and its essential principle was the regrouping of the rural population in order to isolate the insurgent forces. But regroupment alone was not enough. Brigadier Clutterbuck, in his study of the Malayan emergency of which he had first-hand experience, emphasized the importance in British policy there of an effective police system, capable of maintaining order in the villages. Without such a network it is unlikely that the government in Malaya could have recovered control of the situation sufficiently to be able to destroy the guerrilla army in the jungle.[5] A police network of this kind did not exist in Viet-Nam in 1954 and has not been created since. Whether it was practically possible to create one, given that the Americans were advisers and not a colonial authority, is debatable.

These organizational factors do not however explain everything, and it is possible that they were of no more than secondary importance. Those who have argued for the comparability of the Malayan and the South Vietnamese situations have tended too often to ignore the great complexity of Cochinchina's rural society: the ubiquity of its secret organizations and sects and the attachment of the peasantry to the land where their ancestors lie buried. The origins and growth of the Liberation Front were essentially political, and whatever one's conclusions about the degree of involvement of the Hanoi government, the Front could not have become strong without favourable political circumstances in the South. The ultimate solution to the problem of control over South Viet-Nam probably did lie in security organizations and efficient government; but to begin with it was a political problem. In the Vietnamese political tradition, control of the principal city had never been enough to guarantee control over the countryside: it was necessary to curb the potentially rebellious activities of secret associations and sects, and this remained true in Cochinchina in the twentieth century. In 1954 such secret organizations were already in existence, and in a strong position in some areas: whether the South was restored to its former stability would depend on how the 'politico-religious sects' were treated by the government in Saigon. As it turned out, the conflict which developed between the Diêm regime and the Cochinchinese peasantry was the principal factor enabling the southern Communists to build up their strength.

Had the Americans truly understood this situation they would surely have done the utmost to prevent such a conflict from breaking out; their actions throughout the Diêm period suggest that their understanding was very limited indeed. It is not easy of course to assess the relative roles of the Vietnamese and their American advisers in the internal politics of South Viet-Nam. But there are strong indications that at some point in the autumn of 1954 the Eisenhower administration made a positive decision to support Diêm against the 'spiritual union' of the sects; and at that stage the prime minister's survival depended a great deal on the American threat to withhold aid from any other party that seized power. It may well be doubted whether in making this choice the Americans realized that they were not merely taking sides in a factional dispute, but were in effect choosing the man upon whose personality would depend the success or failure of their plans for Viet-Nam. Diêm had many good qualities, but his inability to win over the sects (and not just defeat them) suggests that he was not really the man the Americans ought to have chosen. To argue that there was no alternative is to forget that Diêm owed a great deal of his own prominence before he became premier to the Americans themselves. Lack of choice is in any case no defence where the charge is inadequate knowledge of a situation.

Sun Tzu's advice to 'know your enemy' would have been a great help to the Americans had they heeded it at this point. Equally relevant might have been the advice to 'know your friend'. For in their relationship with Diêm himself the Americans made further errors of judgment. They failed to appreciate that in Vietnamese eyes loyalty should be to the person, not to his ideas or opinions. Their support was based on the belief that Diêm shared their own ideals: but when it became increasingly apparent that he did not, a loud debate began in American circles as to whether they should continue their support or not. Relations between Saigon and Washington were strained by the knowledge that this debate was going on, and Diêm seems never to have wholly trusted his allies despite his initial dependence on them. In the end his doubts proved justified, when the Kennedy administration finally decided to abandon its former protégé to the wolves. In so doing they showed themselves surprisingly unaware of what was actually happening in the country. A good many Cochinchinese had by this time joined the Liberation Front; and a good many other Vietnamese (including those of Central Viet-Nam and some of the Tongkingese refugees) belonged to political groups opposed to both Communism and Diêm. But it was only the intervention of the Buddhist monks of Central Viet-Nam in the summer of 1963 that made any serious impact on American policy: it was their demonstrations, and their skill in playing off the journalists against the diplomats in Saigon, that turned American officialdom against Diêm. Few if any Americans at this point understood the Buddhism of the Lotus School in Viet-Nam, and consequently they over-estimated its importance in relation to the country at large. Perhaps it was no more than an unfortunate coincidence, made possible by limited intelligence about Communist planning, that their change of attitude occurred just at the moment when the Liberation Front was preparing to switch its tactics from the general uprising to the armed revolt.

These mistakes of political judgment stemmed from ignorance, which was the bane of American policy in Viet-Nam throughout the Diêm period: ignorance not so much of current facts as of their significance in terms of an unfamiliar cultural framework. The most surprising thing is that the ignorance did not decline: it was so great that most policy-makers seem almost to have been unconscious of it. A small number of Americans became familiar with the Vietnamese ways of thought and behaviour, and with the working of their institutions; but their number was not sufficiently great to change the attitudes prevailing in the corridors of power. As for academic study of Viet-Nam, the subject was all but ignored by most American universities. As late as 1967 Professor Fairbank was lamenting that it would be another ten years before academic understanding of Vietnamese society and culture in the English-speaking world reached the same level as that already attained in the fields of China and Japan.[6] But in the difficult task of working out viable policies towards the countries of Asia, knowledge and cultural understanding are not merely luxuries in which Westerners may or may not choose to indulge. They are a necessity.

In Viet-Nam the 'organization man' went to war, expecting his statistical superiority to bring speedy victory. Characteristic of this approach was a remark of the Secretary of Defence in 1962, on his return from a visit to Saigon: 'Every quantitative measurement we have shows we are winning this war'.[7] Nowhere indeed has the occidental mania for measurement and precise calculation gone further than in North America. The United States, it is true, could never have become the dynamic nation it now is without a large-scale mechanization of its material life. But side by side with that process has gone the tendency for men's thought to become mechanized too: the invention of interchangeable parts has found its spiritual parallel in a desire to turn knowledge about societies into the concepts and statistical data of a computerized social science. The tendency is not, of course, shared by all Americans; but it is very evident both in the study of politics

and in the practice of government. Such mechanistic generaliza-
tion is often fatal to the deeper understanding of other men's
cultures and ways of thought, which in Asia have not undergone
the same process of mechanization. Unfortunately when the
crucial factors in a situation are political psychology and the
ability to manipulate unfamiliar institutions, quantitive measurement is not enough.

The dictum of Clausewitz (quoted, incidentally, by Truong
Chinh in his pamphlet of 1947) was that 'War is the continuation
of politics by other means'. One of the mistakes of the Americans
in Viet-Nam was to suppose that the reverse can be true: that
politics in such situations is no more than an extension of war.
War is very often a matter of statistics; but politics very definitely
is not. Political success depends on judgment, which in a situation
of cultural confrontation involves the understanding of an alien
psychology. In this the Asians very often have the advantage, for
many of them are more familiar with Western ways of thought
than Westerners are with their Asian cultures. This is not merely
a matter of knowing languages, but one of understanding people.
Communism is said to be a force which holds itself aloof from
cultural differences, employing tactics that are essentially the
same wherever they appear in the world. This may be so, but
it remains true that in Viet-Nam or anywhere else the rest of
society has its own cultural and psychological peculiarities. And
how Communists fare in any society depends on their own
capacity for political manoeuvre within a cultural and institutional
framework already in existence. The shortest answer to the
question why American power failed the Vietnamese after 1954
is that the men responsible for making policy in Washington
ignored the cultural factor in the situation with which they were
dealing.

What after all *is* power? Since the rise of mercantilism and the
discovery of 'political arithmetick' in the seventeenth century, it
has become a habit in the West to assume that power can always
be measured by means of military and economic statistics. But in
practice the only measure of power is success. Economic capacity
and technology can add greatly to a nation's strength in certain
circumstances; but they can be effectively utilized only to the
extent that a situation has been correctly assessed and specific
objectives properly identified. The potential for military victory

cannot always be assumed to give power in and of itself. The mercantilist illusion works only so long as men are prepared to say, with Metternich *apropos* of the armies of Alexander I: 'One cannot argue with so many hundred thousand men.' The Chinese and Vietnamese Communists have rejected this equation that wealth equals power, at least as far as warfare on their own soil is concerned. The underlying supposition of 'guerrilla strategy' and 'people's war' is that no matter how powerful a Western army might be in theory, it must prove its power in practice by fighting on the ground. Against such an enemy there are no victories to be had by the mere possession of powerful weapons: either they must be actually used, or he must be defeated by some other means. It was because the Americans failed to understand this that in Viet-Nam the weapons had to be used.

To say these things is not to deny the virtues of democracy itself. To recognize that the rule of law and representative government are ideas alien to the tradition of Viet-Nam need not imply that there was never any possibility of their developing in that country. By the time Viet-Nam became independent the traditional system was dead, and whatever replaced it (and replaced also the colonial system) would be to some extent alien and new. Communism was in many of its features every bit as alien as were the principles of democracy, and there was no inherent reason why Communism should prove more appropriate to Viet-Nam's needs than a system incorporating Western ideas about government and economic growth. But that could only happen if the Vietnamese who wanted such a system were capable of bringing it about, and if their American allies appreciated the immensity of the problems involved. The Americans failed in understanding, just as their power failed to guarantee peace and stability: the consequence was the war of escalation which became a dominant factor in the world scene during the 1960s.

What had initially been a political and financial commitment to support South Viet-Nam became, step by step, a military one involving the use of America's own forces. For the majority of those who feel most strongly about it, this conflict has become a symbol of the world-wide confrontation between Communism and the Free World. But at a deeper level it is also a symbol of the cultural confrontation between East Asia and the West, and of the tragic failure of a Western power to deal effectively with an oriental situation. As far as South Viet-Nam itself is concerned, the war may well sweep away so completely the traditional framework that whatever emerges from it will have to be modern, whether Communist or Democratic. But elsewhere the extreme violence and the scale of the war is likely to damage faith in the Western achievement throughout Asia. There is a danger that because of it the West will in future be respected only for its power and not at all for its civilization: and when that power fails, as it sometimes will, the damage may be reflected in a declining sense of purpose in the West itself.

Meanwhile, in the villages of South Viet-Nam where the ravages of war are most keenly felt, it is not to be wondered at if the peasant still clings to his belief in Fate at a time when no other set of beliefs or explanations is enough to make sense of the sufferings he has to bear.

EPILOGUE

Toujours l'esprit de l'Occident s'efforça de donner aux choses auxquelles il attribuait de valeur un caractère durable. Il y a en lui une tentative de conquérir le temps, d'en faire prisonnier des formes. Mais cette tentative même n'est possible que dans un monde organisé par lui. C'est lui qui se couronne et réduit au néant l'existence de ce qu'il ne doit pas élire.

André Malraux: Tentation de l'Occident.

Epilogue

In the year 1862 the inhabitants of the Cochinchinese province of Go-Cong composed a declaration against the French, warning the invaders that they would fight to the death for the return of the territory ceded the previous year. It included an eloquent summary of their attitude to the foreigners:

> Your country belongs to the Western seas, ours to the seas of the East. Just as the horse and the buffalo differ between themselves, so do we differ by our language, our writings and our customs. Man has been created in different races. Everywhere man has the same value, but his nature is not the same.[1]

As conquerers the French were very much aware of their mission to civilize the Vietnamese: to make their nature as well as their humanity conform to the ideals of the West. Yet despite several generations of French rule, the Vietnamese are still for the most part conscious of being separated from Westerners by an invisible but very real cultural barrier. Have they not changed at all under the impact of the occidental challenge?

The question is less easily answered than one might imagine. In some respects they have changed a great deal. Materially they have added considerably to their technical skills, from the ability to drive a pedicab to piloting an aeroplane. Their country was made smaller by the introduction of modern communications and transport, and their educational system was transformed by the intrusion of practical subjects like mathematics, chemistry and engineering. They even changed their writing system, so that most of them no longer read Chinese characters. On the intellectual plane, the 'opening up' of Viet-Nam forced them to adjust to a new and wider view of the world. The traditional Vietnamese conception of a world dominated by China, in which they themselves occupied perhaps the second most important place, was shattered by their discovery of the West. New lines of political and social thought led to a new sense of nationality and the idea of the nation as the proper framework for political activity. For many, not only Communists, the idea of revolution replaced that of Fate or the Mandate of Heaven as the proper basis of political power. And the Confucian-Taoist idea of a universe governed by the principles of harmony gave way to a cosmology derived from Western natural science. For all those Vietnamese who have participated in this brave new world of occidental techniques and learning, some measure of change has been inevitable.

But when it comes to that deeper and more nebulous thing usually called 'personality' or sometimes 'social character', that something which distinguished the traditional Vietnamese as a person from the modern European, the changes are more difficult to measure. Even those Vietnamese most thoroughly educated in French learning had their roots in a family life which was, and still is for the most part, very different from the family life of Europeans. Complete personal transformation was rare, if not impossible; yet some measure of change was likely, and was made more so when young people moved from the environment of the village to that of the Westernized urban centres of Hanoi or Saigon. Family discipline was often reduced, and to their own children such people often allowed greater freedom than had ever been tolerated in the past.

Some people—not usually the most educated in either Vietnamese or French learning—allowed their children to concentrate so hard upon acquiring Western techniques that they lost touch completely with their own tradition. This represented change indeed. But these young people were seldom able to arrive at a true understanding of the spirit of the West. The contemporary writer Thu Van, in a 'Vietnamese Letter to President Johnson' composed in 1967, characterized such people as 'native strangers'.[2] In their approach to the West 'they sought not a culture but a means to become wealthy and powerful as the foreigner'. She drew a contrast between them and another, much smaller group of Vietnamese students of the West whom she called 'occidentalists': men and women who were masters of their own culture and were thereby enabled to appreciate the culture and vastness of the West as well as its techniques. Such people were rare, but their role in Vietnamese society was nevertheless very great, for they were the people who could lead the way in bridging the gulf between two different civilizations, and so explain the brave new world in terms that their own people could understand. Very often they played a leading part in the religious revival. Some became Catholics (though only a minority of converts were of this kind) and their presence in the Church made it possible for Vietnamese priests to take over from missionaries long before political independence was achieved. Others made a reappraisal of traditional religions, and participated in the Buddhist revival or else in the growth of Caodaism, the one religion which tried to unite the faiths of East and West. And there were some who rejected all religion, but adopted with a comparable religious fervour the political creed of Marxism. Thu Van's examples of the occident-alists are not at all a politically oriented list: they include Hô Chi Minh, as well as Ngô Dinh Diêm, the novelist Nguyên Tuong Tam (Nhât Linh) and also the Caodaist Nguyên Ngoc Bich.

Those who tried to blend the culture of East and West were deliberately eclectic. But those whose discovery of revolutionary political philosophies led them to reject tradition entirely did not always escape traditional habits of thought. Even the Marxist philosophy as it is interpreted by the Vietnamese mind may have its links with the past. For there is a sense in which Communism might be said to strengthen rather than to undermine belief in Fate. In day-to-day policy decisions, the Marxist idea of *praxis* demands a study of concrete conditions and a determination to change the world instead of being dominated by it; but when it comes to the dialectics of history there is room for a less practical view. The historical process itself is the guarantee of eventual success: in this, History has taken on the role of Heaven. Just as the Mandate of Heaven could in the old days pass from one dynasty to another, now the Mandate of History is held to be passing from one class to another. This is hardly an aspect of Vietnamese Marxism that would find its way into documents published in Hanoi, but it seems possible that some Communist cadres see in this way the philosophy they have been taught. As for the ordinary peasant, does he make any sharp distinction in his mind between the 'sorcerer' or 'bonze' who once claimed to know the future decreed by Heaven, and the party cadre who now insists that he knows what has been decreed by History? Whenever ideas are translated from one language and culture to another it is impossible to be sure that the words have precisely the same meaning for the two peoples involved. Where the languages differ as greatly as do French and English from Vietnamese and Chinese, it seems almost inevitable that there will arise subtle changes of meaning and usage. And if words are difficult to translate, then customs, institutions and attitudes are even more so.

Those colonists who wanted to make Vietnamese into Frenchmen were setting themselves an impossible task. The Vietnamese, with their tradition of eclecticism, might wish to borrow some things from the West; but they would always wish to remain Vietnamese. It was the misfortune of Viet-Nam that the French did not begin to appreciate the impossibility of their 'mission civilisatrice' until after 1945. For the most part indeed, they did not do so until brought up against the difficulties of reconquest during the war against the *Viêt-Minh*. Amongst the small minority of Frenchmen who did appreciate it at an earlier stage was the young art critic André Malraux, who spent some time in Indochina during the years 1923–5. Unlike most of his compatriots, he went there not to educate or govern others but to achieve a greater understanding of himself. The year before, he had written:

> We can feel only by comparison. . . . The Greek genius will be better understood through the contrast of a Greek statue with an Egyptian or Asiatic statue than by the examination of a hundred Greek statues.[3]

His whole attitude to both his own civilization and those of Asia was different from that of the colons of Saigon, and very soon he found himself at loggerheads with the French authorities. They accused him of stealing sculptures from the ancient monuments of Cambodia, which were theoretically protected by a government decree: as a result he was sentenced to three years' imprisonment by a court at Phnom Penh, though later the charges were quashed by an appeal to Paris. In retaliation, Malraux took up journalism in Saigon, and in the pages of *Indochine* lambasted the colonial authorities for failing to live up to the ideals of the politicians at home. He consequently made a personal enemy of the Governor of Cochinchina, Maurice Cognacq, who after a couple of months brought about the closure of the paper by intimidating the printers. What distinguished Malraux's subsequent writings in the period down to 1933 was his willingness to treat Asians as culturally the equals of Westerners, and to recognize in their desire for revolution one of the fundamental themes of the modern world. Asia, he found, was more than a mere foil for the understanding of Greek art.

Nevertheless the arrogance of the colon struck him as a manifestation of his own civilization just as important as the Greek statue, and in his short book *La Tentation de l'Occident* (1926) he explored the relationship between the two. It took the form of an exchange of letters between an imaginary Chinese visitor to Europe and a (possibly less imaginary) Frenchman who knew something of China. The thing that impressed his Chinese most about Western civilization was its endless activity. Whereas the Chinese ideal was one of harmony with the world, the Westerner seemed constantly to assert himself against it. In Europe everyone seemed to be directed by a consciousness of his own individual existence, apart from the universe and apart from God; and from this arose a desire to shape the universe according to his will. In art—the Greek statue for example—the occidental tradition was dominated by representation, the desire to capture active reality in plastic form. The Chinese painter was not concerned with such an impossible task, but sought only to express in art his own sympathy for what he saw. In politics Malraux's imaginary Chinese found a symbol of Western aspiration in the ruins of ancient Rome: the vestiges of an empire founded upon self-sacrifice, but whose only claim to grandeur lay in the sacrifice itself. Vast numbers of slaves were called upon to expend themselves in the interests of sheer power: but what good is power, asks the Chinese, unless one is the emperor? Despite the violence and cruelty that have characterized Chinese and Vietnamese history, the traditional values of those countries never glorified power for its own sake. Neither their Gods nor their rulers were invested with absolute omnipotence.

It was the Westerners' quest for power that took them to the ends of the earth in the era of capitalism and colonization, and led the French to conquer Viet-Nam. In his finest novel *La Condition Humaine* (1933) Malraux epitomized this occidental approach to Asia in the character of Ferral, the French banker whose philosophy is summed up in his assertion:

> A man is the sum total of his actions, of the things he has done and of the things he may do yet. . . . I am my roads, my work.[4]

Indochina was but one more of the things the French mind sought to transform into something it was not. They did indeed transform it, but not into anything they could have foreseen or desired. Malraux was conscious of the inevitable failure of the West, of the impossibility of remaking Asia in its own image. He was conscious too of the agony of the Westerner who discovered his own limitations. He placed into the mouth of another character in the same novel words which sum up his sense of the futility of Western endeavour:

> Each man suffers because he thinks. Fundamentally the mind only conceives of man as eternal, and so all consciousness of this life can be nothing but an agony. . . . Every man dreams of being God.

Malraux was not advocating that Westerners should prefer the traditional values of China to their own. The Asians were themselves rejecting those values in the course of a revolution of world-wide significance. What the twentieth century needed was some new set of values that would transcend all traditional cultures, East and West alike. Malraux himself never solved the problem which he identified in his earlier works. In *La Condition Humaine* he seemed at times to suggest that the answer lay in Marxism, and the Communist form of revolution. But he never wholly committed himself to that view, and ultimately he retreated from international idealism into a nationalism (though not a traditionalism) of his own. What he recognized very clearly was that the claim to final and ultimate cultural superiority, the claim to have a 'mission civilisatrice', was no more than a temporary escape from the problem. The West must not be afraid to look the East squarely in the face and accept its cultural challenge.

There are no easy formulae that will enable us to transcend the cultural differences between Viet-Nam (or any other Asian country) and the West. The only thing that will serve is cultural understanding, slowly and painfully arrived at through study and experience. Greater knowledge of Asia on the part of a handful of specialists is an important pre-requisite for this, and we shall need to move beyond the point where only a tiny minority of Westerners have any knowledge of an Asian language and its culture. But more important still is the need for a fundamental change of attitudes in the Western world, for only that will enable a change in the basis of political decisions. Until the present decade this need could be ignored. It was enough to make speeches about the equality of races and the desirability of mutual understanding, and to treat Asian equality as a matter for politeness rather than action. But in Viet-Nam the consequences of inadequate cultural understanding have begun to materialize. The United States has not over-reached its physical resources: but its knowledge of Asians has proved too limited to support the ambitions of its policy.

It lies beyond the scope of this short essay to determine whether future policies of the West in Asia should be directed towards maintaining power and influence, or whether it is possible to concentrate solely on the provision of material and technical aid. If the lesson of Viet-Nam has any bearing on these larger issues, it is that events there demonstrate how sadly ill-equipped the West at present is to play any part at all in the East. A century ago the Europeans forced East Asia to respond to the challenge of technological superiority. That superiority still exists and many Asians are still eager to learn the skills and techniques of the West. But politically they have found the measure of Western civilization and power. In place of the old challenge, a new one has developed: a challenge from Asia to the West, of a different and more complicated kind. Whatever our future aims may be, we can no longer rely upon our own achievements and superiority being taken for granted by Asians. The Westerner in the East must now be culturally on the defensive: if he wishes either to influence or to help, he must first be prepared to learn.

Notes

PROLOGUE

1. On traditional Vietnamese chronology see P. Huard and M. Durand: *Connaissance du Viet-Nam* (Hanoi, 1954), pp. 75–77.
2. Trân Van Giap: 'Le Bouddhisme en Annam des Origines au XIIIe Siecle', *Bull. de l'Ecole Française d'Extrême-Orient*, vol. xxxii (Hanoi, 1932), p. 259; R. Lingat: 'Les Suicides Religieux au Siam' in *Felicitation Volumes of South East Asian Studies presented to His Highness Prince Dhaninivat*, vol. i (Bangkok, 1955), pp. 71–5; and *Echo Annamite* (Saigon newspaper), 31st March 1930.

   On Buddhist scriptures relating to this practice, see J. Filliozat: 'La Mort Volontaire par le Feu at la Tradition Bouddhique Indienne', *Journal Asiatique*, vol. ccli (Paris, 1963), fasc. i, pp. 21–51.
3. Contrast, for example, the interpretation in Marguerite Higgins: *Our Viet-Nam Nightmare* (New York, 1965), with that of David Halberstam: *The Making of a Quagmire* (New York, 1964). Both these correspondents were in Saigon in the summer of 1963.
4. The best available introduction to Vietnamese history in the pre-French periods, in a Western language, is Lê Thanh Khôi: *Le Viet-Nam: Histoire et Civilisation* (Paris, 1955). See also Joseph Buttinger: *The Smaller Dragon* (New York, 1958).
5. For a survey of the traditional Vietnamese system of government see R. Petit: *La Monarchie Annamite* (Paris, 1931).

PART ONE

Chapter I

1. Accounts of the traditional Chinese background are innumerable and too well known to cite here. Comparable works on Viet-Nam are less numerous. See P. Huard and M. Durand: *Connaissance du Viet-Nam* (Hanoi, 1954), and also M. Durand: 'Quelques eléménts de l'Univers moral des Vietnamiens', *Bulletin de la Société des Études Indochinoises*, new series, vol. xxvii (Saigon, 1952).

2. Quoted from the translation by D. C. Lau (Penguin Books, Harmondsworth, 1963), p. 105. On Nguyên Binh Khiêm, see Duong Dinh Khuê: *Les Chefs d'Oeuvre de la Litterature Vietnamienne* (Saigon, 1966), pp. 67–8.

3. Quoted from the translation by Lin Yu-tang, *The Wisdom of Confucius* (London, 1958), p. 123.

4. For a long discussion of the importance of this idea of God as law-maker in the development of Western thought see Joseph Needham: *Science and Civilisation in China*, ii (Cambridge, 1956), ch. 18.

5. Cf. H. J. R. Murray: *A History of Chess* (Oxford, 1913), pp. 121 ff.

6. The by now classic example of this comparison is that of K. A. Wittfogel: *Oriental Despotism, a Comparative Study of Total Power* (Yale, 1957).

7. This absence of an orthodox *Sangha*, rather than any specific difference of belief, is probably the most important distinction between the (Mahayana) Buddhism of Viet-Nam and the Theravada Buddhism of Cambodia, Siam and Burma. The nature of Vietnamese Buddhism in the twentieth century will be discussed in Chapter V below.

8. The story is recounted in Nguyên Dang Thuc: *Asian Culture and Vietnamese Humanism* (Saigon, 1965), pp. 126–38.

9. Cf. J. Chesneaux: *Les Sociétés Secrètes en Chine* (Paris, 1965); Georges Coulet: *Les Sociétés Secrètes en Terre d'Annam* (Saigon, 1926); and also Leon F. Comber: *Chinese Secret Societies in Malaya* (New York, 1959).

10. On persecution in China see J. J. M. De Groot: *Sectarianism and Religious Persecution in China* (Leiden, 1901); but de Groot's implication that the Confucian motive for persecution was a desire for religious as well as political orthodoxy is not now accepted. On Vietnamese persecutions of Christianity, see G. Taboulet, *La Geste Française en Indo-chine*, vol. i (Paris, 1955).

11. The poem was composed by Nguyên Du about 1813, but was based on an earlier Chinese novel. The Vietnamese poem has been translated into French more than once, most recently by Xuân Phuc and Xuân Viêt in the series 'Connaissance de l'Orient' (UNESCO, Paris, 1961). The quotation below is rendered into English from the latter French edition. Cf. Duong Dinh Khuê, *op. cit.*

12. G. Coulet, *op. cit.*, contains a general discussion of the *thây-phap*, as well as documentary evidence of the activities of such men in the secret society movements of 1913–16.

13. On Phan Dinh Phung, see Nguyên Phut Tân: *A Modern History of Viet-Nam* (Saigon, 1964), pp. 241–79.

Chapter II

1. Some of these poems are translated in Duong Dinh Khuê: *Les Chefs d'Oeuvre de la Litterature Vietnamienne* (Saigon, 1966), pp. 320–328.
2. It has been translated into French: Ngô Dinh Diêm, Nguyên Dinh Hoe and Trân Xuân Toan: 'L'Ambassade de Phan Thanh Gian, 1863–4', *Bull. des Amis du Vieux Huê*, 1919 and 1921 (Huê).
3. A list of his writings together with a biographical note will be found in A. Brébion and A. Cabaton: *Dictionnaire de Bio-bibliographie de l'Indochine Française* (Paris, 1935).
4. No adequate account of Tô's career or memorials exists in a Western language. The brief summary here is based on Pham Van Son: *Viêt-Su Tân-Biên*, vol. v, pt. i (Saigon, 1962), pp. 263–72. There had been an embassy to Paris earlier, but the French government refused to receive it. See also Pierre Daudin and Lê Van Phuc: 'Phan Thanh Gian et sa Famille', *Bull. de la Société des Études Indochinoises*, n.s. xvi (Saigon, 1941).
5. Thai Van Kiêm: 'Les Premières Relations entre le Viêt-Nam et les États-Unis d'Amérique', *Bull. de la Soc. des Études Indochinoises*, n.s., xxxvii (1962), pp. 302ff.
6. J. R. Levenson: *Confucian China and its Modern Fate*, 3 vols. (London, 1958–65).
7. Duong Dinh Khuê, *op. cit.*, pp. 266–75.
8. See J. R. Levenson: *Liang Ch'i-ch'ao and the Mind of Modern China* (Harvard, 1954), for a thorough analysis of Liang's ideas.
9. See Pham Van Son: *Viêt-Su Tân-Biên*, v, pt. ii (*Viêt-Nam Cach-Mang Cân-Su*) (Saigon, 1963), pp. 362–7, for a full account of Phan Bôi Châu's life; cf. below, Chapter VII.
10. Benjamin Schwarz: *In Search of Wealth and Power: Yen Fu and the West* (Harvard, 1964).
11. The best available biography of Sun Yat-sen is M. L. Sharman: *Sun Yat-sen, a Critical Biography* (New York, 1934). I have not been able to discover the date of the first translation of Sun's writings into Vietnamese; but there was a French translation published in 1929, which would be available at least to Vietnamese students at that time studying in Paris.
12. This and other Vietnamese political movements of the 1920s will be discussed in Chapter VII below.
13. J. Needham: *Science and Civilisation in China*, vol. ii, ch. 10, pp. 89–98. On the problem of Chinese and Vietnamese methods of logic see, for example, P. Huard: 'Les Chemins du Raisonnement et de la Logique en Extrême-Orient', *Bull. de la Société des Études Indochinoises*, n.s., vol. xxiv, pt. 3 (1949).

Chapter III

1. The literature of French colonial theory is immense; for an introduction to it see R. F. Betts: *Assimilation and Association in French Colonial Theory, 1890–1914* (New York, 1961).
2. Cf. Nguyên Huu Khang: *La Commune Annamite, Étude historique, juridique et economique* (Paris, 1946), pp. 51–7.
3. The best introduction to the Vietnamese village is G. C. Hickey: *Village in Viet-Nam* (Yale, 1964), but it must be remembered that it relates specifically to a village in Cochinchina. Another useful study, giving the picture for Tongking in a more generalized way, is P. Ory: *La Commune Annamite au Tonkin* (Paris, 1894). On the Chinese background, and especially the importance of the clan in South China, see M. Freedman: *Lineage Organisation in Southeastern China* (London, 1958).
4. Phan Huy Chu: *Lich-Triêu Hiên-Chuong Loai-Chi*, compiled about 1820 and surviving in several copies (in Chinese); it was extensively used by Nguyên Huu Khang, *op. cit.* For a summary of traditional village legislation over the centuries, cf. Nghiêm Dang: *Viet-Nam, Politics and Public Administration* (Honolulu, 1966), pp. 146–50.
5. Môc-Hoa is now in Kiên-Tuong province; many of the South Vietnamese provinces were renamed, with new boundaries, by Ngô Dinh Diêm.
6. 'Rapport du Gouverneur de la Cochinchine sur la Situation Politique du Pays, 1922.' (National Archives, Saigon.)
7. Cf. Chapter I, note 9, above. Coulet's work gives the only detailed account of the secret society revolt of 1916 in Cochinchina.
8. 'Rapport du Gouverneur de la Cochinchine, etc., 1917.' (National Archives, Saigon.)
9. The statistics for 1930 were published in Yves Henri: *Economie Agricole de l'Indochine* (Hanoi, 1932).

Chapter IV

PART TWO

1. The Chinese tribute system from the seventeenth to the nineteenth century has been analysed in detail by J. K. Fairbank and S. Y. Teng: 'On the Ch'ing Tributary System', *Harvard Journal of Asiatic Studies*, vol. vi (Harvard, 1941). On the history of Viet-Nam's relationship with China see Lê Thanh Khôi: *Le Viet-Nam: Histoire et Civilisation* (Paris, 1955).
2. *The Dynastic Chronicles of the Bangkok Era: The Fourth Reign.* Translated by Chadin Flood, vol. ii (Tokyo, 1966), pp. 300–4.
3. There is a detailed study of this division of Dai-Viêt between the

Trinh and the Nguyên, and of the subsequent wars between the two families, in L. Cadière: 'Le Mur de Dông-Hoi, Étude sur l'Établissement des Nguyên en Cochinchine'. *Bull. de l'École Française d'Extrême-Orient*, vi (Hanoi, 1906).

4. M. Gaultier: *Minh Mang* (Paris, 1935).

5. For a good, detailed account of this period, and of French activity in Viet-Nam generally down to about 1885, see A. Schreiner: *Abrégé de l'Histoire d'Annam* (Saigon, 1906).

6. Cf. L. Finot: 'L'Archéologie Indochinoise, 1917–30', *Bull. de la Commission Archéologique de l'Indochine* (Paris, 1931); there is of course a large quantity of academic literature on the subject.

7. O. Mandelshtam: *Collected Works*, edited by G. P. Strune and B. A. Filipoff (New York, 1966).

I owe this reference to Mr Robin Milner-Gulland of the University of Sussex.

8. Alexandre de Rhodes: *Dictionarium Annamaticum, Lusitanum et Latinum* (Rome, 1651). De Rhodes had been in Viet-Nam for long periods between 1615 and 1645; but the long-accepted version that he was the first to create a Romanized script for Vietnamese has been challenged by Father Thanh Lang. For a good account of the development of *quôc-ngu* writing see Dinh Xuân Nguyên (Thanh Lang): *Apport Français dans la Littérature Vietnamienne* (Saigon, 1962), pp. 26–30.

9. On the development of Vietnamese literature in the 1920s and 1930s, see Dinh Xuân Nguyên, *op. cit.*; Pham Thê Ngu: *Viêt-Nam Van-Hoc Su Gian-Uoc Tân-Biên*, vol. iii (Saigon, 1965); and also S. D. O'Harrow: *The Growth of Modern Vietnamese Prose Fiction* (unpublished thesis, M.A., University of London, 1965).

10. In the sixty years before the French annexed Saigon, the capital had been at Huê; before that the Saigon area had been within the virtually independent kingdom of the Nguyên princes (also ruled from Huê) ever since its first settlement by Vietnamese in the mid-seventeenth century. Earlier than that, Cochinchina had been part of Cambodia. Under French rule, although Hanoi was the capital of the whole Union Indochinoisc from 1887 Cochinchina still had considerable autonomy thanks to the fact that it was a colony with a direct relationship to Paris, whereas the rest of the Union consisted of protectorates.

Chapter V

1. J. R. Levenson: *Confucian China and its Modern Fate*, vol. ii, pp. 14 ff.; cf. Review of Trân Trong Kim's volumes by E. Gaspardone, *Bull. de l'École Française d'Extrême-Orient*, 1930 and 1933.

2. Figures from *The Religions of Viet-Nam in Faith and Fact* (San Francisco, 1966; published for U.S. Navy). This is a minimum figure for the Caodaists; other sources give one million or more adepts.

3. G. Coulet: *Cultes et Religions de l'Indochine Annamite* (Saigon, 1929), pp. 179–86. I am indebted to Mrs Marjorie Topley for information about the *Tao-Yuan*, which is also known as the 'Red Swastika Society'.

There is no satisfactory account of the development of Caodaism in any Western language, but see Gouvernement-Général de l'Indochine: *Contribution à l'Histoire des Mouvements Politiques de l'Indochine Française*, vol. vii, *Le Caodaisme* (Hanoi, 1937); also G. Gobron: *Histoire du Caodaisme* (Paris, 1948); and G. C. Hickey, *Village in Vietnam* (Yale, 1964), Appendix B. The account here is based on these works and also conversations with Caodaists in Saigon.

4. On the role of the medium (*đồng*) in some North Vietnamese sects, see M. Durand: *Technique et Panthéon des Médiums Vietnamienne* (Paris, 1959).

5. There is an account of *Hoa-Hao* Buddhism in B. B. Fall: 'The Political-Religious Sects of Viet-Nam', *Pacific Affairs*, September 1955, later reprinted in his *Viet-Nam Witness, 1953–66* (New York, 1966), pp. 148–54. *Hoa-Hao* (like the Chinese *Tai-Ping*) means literally 'Great Peace'.

6. Donald Lancaster: *The Emancipation of French Indochina* (London, 1961), pp. 89–90. The best account of Japanese policy towards Vietnamese nationalist and religious groups is in P. Devillers: *Histoire du Viet-Nam de 1940 à 1952* (Paris, 1952), pp. 88 ff.

7. Phan Xuân Hoa: *Tam-Muoi-Bây Nam Cach-Mênh Viêt-Nam* (Hanoi, 1949), p. 100.

8. Cf. Donald E. Smith: *Religion and Politics in Burma* (Princeton, 1965).

9. For an introduction to Japanese Buddhism, see M. Anesaki: *Religious Life of the Japanese People* (Tokyo, 1938).

10. Cf. Wing-tsit Chan: *Religious Trends in Modern China* (New York, 1953).

11. The best introduction to Vietnamese Buddhism is in Mai Tho Truyên: *Le Bouddhisme au Viet-Nam* (Saigon, 1962), originally published in 'Présence du Bouddhisme', *France-Asie*, xvi (Saigon, 1959).

The attempt here to compare Vietnamese and Japanese Buddhism is based on the author's own observations in Saigon and Huê in 1966; the Vietnamese Buddhists do not openly admit that there are two separate sects amongst them, but the differences between Lotus Buddhism and Amidism are evident to the informed observer.

12. Trân Van Giap: 'Le Bouddhisme en Annam', *Bull. de l'École Française d'Extrême-Orient*, xxxii, 1932.

13. On the early history of Christianity in Viet-Nam see G. Taboulet, *La Geste Française en Indochine*, vol. i (Paris, 1955); and also G. Coulet, *Cultes et Religions* (cited above). The figures for 1966 are from the source cited in note 1 (Chapter V), above.

Chapter VI

1. The principal Western account of the Constitutionalist Party after 1917 is that of I. Milton Sacks: 'Marxism in Viet-Nam' in F. N. Trager: *Marxism in South East Asia* (Stanford, 1959), but it is very brief (not being an integral part of Professor Sacks' subject in that article). All accounts of the party give its date of foundation as 1923, and therefore ignore completely its early development between 1917 and that year.

2. On the ideas of Chailley-Bert and Harmand see, to begin with, R. F. Betts: *Assimilation and Association, etc.* (cited in note 1, Chapter III, above).

3. Quoted from T. F. Power: *Jules Ferry and the Renaissance of French Imperialism* (New York, 1944).

4. On this movement see Nguyên Phut Tan: *A Modern History of Viet-Nam* (Saigon, 1964), chapters on Phan Châu Trinh and Phan Bôi Châu; cf. also note 9, Chapter II, above.

5. Most of the information given here about the Constitutionalist Party is derived from this newspaper, published in Saigon between 1917 and 1925; and from its successor *La Tribune Indochinoise* (Saigon, 1926–42). See also Georges Garros: *Forceries Humaines: L'Indochine litigieuse, Esquisse d'une Entente Franco-Annamite* (Paris, 1926).

6. Nghiêm Dang: *Viet-Nam, Politics and Public Administration* (cited above), pp. 59, 133; and 'Rapport du Gouverneur de la Cochinchine sur la Situation Politique du Pays, 1922' (National Archives, Saigon).

7. Quotation translated from *La Tribune Indochinoise*, 29th June 1929; cf. Nguyên Dang Thuc: *Asian Culture and Vietnamese Humanism* (Saigon, 1965), pp. 54 ff.

Chapter VII

1. Nguyên An Ninh: *La France en Indochine* (Paris, 1925).
   No Western source has a full account of the career of Nguyên

An Ninh: see *Dân-Quyên* (Saigon newspaper, in Vietnamese), 16th August 1964; *L'Avenir du Tonkin*, 5th May 1926; and *La Lutte*, 1936–7 *passim*, for the Congress movement of those years.

2. Nguyên Phut Tan: *A Modern History of Viet-Nam* (cited above, note 4, Chapter VI).

3. The only full-length biography of Hô is Jean Lacouture: *Hô Chi Minh* (Paris, 1967); it includes references to other available sources.

4. The Governor-General was Klobukowski; the speech from which the quotation is translated was printed in *Le Courrier Saigonnais*, 27th November 1909.

5. Gouvernement-Général de l'Indochine: *Contribution à l'Histoire des Mouvements Politiques de l'Indochine*, vol. i: *Le 'Parti Revolutionnaire du Jeune Annam'* (Hanoi, 1933).

6. Same series, vol. ii: *Le 'Parti National Annamite' au Tonkin* (Hanoi, 1933).

7. Same series, vol. iv: *Le Parti Communiste Indochinois* (Hanoi, 1934).

8. On the Trotskyists in this period, see I. M. Sacks, 'Marxism in Viet-Nam' in F. N. Trager: *Marxism in South-East Asia* (Stanford, 1959).

9. For the composition of this government see P. Devillers: *Histoire du Viet-Nam de 1940 à 1952* (Paris, 1952), pp. 125–7. No detailed account of its short history has been written.

10. On the development of the *Viêt-Minh* Front see B. B. Fall: *Le Viet-Minh* (Paris, 1960); also J. Lacouture, *op. cit.*

Chapter VIII

1. Quoted by Jerome Ch'en: *Mao and the Chinese Revolution* (London, 1965), p. 223.

2. Truong Chinh: *The Resistance will Win* (Hanoi, 1960), reprinted in *Primer for Revolt* (New York, 1963); originally published in a Vietnamese Communist journal, 1946–7.

Vo Nguyên Giap: *People's War, People's Army* (Hanoi, 1961), also reprinted in an American edition with an introduction by B. B. Fall (New York, 1962).

3. A number of books and articles in Vietnamese dealing with such heroes appeared in the early 1940s. They included a new translation by Mac Bao Tiên of Nguyên Trai: *Lam-Son Thuc-Luc* (1944), which was a contemporary account of Lê Loi's struggles against the Chinese; and Hoa Bang: *Quang-Trung Anh-Hung Dân-Tôc* (Hanoi, 1944), dealing with the career and victories of Quang-

Trung, 'hero of the people'; the latter author also published essays on Lê Loi and Trân Hung Dao about this time.

4. Cf. L. Cadière: 'Le Mur de Dông-Hoi, Étude sur l'Établissement des Nguyên en Cochinchine', *Bull. de l'École Française d'Extrême-Orient*, vi (Hanoi, 1906).
5. Bernard B. Fall: *Street without Joy* (Harrisburg, 1961).
6. The text of the Geneva Agreement and Declaration is reprinted in Marvin E. Gettleman: *Viet-Nam, History, Documents and Opinion on a major World Crisis* (Penguin Books, Harmondsworth, 1965), pp. 144–68.
7. This too is reproduced in Gettleman, *op. cit.*, pp. 64–7.
8. D. Lancaster: *The Emancipation of French Indochina* (London, 1961), citing for the full text of the 4th June treaty, *L'Année Politique, 1954*, pp. 572–3.

PART THREE

Chapter IX

1. The text of this speech, from which the quotation at the beginning of Part Three is taken, is also reproduced by Gettleman, *op. cit.*, pp. 341–7.
2. Cf. W. J. Buch: 'La Compagnie des Indes Néerlandaises et l'Indochine', *Bull. de l'École Française d'Extrême-Orient* (Hanoi, 1936).
3. Samuel Baron: *A Description of the Kingdom of Tonqueen* (original edition 1686; reprinted in John Churchill: *Collection of Voyages and Travels*, vol. iv, London, 1732).
4. Charles Robequain: *L'Evolution Economique de l'Indochine Française* (Paris, 1939; English translation, 1944) gives the best account of French economic achievement in Indochina.
5. Cf. Donald Lancaster, *op. cit.*, pp. 98–101.
6. P. Gourou: *Les Paysans du Delta Tonkinois* (Paris, 1936).
7. In his contribution to P. J. Honey: *North Viet-Nam To-Day* (New York, 1962), originally published in *China Quarterly*, no. ix, January–March 1962, p. 109. Dr Bich argued that the Diêm government, at that time still in power, should trade with North Viet-Nam.
8. W. W. Rostow: *The Stages of Economic Growth* (Cambridge, 1960), pp. 19, 26.
9. Trân Quôc Vuong, Ha Van Tan, *et al.*: *Lich-Su Chê-Dô Phong-Kiên Viêt-Nam* (Hanoi, 1960): introduction by Trân Van Giau, in vol. i, p. 4.
10. Lê Duân: 'Socialist Industrialisation', a speech at the seventh

session of the Central Committee of the *Lao-Dông* party, 1963, in *On the Socialist Revolution in Viet-Nam*, vol. ii (Hanoi, 1965), p. 14.

Chapter X

1. Mao Tse-tung: *On Contradiction* (English translation, Peking, 1960), p. 1. The original was written in 1937.
2. Appendix to F. Engels: *Ludwig Feuerbach and the End of Classical German Philosophy* (English edition, Moscow, 1950).
3. R. Deloustal: 'Ressources financières et economiques de l'État dans l'Ancien Annam', *Revue Indochinoise*, n.s. xlii–xliii (Hanoi, 1924–25).
4. Hoang Van Chi: *From Colonialism to Communism, a Case History of North Viet-Nam* (London, 1954).
5. *The Quynh-Luu Uprisings* (Saigon, 1958).
6. These figures are given in the Resolution of the Fifth Plenum of the Central Committee of the *Lao-Dông* party, July 1961, translated in *Vietnamese Studies*, no. 2; *Agricultural Problems* (Hanoi, 1964); see also V. P. Karamyshev: *Agriculture in the Democratic Republic of Viet-Nam* (Russian edition, Moscow, 1959; English translation by U.S. Joint Publications Research Service, Washington, 1961).
7. Cf. Chapter IV, note 9, above. The study by S. D. O'Harrow is particularly concerned with the work of Nhât Linh. It should be compared with the translations of early socialist and Marxist writing in Viet-Nam, such as that of Ngô Tât Tô, in 'Littérature du Viet-Nam', *Europe*, nos. 387–8 (Paris, 1961).
8. Huu Mai: *The Last Stronghold* (English translation, Hanoi, 1963); the novel itself is dated April 1961.
9. Hoang Van Chi: *op. cit.*, Part iv.
10. Quoted by Nguyên Dang Thuc: *Asian Culture and Vietnamese Humanism* (Saigon, 1965), p. 96, in an article on the *Nhân-Van* affair.

Chapter XI

1. One of the clearest accounts of Diêm's struggle for power in the years 1954–5 is that of Donald Lancaster: *The Emancipation of French Indochina* (London, 1961), chapters xviii and xx. See also Joseph Buttinger: *Viet-Nam, a Dragon Embattled* (New York, 1967), vol. ii, chapter xi.
2. Denis Warner: *The Last Confucian* (London, 1963), which gives a useful insight into the Diêm period despite its evident bias against the government. A less hostile general survey is Robert Scigliano:

South Viet-Nam, Nation under Stress (Boston, 1963). The fullest biographical details on Diêm and Nhu are to be found in Bernard B. Fall: *The Two Viet-Nams, a Political and Military Analysis* (New York, 1963), ch. xii. To these studies of the Diêm administration may now be added Dennis J. Duncanson: *Government and Revolution in Viet-Nam* (London, 1968).

3. Emmanuel Mounier: *Personalism* (English translation, London, 1952), p. xix. The best account of Vietnamese Personalism is that by John C. Donnell: 'Personalism in Viet-Nam' in Wesley R. Fishel: *Problems of Freedom: South Viet-Nam since Independence* (Michigan S.U., East Lansing, 1961).

4. Cf. Nghiêm Dang: *Viet-Nam, Politics and Public Administration* (Honolulu, 1966), pp. 157–9.

5. For a critical assessment of the South Vietnamese economy in the first half of the Diêm period see B. B. Fall: 'South Viet-Nam's Internal Problems', *Pacific Affairs*, September 1958, summarized in the same author's *Viet-Nam Witness* (New York, 1966), pp. 169–189.

6. The activities of these movements in one particular village are indicated by G. C. Hickey: *Village in Viet-Nam* (Yale, 1964), pp. 10, 202, etc.; see also Nghiêm Dang, *op. cit.*, pp. 198–9.

7. For a damming account of the *Cân-Lao* party, see D. Warner, *op. cit.*, pp. 116 ff.

8. The official version is given most fully in the 'White Paper', U.S. Department of State: *Aggression from the North* (Washington, 1965).

9. G. C. Hickey, *op. cit.*, pp. 58–73.

10. Cf. G. M. Kahin and J. Lewis: *The United States in Vietnam* (New York, 1967), p. 100.

11. Douglas Pike: *Viet-Cong: the Organisation and Techniques of the National Liberation Front of South Vietnam* (M.I.T. Press, Cambridge, Mass., 1966).

12. *Ibid.*, pp. 154–65, etc. This interpretation of Mr Pike's data, which he himself does not pursue vigorously, should not be taken to imply that Hanoi had *no* influence in the South before 1963; it is a question of the tightness of the control.

13. *Ibid.*, p. 162; and *Sunday Times*, 23rd February 1964.

14. The policy of the Democratic Republic of Viet-Nam towards the Sino-Soviet dispute down to 1963 has been studied in detail by P. J. Honey: *Communism in North Viet-Nam* (M.I.T. Press, 1963). Indications of a hardening of the line by Hanoi towards the struggle in the South about the middle of 1963 are contained in Nguyên Chi Thanh: 'Who will win in South Viet-Nam?', *Hoc-Tâp*, July 1963; English translation in *Vietnamese Studies*, no. 1 (Hanoi,

1964). General Thanh was later in command of North Vietnamese troops in the South, until his death (apparently in action) in the summer of 1967.

Chapter XII

1. Cf. R. Scigliano: *South Viet-Nam, Nation under Stress* (Boston, 1963), p. 49.
2. *Public Papers of the Presidents: Dwight D. Eisenhower 1954* (Washington, 1960), no. 306 (p. 949).
3. Dean Acheson: 'Crisis in Asia, an Examination of United States Policy', *Department of State Bulletin*, xxii (Washington, 1950), pp. 111–18.
4. Speech to the University of Washington, quoted in Theodore C. Sorenson: *Kennedy* (London, 1965), p. 511.
5. Richard Clutterbuck: *The Long, Long War: the Emergency in Malaya* (London, 1967), especially ch. viii.
6. In a speech at the International Congress of Orientalists, Ann Arbor (Michigan), August 1967.
7. A. M. Schlesinger, jr.: *The Bitter Heritage* (Boston, 1966), p. 31.

EPILOGUE

1. Admiral Reveillère: 'Patriotisme Annamite', *Revue Indochinoise*, 6th year, no. 190, 9th June 1902, pp. 515–17. I am indebted to Dr Milton Osborne of the University of Monash for this quotation.
2. Thu Van: 'A Vietnamese Letter to President Johnson', *Michigan Quarterly Review*, vol. vi, April 1967.
3. Quoted from Malraux's preface to the catalogue for the 'Exposition D. Galanis' (Paris, 1922), by W. G. Langlois: *André Malraux, the Indochina Adventure* (London, 1966). The latter is a detailed account of Malraux's experiences in Saigon and Cambodia; it also throws valuable light on the political atmosphere of Cochinchina in 1923–5.
4. Quoted from the English translation: André Malraux: *Man's Estate* (Penguin Books, Harmondsworth, 1961), p. 215; the second quotation is ibid., p. 316.

Index

Agrovilles, 157
Acheson, Dean, 171
Archaeology of Viet-Nam, 65
Assimilation and association, 40–1, 88, 89
August Revolution, 111

Bao-Dai, abdication, 11, 111; becomes head of Associated State, 120
Bert, Paul, 88
Binh-Xuyên secret society, 119, 153
Buddhism, 3; Amidist, 16, 79; in Burma and Ceylon, 78; in Japan, 79; Mahayana, 78, 79; Theravada, 78, 80

Cach-Mang Dang, and *Thanh-Niên,* 103
Cambodia, 63, 64
Cân-Lao Nhân-Vi Dang, 160–1
Cao-Dai religion (Caodaism), 71–4, 75, 77, 151–2
Cap, Trân Quy, 91
Catholicism, 21, 26, 83
Chang Fa-kwei, 110
Châu, Phan Bôi, 33, 90, 99
Chiêu, Bui Quang, 92, 96, 139; killed by Communists, 97, 111
Chiêu, Gilbert Trân Chanh, 91
Chiêu, Ngô Van, 74
China, 6–7, 30, 57–9, 118–19, 166
Chu nôm (characters), 66
Cochinchina, 60, 63, 65, 68; French assimilation in, 41–2; obstacles to Communism in, 108; religious movements in, 71; rise of political societies, 51
Communist Party, 112, 115

Communist revolt, 1930, 106–7
Confucian ideals, 12–14
Confucianism, revival of, 70–1
Conseil Colonial (Cochinchina), 94, 159
Constitution of 1956, 156, 160
Constitutionalism, 95
Co-operatives, 145
Cuong-Dê (Prince), 76, 90

Da-Nang, attack on, 6
Dai-Dao Tam-Ky Phô-Dô (Caodaism), 72
Dai-Viêt party, 92, 110, 112, 147
Dang Lao-Dông, 115
Dang Nhân-Dân Cach-Mang Viêt-Nam, 165
Dao, Trân Hung, 13, 15
Dao-Lanh religion, 72
De Rhodes, Alexandre, 66
Democratic Republic of Viet-Nam, 111
Descartes, influence of, 38
Diêm, Ngô Dinh, 4, 85, 152, 154, 175–6, 185
Diên Biên Phu, 119
Doan-Tuyêt, 147
Doctrine of the Mean, 46
Dông-Kinh Nghia-Thuc, 91
Dông-Son, 65
Doumer, Paul, 128
Duân, Lê, 136
Duy-Tân Hôi, 90; plot to abduct Emperor, 92

Eisenhower, President, letter to Ngô Dinh Diêm, 169–70
Elections of 1926, 93–4
Examination system, 20; abolished, 89, 96

Fate, concept of, 22 ff.
Ferry, Jules, 88; on colonies, 128
French conquest, 29, 64–5

Geneva Agreement, 120–1
Gia-Long, 64
Gian, Phan Thanh, 26, 28
Giao, Duong Van, 96
Giap, Trân Van, 81
Giap, Vo Nguyên, 112, 115, 118
Giau, Trân Van, 109, 136
God, concept in China and Viet-Nam, 15
Great Learning, 14

Hanoi, Chinese occupation, 111
Heaven and Earth Society, 21
Hô Chi Minh, 34, 66, 100, 106, 185; arrest, 107; imprisonment and release, 110–11
Hoa-Hao Buddhism, 71, 76, 151, 160
Hobbes, Thomas, 46
Hoc, Nguyên Thai, 106
Hope of Youth Party, 98
Huê, 11–12
Hugo, Victor, 74, 152
Hundred Flowers period, 143, 144
Huu Mai (The Last Stronghold), 148

India, constitutionalism in, 86
Industrialization, 133
Irrigation, 31

Japanese occupation, 109; of Cochinchina, 76
Johnson, L. B., 126

K'ang Yu-wei, 31, 32
Kennedy, John F., 171–2, 174
Khiêm, Nguyên Binh, 13; hero cult, 15
Khmers, 60, 63
Khôi, Ngô Dinh, murder of, 111, 154
Khôi, Phan, 149
Khoi-nghia, 166
Khuyên, Nguyên, 24
Kiêm, Mai Van, 50
Kierkegaard, 154
Kim, Trân Trong, 71, 109

Kim Vân Kiêu (poem), 22, 140
Ky, Petrus Truong Vinh, 26, 27

Land, expropriation, 142–3; ownership in Cochinchina and Tonking-Annam, 53; policy of Diêm, 156
Land reform, 141–5
Language reform, 66
Lao-Dông party, 104, 141
Lê dynasty, 60–63
League of Nations, 34
Li T'ai-po, 74
Liang Ch'i-ch'ao, 32, 33, 36, 90
Liên-Doan Công-Chuc Cach-Mang Quôc-Gia, 160
Liên-Viêt Quôc-Dân Hôi, 115
Liu Shao-ch'i, in Hanoi, 166
Logic, East and West, 17
Long, Nguyên Phan, 93, 94, 96
Lotus school, 81
Lutte, La, 99, 109

Mai, Duong Bach, 109
Malaya, comparison with, 175
Malraux, André, 186 ff.
Mao Tse-tung, 114, 116, 138, 148
Marxism, Vietnamese, 185
Mat-Trân Dân-Tôc Giai-Phong Miên-Nam Viêt-Nam, 162
Migration from North to South, French proposals, 132
Minh-Mang, 31, 64, 85
Mining, in Viet-Nam, 128–9
Môc-Hoa, l'affaire de, 46 ff.
Monarchy, collapse of, 12
Mounier, Emmanuel, 154–5
Movement for National Revolution, 160, 161

Nam-Phong Tap-Chi (periodical), 67
Nation, concept of, 34, 57
National Front for the Liberation of the South of Viet-Nam, 162, 164
National League of Revolutionary Civil Servants, 160
National People's Party, 104, 112
Nguyên Ai Quôc, see Hô Chi Minh
Nguyên Du, 23

Nguyên and Trinh clans, rivalry, 60–63
Nguyên and Vo clans, rivalry, 47–8
Nhân-Van, 149
Nhât Linh (Nguyên Tuong Tam), 5, 147, 185
Nhu, Madam, 155
Nhu, Ngô Dinh, 152, 153, 154
Nineteenth Century (McKenzie), 32
Ninh, Nguyên An, 98

'Oriental despotism', 17

Parti Constitutionaliste, 93
Party of the Workers, 115
Peasant demonstrations, 91
People's War, People's Army, 116
Personalism, 154–5, 173
Phat, Cao Triêu, 77
Phong-Trao Cach-Mang Quôc-Gia, 160
Phuc-Quôc movement, 110
Phung, Phan Dinh, 24
Phuong, Nguyên Tri, 28
Population, imbalance of, 132

Quan-Công, 74
Quang Duc, 3–5
Quôc-Dân Dang party, 37, 104; and Communists, 112
Quôc-ngu script, 67
Quynh-Luu revolt, 144
Quynh, Pham, movement for education, 96; murder of, 111

Railways, 128
Rectification campaigns, 148, 149
Regionalism, in South Viet-Nam, 163–4
Religious persecution, 20
Robequain, Charles, 129–30
Rostow, Walt W., 133–4
Rousseau, J. J., 146

San-Min Chu-I, 37
Sanh, Phan Phat, 66
Sarraut, Albert, 89

Secret societies, 20, 21, 50–1
Siam, 58, 59, 64, 78
Silk, 126, 130
So, Huynh Phu, 76–7
Société d'Enseignement Mutuel, 92
Sun Yat-sen, 36, 87, 97, 136

Tac, Pham Công, 76, 153
Tagore, Rabindranath, 37, 96–7
Tân-Viêt Cach-Mang Dang, 103
Tân-Viêt Dang, 103, 107
Tao-Yuan religion, 73
Tây-Son dynasty, end of, 64
Tây-Son rebels, 63
Thai-Tong, Trân, Emperor, 19
Tham, Hoang Hoa (Dê Tham), 100
Thanh-Niên, see Viêt-Nam Cach-Mang Thanh-Niên Hôi
Thâu, Ta Thu, 95, 100, 111
Thây-phap, 23, 74
Thê, Trinh Minh, 77
Thu Van, 184–5
T'i-yung, philosophy of, 30, 172
Tientsin, Treaty of, 59
Tô, Nguyên Truong, 27
Tô-Tam (novel), 147
Tri, Phan Van, 25, 29
Tribune Indigène, 92, 93
Tributary system, 58–9
Trinh, Phan Châu, 90, 91
Trinh clan, 60–63
Truong Chinh, 116, 117, 143, 178
Trotskyist movement, 109
Tru, Nguyên Công, 31
Trung, Lê Van, 75
Tu, Dao Duy, 118
Tu, Lê Huu, 84
Tu-Duc, 26
Tu-Luc Van-Doan group, 147
Tuong, Hô Huu, 109
Tuong, Nguyên Ngoc, 74
Tuong, Tôn Tho, 95

United States, attitude to sects, 152, cultural confrontation with Vietnamese, 169; ignorance of Viet-

Nam, 175, 177; objectives, 170; relationship with Diêm, 175-6
University of Hanoi, 89, 91, 96

Van, Trân Cao, 92
Varenne, Alexandre, 55, 89
Viên, Bui, 28, 168
Viêt-Công, 162 ff.
Viêt-Minh, 77; Front, 95, 110; military strategy, 117–18
Viêt-Nam Cach-Mang Dông-Minh Hôi, 110
Viêt-Nam Cach-Mang Thanh-Niên Hôi, 101–6
Viêt-Nam Dôc-Lâp Dông-Minh, see Viêt-Minh

Viet-Nam People's Revolutionary Party, 165
Viêt-Nam Phuc-Quôc Hôi, 99
Vietnamese Independence Association, 99
Villages, administration, 42 ff.
VNQDD, see Quôc-Dân Dang

World Fellowship of Buddhists, 80
Women's Solidarity Movement, 160
Workers' Personalism Party, 160

Xa (she), 43–4

Yên-Bay mutiny, 106
Yen Fu, 35